Proud to Live Here

PROUD
to
Live Here

*in the
Connecticut River Valley of
Vermont and New Hampshire*

Richard J. Ewald
with Adair D. Mulligan

Edited by Sharon F. Francis

CONNECTICUT RIVER JOINT COMMISSIONS
CHARLESTOWN, NEW HAMPSHIRE

Connecticut River Joint Commissions
Charlestown, New Hampshire 03603
© 2003 by the Connecticut River Joint Commissions
Printed in Lebanon, New Hampshire

ISBN: 0-9728056-0-5

This publication has been funded in part by grants
from the National Trust for Historic Preservation,
the Windham Foundation, the Crosby Foundation,
and the National Oceanographic and Atmospheric
Administration of the U.S. Department of Commerce.

Cover illustrations
Front: "Turkeys on Washburn Hill"
Woodblock print by Matt Brown, Lyme, New Hampshire

Back: Two special places in the northern Connecticut River
Valley, both protected and conserved by their forward-
thinking owners. Top photograph by Adair D. Mulligan,
bottom photograph by Bob Green.

Printed on recycled paper

❧ Table of Contents ❧

PREFACE vii

INTRODUCTION: Where We Are: *Between the Source and the Sea* 1
How to Travel Around in This Book 7

CHAPTER 1. Ancient Waterway: *Written in the Rocks & Sand* 8
Landscape Formation, Plate Tectonics, Erosion, Quarries, Minerals, Glaciers,
The Legacy of Lake Hitchcock, Terraces, Floodplain Soils

CHAPTER 2. Natural Communities: *The Wild Things* 19
Trout, Salmon, Mussels; Insects, Amphibians, Reptiles; Migration Corridor, Birds of Prey;
Mammals; Forest History; Wetlands, Riparian Habitats, Floodplain Forests; Species of
Concern; Conservation Pioneers, Conte Refuge, Landscape Scale Conservation, Economics

CHAPTER 3. Amerindians: *Early Life on the Long River* 46
Paleo-Indian Period, Archaic Period, Woodland Period, Contact Period,
Archeological Sites, Petroglyphs, Historic Markers, Cultural Borrowings

CHAPTER 4. Settlement: *The Shape of Community in Town & Countryside* 55
Settlement Patterns, Frontier Forts, Indian Raids & Captives, Town Commons & Greens,
Hill Towns, Cellar Holes, Agricultural Villages, River & Confluence Towns,
Historic Districts, Community Character

CHAPTER 5. Agriculture: *Our Roots in the Soil* 71
Soils, Stone Walls, Morgan Horse, Merino Sheep & Animal Breeding, Dairy Farming,
Farmstead Architecture, The Grange, Working Farms Open to the Public, Maple Sugar,
Roadside Stands, Farmers' Markets & CSAs

CHAPTER 6. Industry & Commerce: *Taking Care of Business* 85
Early Industries, Mining, Water-Powered Mills, Hydroelectric Power, Logging,
Paper & Textile Manufacturing, Precision Manufacturing, Science & Inventions,
Local Industries, The General Store, Downtown Revitalization

CHAPTER 7. Transportation: *Traveling Places* 101
Indian Trails, Early Roads and Turnpikes, Canals & River Boats, Steamboats,
Railroads, Light Rail Trolleys, Fords & Ferries, Bridges, Air Travel,
Interstate Highways, Archeological Features

CHAPTER 8. Architecture: *Narrators in Stone & Wood* 121
What Makes Something Historic?, Building Types, Historic Properties, National Historic
Landmarks, Notable Architects, Some Notable Buildings, Historic Districts,
Meeting Houses, Religious Buildings, Industrial Buildings, Farmstead Architecture

CHAPTER 9. Civic Life & The Arts: *Public Agreements & Personal Achievements* 141
"New Connecticut," State Boundaries, Political Touchstones, Political Personalities,
Town Meeting, Education, Religion, Artists & Authors, Cultural Centers

CHAPTER 10. Tourism & Recreation: *Getting Away Means Going Back* 157
Inns & Taverns, Mineral Springs, Grand Hotels, Tourist Cabins & Roadside Attractions,
Summer People, Winter Sports, Old Home Day, Outdoor Recreation Today, Summits,
State Parks, Bicycle Trails, The Connecticut River, Connecticut River Byway

CHAPTER 11. Community Profile: *A Constellation of Places, Images and Stories* 177
Community Profile Checklist

APPENDIX A. Towns of the Connecticut River Watershed 183

APPENDIX B. Agencies & Organizations 185
Environmental Quality & Conservation, Agriculture, The Arts,
Historical Resources & Preservation, Planning, Transportation & Community
Development, Tourism & Recreation

APPENDIX C. A Sampler of Domestic Architectural Styles 192

APPENDIX D. National Register Historic Districts 202

PHOTO CREDITS 203

INDEX 207

❊ Preface ❊

FOR weeks, chorus lines of geese have been winging high overhead on their ancient autumnal journey southward. Sometimes low and raucous, sometimes high disembodied voices, the geese follow the Connecticut River as they have for thousands of years.

On earth below them, another winging has been taking place for several seasons. Thanks to the Internet, author Richard Ewald in Putney, Vermont, has been able to wing chapters of this book to Adair Mulligan in Lyme Center and to me in Charlestown, New Hampshire, for a trialogue that has covered many drafts and many months of mutual creativity on the part of three people who share a love of history, nature, and language, and appreciate each other's insights. We have added and subtracted, refined and polished the manuscript with the single aim of giving wings and purpose to the reader's love of the northern Connecticut River Valley.

Proud to Live Here grew out of an earlier publication, a study of the cultural landscape of the northern valley conducted by the Connecticut River Joint Commissions for the National Park Service, and written by Richard Ewald. Published in 1995, the study touched a popular chord. We soon ran out of copies. Rather than republish, we agreed with Rich to expand the ideas he had so elegantly set forth, to embark on a new publication with a shift in audience to the people, organizations, and communities that share the valley, its past and its future.

Over the last few years, the Connecticut River watershed has received increased recognition for its outstanding natural, historic, and cultural heritage. Congress honored the valley by establishing the Conte National Fish and Wildlife Refuge. The President named it as one of fourteen American Heritage Rivers. The States of New Hampshire and Vermont designated a Connecticut River Byway from the Canadian border to the Massachusetts line. Each honor attests to the intrinsic qualities of this place, and also challenges people of the valley to expand what it means to live within and be stewards of a cultural and environmental treasure.

Proud to Live Here is a gift from the Connecticut River Joint Commissions to our friends, neighbors, and visitors. The book is designed to provide inspiration, information, ideas and suggestions. We hope it stimulates new appreciation for the natural and cultural heritage of this remarkable place, and new motivation to learn and to act.

The Connecticut River Joint Commissions is a unique institution, an outgrowth of this unique place. While the Connecticut River might be at the far edge of the each state's map, Vermont and New Hampshire both paid tribute to the river and its watershed in the 1980s by establishing commissions to preserve and protect its resources, advise on growth and development, and cooperate with the other state. Working together since 1990 as the Connecticut River Joint Commissions, they continue a tradition of bi-state friendship and cooperation in the valley that echoes its early history. Both commissions are advisory and have no regulatory powers, preferring instead to promote public involvement in decisions that affect the river and its watershed.

Proud to Live Here joins other publications from CRJC: the six volume *Connecticut River Corridor Management Plan*, written with our five local river subcommittees; facts sheets on *The Challenge of Erosion* and *Riparian Buffers;* a booklet on *Boating on the Connecticut River;* and more. Each is part of our conversation with people in the valley about how to be good neighbors to a great river.

The Connecticut River Joint Commissions were immensely fortunate to be able to work with Richard Ewald, principal author of *Proud to Live Here*. His experience in historical and architectural subjects and his graceful prose and photography will be apparent as the reader turns the pages of this volume. CRJC's Communications Director, Adair Mulligan, brought her indefatigable energy, knowledge of the river valley, and publication experience to the project. When reviewers recommended adding a chapter on natural communities, Adair quickly volunteered to apply her professional background in environmental biology, and wrote the new chapter.

River commissioners Nathaniel Tripp of Barnet, Mary Sloat of Northumberland, Cheston Newbold of Cornish, and David Deen of Westminster reviewed the manuscript, and contributed generously of their fresh perspective and ideas.

Others who read manuscript chapters and added invaluable expertise are Stephen Taylor, Commissioner of Agriculture, Richard Boisvert, Deputy State Archeologist, James Garvin, State Architectural Historian, and Carl Schmidt, Historical Resources Council, all of New Hampshire, and Elsa Gilbertson, former Vermont State Architectural Historian, Jenny Tollefson, The Nature Conservancy, Richard Little, Greenfield Community College, and Dr. Jack Ridge, Department of Geology, Tufts University.

Proud to Live Here contains hundreds of images, each illuminating the story in a special way. None is more special than the cover wood block print created by Lyme, New Hampshire, artist Matt Brown. When Matt heard about the book, he set aside other projects to work on the image that goes to the heart of why people are so proud to live in the Connecticut River Valley.

Credits appear separately, but several image sources deserve special mention. Frank J. Barrett, Jr., Chair of the Connecticut River Byway Council, opened his extensive collection of historic postcard images, which appear throughout the book. Norwich, Vermont, photographer Rosamond Orford made available her breathtaking color images. Susan Morse, nationally recognized wildlife ecologist, provided her engaging wildlife photographs. The tal-

ented staff of the *Coos County Democrat* contributed a number of images, as did the Audubon Society of New Hampshire, The Nature Conservancy, and the Upper Valley Land Trust. Katharine Blaisdell offered her historic photos of the Wells River-Woodsville area. Archeologists Richard Boisvert and Wesley Stinson provided images. Many of Richard Ewald's and Adair Mulligan's photographs also appear. We print their work, and all the other images in these pages with profound admiration and appreciation.

The Connecticut River Joint Commissions appreciate support for *Proud to Live Here* from the National Trust for Historic Preservation, the Windham Foundation, the Crosby Foundation, and the National Oceanographic and Atmospheric Administration of the U.S. Department of Commerce. We are also grateful for the sustaining support of the States of New Hampshire and Vermont.

Manuscript and images became a book through the talented ministrations of May 10 Design and the printing skills of Whitman Press, both of Lebanon, New Hampshire. The type face is Winchester. We hope you like it as much as we do.

The Connecticut River Valley of Vermont and New Hampshire is a distinctive place, shaped by a mighty river, and further formed by stalwart people whose hands, heads, and hearts have created an admirable culture and landscape. We who live here and our visitors are stirred by the sheer beauty of the valley, the charm of our villages, and the productivity of our farms and businesses, the civic vitality of our communities.

We have thousands of reasons to be proud of this place. We have thousands of things to do to pass on the legacy we have inherited.

—Sharon F. Francis
Executive Director
Connecticut River Joint Commissions
Charlestown, New Hampshire

December, 2002

Introduction
Where We Are:
Between the Source and the Sea

THE ground outside my window slopes down to a little stream too small to earn a name on the maps. Several hundred feet to the east, the stream joins Beaver Brook which, a couple of miles to the north, spills into the Saxton's River. To the east, at a confluence braided with gravel, the Saxton's River empties into the Connecticut River. That's my watershed address—three tributaries removed from the Connecticut.

If you live in one of the 93 towns in New Hampshire or 114 towns in Vermont whose lands lie within the drainage area of the Connecticut River, its watershed, then we share an address common to 41 percent of Vermont's total area, and 33 percent of New Hampshire's. We are each one long, wet, gliding step from home to Long Island Sound. That's true whether you live in riverfront towns like Brattleboro or Lebanon, or amid tributary networks in Readsboro or Victory, Vermont, in Keene or Dixville, New Hampshire. It's true for Randolph, Vermont and Randolph, New Hampshire. Between the eastern slopes of 4,235-foot Killington Peak in

Ready to explore the river.

1

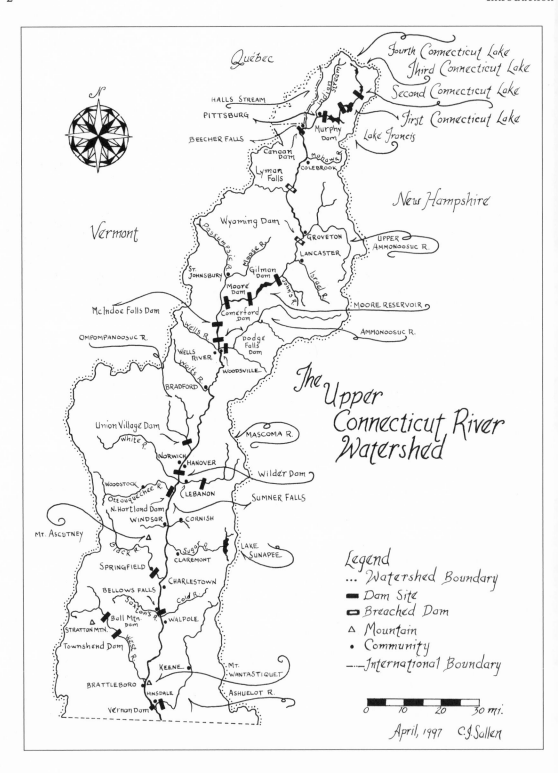

Québec

HALLS STREAM
PITTSBURG
BEECHER FALLS

Indian Stream

Fourth Connecticut Lake
Third Connecticut Lake
Second Connecticut Lake
First Connecticut Lake
Lake Francis

N

Canaan Dam
Lyman Falls

Murphy Dam

Mohawk
COLEBROOK

New Hampshire

Vermont

Wyoming Dam

Passumpsic R.

Moore R.

GROVETON
LANCASTER

UPPER AMMONOOSUC R.

ST. JOHNSBURY

Gilman Dam

John's R.

Israel R.

Moore Dam
Comerford Dam

MOORE RESERVOIR

McIndoe Falls Dam

Wells R.

Dodge Falls Dam

AMMONOOSUC R.

OMPOMPANOOSUC R.

WELLS RIVER
Wells R.

WOODSVILLE

BRADFORD

The Upper Connecticut River Watershed

Union Village Dam

White R.

MASCOMA R.

NORWICH
HANOVER

Woodstock
Ottauquechee R.

LEBANON

Wilder Dam

SUMNER FALLS

N. Hartland Dam
WINDSOR

CORNISH

Mt. Ascutney

Black R.

Sugar R.
CLAREMONT

LAKE SUNAPEE

SPRINGFIELD

CHARLESTOWN

Legend

BELLOWS FALLS

Cold R.

Sartons R.

Ball Mtn. Dam

WALPOLE

STRATTON MTN.

Townshend Dam

West R.

KEENE

BRATTLEBORO
HINSDALE

Mt. WANTASTIQUET

ASHUELOT R.

Vernon Dam

... Watershed Boundary
▬ Dam Site
⬭ Breached Dam
△ Mountain
• Community
---- International Boundary

0   10   20   30 mi.

April, 1997   C.J. Sallen

Vermont and the western slopes of 6,288-foot Mount Washington in New Hampshire, we are all gathered into a single flow.

The Connecticut River is the heart of our place and our story. It flows through space, and it flows through time, connecting us as communities that share both a common heritage and prospects for the future. It is a river valley of breathtaking beauty.

The map of the Connecticut's watershed reveals some basic truths. We live in what we might call the northern val-

The Connecticut River flows south in a broad sweep between Guildhall, Vermont, and Lancaster, New Hampshire.

ley, where the river and most of its tributaries originate. Of the Connecticut's 410 miles, our two northern states share some 270 miles, or 68 percent of its total length. Our lands total about 4.5 million acres, 63 percent of the whole four-state watershed. In other words, the geographic area we call home in Vermont and New Hampshire makes up the majority of the Connecticut River Valley. We are therefore responsible for a major share of its character, not to mention the quality of the water as it enters Massachusetts.

What this map doesn't reveal is also important. The way things here in the northern valley *are now* — settled later than Connecticut and Massachusetts, less densely populated, less "malled"—is closer to the way things *used to be* in all of New England. About 85 percent of our region is now forested. The portion of the river from Canaan to Gilman, Vermont, is the longest undeveloped segment of a major river in that state. What we share in the northern valley is special.

However, for the past two centuries, the Connecticut River has divided New Hampshire from Vermont, forming the entire length of the political boundary between them. The two states' cross-river

cooperation has been the exception rather than the rule. Today New Hampshire maintains jurisdiction of the Connecticut to the ordinary low-water mark on the Vermont shore. But before it was a political divider, the river was a political unifier. Before Vermont and New Hampshire were admitted to the Union, around 1780, a number of towns on both sides of the river in the upper valley attempted to form a separate state, with the river at its center.

Today we envision another kind of unity, reaching over boundaries to see and seek relationships. We see the river as the seam between the states, a seam that binds them together. On each side of the river, we are more like each other than the rest of our separate states, whose capitols, in Montpelier and Concord, are outside our watershed. We share a natural, historic, and cultural landscape that transcends the political border.

The natural and cultural unity of the Connecticut River Valley has been celebrated or expressed recently in a number of ways:

➔ The Legislatures of both states recognized the special qualities of the Connecticut River watershed by establishing a pair of commissions to cooperate together to preserve and protect valley resources and guide growth and development.

→ Many individuals and organizations from both states came together to advise Congress on the creation of the Silvio O. Conte National Fish & Wildlife Refuge, which covers the entire watershed.

→ The National Park Service conducted a special study of the heritage of the four-state watershed, treating it as a distinct entity.

→ Local citizens from New Hampshire and Vermont joined with the Connecticut River Joint Commissions to create a comprehensive *Connecticut River Corridor Management Plan* for the river and their riverfront towns.

→ The Connecticut was designated an American Heritage River, one of the first 14 rivers selected from among 124 others for its significant contributions to American history.

→ A Connecticut River Byway has been developed to promote the northern valley river corridor as a heritage tourism destination, for both residents and visitors. Ten "waypoint communities" along the corridor are creating centers to interpret and promote natural, cultural, historic, and farm heritage-related features of their region and the entire Byway.

The American Heritage River designation recognizes that people up and down the river already are hard at work to improve their communities by combining economic development, environmental protection, and historic preservation. The Connecticut River Byway is a timely opportunity to re-educate ourselves about our place, stimulate community pride, and work cooperatively for economic development. All of this is best accomplished when it

builds on each community's authentic history, its individual identity, and its place in the natural and cultural landscape.

This book is intended to assist that work in communities in the Connecticut River Valley in New Hampshire and Vermont, and to help all of us open our eyes to the places where we live. It is not meant to be a comprehensive history or inventory. Even if you find that a distinctive aspect of your own town is not mentioned, this book will enable you to place it in context and identify the steps that will help keep it a contributing part of your local cultural landscape.

This approach to preserving a cultural landscape can be applied anywhere. Wherever you live, outside your window likely will be a thread of moving water—even if it's a no-name little stream—that will provide you with a watershed address and the means to enter more deeply into the nature and history of your place.

WHAT IS OUR CULTURAL LANDSCAPE?

At the beginning of a new century and new millennium, we are witnessing two profound trends. One is the generic "sprawl" that continues to rise like a storm tide here in the northern Connecticut River Valley. After a half-century of accumulating

Out for a Sunday drive along the Sugar River in West Claremont.

momentum, automobile-oriented commercial and residential growth drives wave after wave of change against our everyday world and special places. It washes away our traditional downtowns and landscapes, soddens our architectural standards, and erodes our confidence in our ability to withstand its momentum.

The other profound development is a response to the first: here in the northern valley, more and more individuals, and more and more groups, are looking for ways to stem the tide, and to reverse it.

Sharon, Vermont, street scene, c.1909.

We've witnessed the loss of landmarks, of natural settings, of the "feel" of our former communities, and it's driven us to take action. We're working to preserve water, air and soil quality, to support agriculture and preserve open space, to find new uses for historic buildings, to insist that roads and bridges maintain a human scale, to celebrate local history. This all involves a reawakening to the importance of *place* in our lives, to an awareness of our daily presence within a living cultural landscape.

So what *is* a cultural landscape? Simply defined, a cultural landscape is the natural environment, evolved over time, inhabited and altered by humans over time. It may be expressed as an equation:

$$\frac{\text{Culture (who we are)}}{+ \text{Landscape (where we are)}}$$
$$\text{This particular place}$$

We live out our lives inside that equation, surrounded by the physical presence of our cultural landscape. It's a topography of hills and rivers in a climate with four seasons, of downtowns and rural open spaces, farms and forests, churches and factories, roads and bridges, small private homes and large public buildings, and much more. These form the tangible basis for our sense of place.

We are equally involved in how we occupy this place every day, in our family and work, in our customs, traditions and festivals, our political agreements and disagreements, our habits of mind. We declare our values in the ways we enact our roles within our communities, taking our place in the continuity of generations here. And in how we treat this cultural landscape as its inheritors, as its caretakers during our lifetimes.

But we are, understandably, so immersed in the details of our daily lives that we don't much think about our cultural inheritance. Then comes a day, like the one in early spring when we look at the dwindled wood pile in sudden surprise. How did it disappear so fast? Where did it all go? Burning it one stick at a time over a long winter, we didn't pause to take stock. Then all at once we see how much has gone up in smoke.

Changes happen to our communities in the same slow, incremental way. One day the farm stand by the side of the road is boarded up, and the next year the whole farm becomes a housing development. One day a fire destroys the upper floors of a 19th century brick commercial block downtown, and the next year it's torn down and replaced with a parking lot.

Perhaps a new shopping mall goes up in a cornfield out by the highway. Then new town offices are built near the mall, with space for the library, fire and police. The next year, the post office moves out there from downtown. Soon, half the storefronts in the historic commercial district are empty, and the windows on the old town hall are broken or boarded up, and the old library's been demolished and replaced with a gas station and mini-mart.

These are small changes, made one by one, over a period of time, not seen as significant by themselves, perhaps not really seen at all when they occurred. But suddenly we look around and ask: What happened to our community? Where did it go? Where in the world are we? Can't we do better than this?

The goal of this book is to take stock of our cultural landscape, our woodpile, and following that, to address some basic questions: What are the layers of change beneath the present moment? How did this place come to be the way it is? What important parts of that story are worth remembering and retelling? What are the special places worth saving? And, most importantly, how do we go about all this?

WHY IT MATTERS AND
WHY WE SHOULD CARE

In the short story "Bedrock," by Annie Proulx, an old man named Perley is said to have granite in his blood from a lifetime of eating potatoes grown in the soil of his New England farm. While that might seem fanciful, we all know intuitively that the places where we live and work really do affect us deeply.

We also know, just from looking around, that we affect our places. So it's clear that our relationship with our surroundings is a circular one: we make places and then the places make us, then we remake places which in turn remake us, and so on, one generation after another. This is how individuals, families and communities share in the evolution of a cultural landscape, influencing it and being influenced *by* it.

If we care about the kinds of communities we're making, and what they're making of *us*, then it's important that we perceive changes as—preferably before—they occur, and influence them for the better, for the sake of our communities' health. For we can also see by

looking around us in the northern river valley, in New England and the United States, that the communities which appear to be thriving, which show signs of social and economic stability, are those which value and embrace their natural and historic resources.

Our old buildings aren't getting any younger. They're standing out in the weather, some of them empty for lack of a good use, or they're being knocked down for no good reason. Our natural places are threatened by pollution, over-use, or ill-conceived development. Our enthusiasm for long-term stewardship of real places is diverted by a 24/7 media drenching in celebrity worship, get-rich-quick stories, and the titillating attractions of "virtual realities" and "reality-based" television shows.

Both historic preservation and environmental protection formerly focused on isolated fragments of our landscape — the endangered species here, the threatened building there. But environmental protection now is understood to involve the preservation of the habitats that support a constellation of

This 1893 church still serves its congregation in Woodsville, New Hampshire, despite losing its elegant steeple to the 1938 Hurricane.

Looking toward a bright future, secure within a celebrated past.

species. Historic preservation is now understood to involve the revitalization of communities that inhabit historic architecture and traditional landscapes. Both historic and environmental protection rely on developing and practicing a sense of place.

The selection of the Connecticut River as an American Heritage River in 1998 strengthened our collective sense of place.

On the same day the designation was reported in a newspaper in our region, however, other articles in the same edition told a different story: someone had dumped old tires and construction trash into one of the Connecticut's tributaries, and four historic homes in a local community were demolished for a parking lot. It was a rainy day, and no doubt leaking roofs in dozens of old granges and town halls let water seep into rafters and soak into plaster. A lot of work has been done; a lot more needs to be done.

But this isn't all a grim, serious business that requires you to sign on to "save the world." It's also interesting, fun, and personally satisfying to perceive the Connecticut River watershed as place and metaphor, to find and value your own place in it. Maybe your part is to wade into the water and really *feel* the tug of gravity for the first time. Or do more shopping downtown. Or just walk through the woods on a hillside and suddenly know yourself to be part of something that's been going on since time began.

The act of investing ourselves in where we live, in whatever way we're called, instills "pride of place." It's not a willful pride of ownership so much as a thankful pride of stewardship. We hold these places in trust for our children and grandchildren.

We're proud to live here.

How to Travel Around in This Book

This book organizes our natural and cultural landscape into themes, and explores each one in a variety of ways. Consider the themes as a framework for placing your own community in context with neighboring communities and the whole watershed.

The Basic Story: An introduction to the theme, and the role it plays in our landscape.

Resources & Revelations: An inventory of local places, events, and people that are significant or typical examples of the theme. "Resources" may be landscape forms, historic or contemporary structures, property types, and sites. "Revelations" may be events or occurrences (historic or contemporary), trends, traditions, stories, and iconographic images. Note features that are important to your community and add your own ideas to the list.

Threats: Specific problems and issues relevant to the theme and its resources. Use these examples to stimulate your thinking about other possible threats.

Actions & Activities: Opportunities for advocacy, preservation, appreciation, interpretation, education, and promotion. Limited only by available space. Think of more to address your community's issues.

Q & A: Questions to ask of ourselves or of students at all educational levels. Can you think of more?

FYI : Sources of information, services and assistance related to the theme. These include a variety of publications, videos, and Internet web sites.

See the appendices for a list of helpful public and private organizations on the federal, state, regional and local levels.

CHAPTER ONE

Ancient Waterway
Written in the Rocks & Sand

The earth beneath our feet is the basis of our cultural landscape. The present moment in the natural environment, down to the latest raindrop or snowflake falling at our feet, has been in preparation for perhaps four billion years. Natural resources are essential to human life. It is important to maintain our soils and forests, and to safeguard the quality of our air, waterways, and underground aquifers.

❋ The Basic Story ❋

SEEN from the air, our region resembles a deeply wrinkled carpet. The Connecticut River is the deepest and longest trough in a vast network of ridges and furrows. It drains a long basin that lies between the spines of two roughly parallel mountain ranges, the Green Mountains of Vermont and the White Mountains of New Hampshire.

Unlike, say, a desert or flat seashore, our spaces have a vertical as well as horizontal scale. Mountains and hills layer the far and middle distance of our perspective. We look up at hillsides from sheltered valleys, and climb to overlooks for longer views. As we move through this landscape, it rearranges itself constantly, reshaping the familiar, revealing something new.

Many of the things deeply ingrained in our lives—maple syrup in early spring, flying V's of migrating geese, colorful autumn foliage, and even the cycle of

The Connecticut River between Thetford and Lyme.

8

Waterfalls and cascades, such as Beaver Brook Falls in Keene, NH, mark the plunges of tributary streams toward the Connecticut River.

the four seasons themselves—are the result of our location on the planet and eons of geologic processes and events. Our crops, our architecture, our clothing, our interactions with nature—all are responses to climate and weather. Apples, steeply-pitched roofs covered with slate, winter skiing, firewood burning in fireplace or stove—these and many other characteristic elements of our regional culture derive from our geography and climate.

The physical shapes of our places themselves—from valley floodplains to hillsides to upland plateaus to mountaintops—narrate a long story of physical changes to the topography. In drier places like the American Southwest, the geologic record is starkly visible in such landmarks as the Grand Canyon. Here in northern New England, our moist, vegetation-rich climate obscures the record.

The evidence around and underneath us suggests that continents collided and mountains tilted up, and that mile-thick glaciers bulldozed and redistributed great masses of earth. It says that water and gravity worked for millions of years to contour the broad outlines and the intimate details of our topography. And it says that about 11,000 years ago, the last gla-

ciers receded and our climate stabilized. Our landscape then changed from an arctic tundra to what is today a boreal forest in the region's north and a northern hardwood forest to the south, that support the current diversity of flora and fauna, among them us, the human species.

Of course, the occasional tremor of a mild New England earthquake reminds us that "terra firma" is still in motion far below our feet. Many of the same slow processes that produced our landscape are still at work. A brook, silt-brown after a rain, demonstrates that flowing water continues to redistribute soil downhill from ancient mountains. The way that gravel and sand are distributed in small streams mirrors larger shapes in the landscape.

What we call pre-history is truly ancient history. Geologists say that the Connecticut River has flowed more or less in its current location for about two million years. Compared to that long a period, what scientists call "deep time" challenges comprehension. The bedrock underlying the river region probably was formed more than 400 million years ago.

A surprising secret beneath our feet was discovered in 1989 by seismic refraction research conducted by the U.S. Geological Survey and the U.S. Air Force. The fly-over confirmed what some geologists had suspected for several decades—the river's bed is consistent with, or roughly parallel to, a discontinuity in the earth's crust that is detectable to a depth of 20 miles! This evidence supports the theory that a continental collision and separation occurred some 600 million years ago.

While some geologists are reluctant to explain the discontinuity, others reason that land masses collided and then separated, leaving attached to North America a portion of the African continent that is much of present-day New Hampshire. If this theory is true, then our two states originated upon different continents.

The theory helps to explain differences between the rock on both sides of the river. Vermont's generally older rocks are metamorphosed sediments deposited as limestone, sandstone and shale, similar to those of the rest of the North American continent. By contrast, New Hampshire's younger rocks—particularly its granite—are mainly crystalline igneous and metamorphic rock types, reflecting an African or European origin.

No matter how our underlying bedrock evolved, the scenes around us were shaped more recently by a series of glaciations. Glaciers last covered New England during a maximum advance at about 23,000 years ago. In places, the ice was one-and-one-half miles thick. The glaciers redesigned our topography, first by their inexorable and massive movement, and then by the prodigious waters released in their melting. The last glacier began to melt during a warming trend about 18,000-20,000 years ago, inaugurating a period that put the finishing touches on our familiar land forms.

One of the most extraordinary features of our late-glacial environment was a long lake, formed

Glacial Lake Hitchcock occupied much of the northern valley from 17,000 to 12,000 years ago. After Rittenour, 1999.

from the waters of melting ice, which occupied the present valley of the Connecticut River. Lake Hitchcock, as it is called, stretched at least two hundred miles from present-day Rocky Hill, Connecticut, to present-day West Burke, Vermont, and Littleton, New Hampshire. Lake Hitchcock existed for about 5,000 years, and was one to twelve miles wide, extending some distance up every one of the tributary rivers and streams that today flow into the Connecticut River. Glacial Lake Hitchcock drained by about 12,000 years ago, and various remnants of the lake persisted in some locations.

So the geologic past has shaped the present landscape on a scale that ranges from our tallest mountains to the stones that turn up in our garden soils. About 11,000 years ago, when the last glaciers receded from northernmost New England and the climate stabilized, an arctic tundra slowly gave way to a landscape that today supports our current diversity of flora and fauna, and the Connecticut River Valley became a habitat suitable for human occupation.

❈ Resources & Revelations ❈

PLATE TECTONICS

When the North American and African plates slowly drifted together, the geological record shows they captured between them material from an ancient sea pockmarked with volcanoes. This formed an island chain known as the Bronson Island Arc, formerly located in the middle of the proto-Atlantic Ocean. These remnants form a series of hills and knobs in New Hampshire extending between Massachusetts' northern border and Lancaster,. They occur along a gently curving line which, generally, both parallels the Connecticut River and corresponds with the plate tectonic boundary.

These features, formed of ancient volcanoes and ocean-bottom muds, include the elevations of Wantastiquet Mountain, in Hinsdale, New Hampshire, immediately across the Connecticut River from Brattleboro, Vermont. Other remnants include Mascoma Dome in Enfield, elevations in Keene, Alstead and Canaan, and portions of Cornish, Plainfield, Lebanon and Hanover.

EROSION

Standing on the rim of the Grand Canyon, it is possible to see how much earth the Colorado River has removed from the flat terrain and get a sense of the "deep time" required for such changes. In our landscape, a similar scale of erosion is implied by "monadnocks," the single mountains that stand above a surrounding plain.

The Connecticut River meanders through a nearly flat section of floodplain at Maidstone, Vermont, and Northumberland, New Hampshire.

Mount Monadnock, (elevation 3,165 ft.) the namesake for this land form in Jaffrey, New Hampshire—along with the peaks of the region's other monadnocks found in Lemington, Stratton and Windsor, Vermont, and in Orange and Sunapee, New Hampshire—are mountains made of resistant rock types that were left standing high as less resistant rocks around them were removed by erosion. Mt. Ascutney, the tallest peak closest to the river, in Windsor, may have originated as a volcano.

The Green Mountains of Vermont and the White Mountains of New Hampshire are the remnants of very ancient mountain ranges that once were several times their present height but have been worn down over millions of years. Bedrock is visible atop mountains and hills, and in road cuts made for highways. A quarry high on a hill above Lebanon Airport has exposed bedrock now visible for miles.

The river and its tributaries continue to erode our landscape. Riverbeds wander within their valleys as currents cut new channels and leave old ones dry. Moving water removes material from one place and deposits it in another, sometimes to the dismay of those holding deeds to the land through which it moves.

QUARRIES, MINES & MINERALS

Very old granite, marble, slate and shale throughout the river valley have been a source of raw materials for buildings, bridges, and street paving. A number of quarries are still actively mined.

Local industries sprang up around deposits of such resources as copper, in eastern Orange County, and talc, in Chester, Vermont and at Cottonstone Mountain in Orford, New Hampshire. Precious metals and minerals have been found in such places

Mount Ascutney, a monadnock, dominates river views from Bellows Falls to Fairlee.

as Ruggles Mine, Grafton, Vermont (pegmatite, including mica, quartz and feldspar, and uranium minerals), the Surry Mountain Gold Mine, Surry, New Hampshire (mica, copper, lead, silver and gold), and silver mines along the Ammonoosuc River. *(For more on the region's mining industry, see Industry & Commerce.)*

Springs of naturally-occurring mineral waters drew Native Americans to a place in present-day Brunswick, Vermont, where European immigrants later erected a series of resort hotels.

GLACIERS

The summit of Mt. Monadnock east of Keene, New Hampshire, and other high elevation bedrock deposits exhibit deep grooves and scratches made by harder rocks carried along by glaciers. "Sheepback" mountain profiles were produced when enormous ice masses scraped the northwest slopes of hilltops into gentle inclines, and broke off their southeast faces to form abrupt profiles that are said to resemble the backs or faces of sheep. Examples are Holt's Ledge in Lyme, New Hampshire, the Palisades in Fairlee, Vermont, and in Carroll, New Hampshire.

As it advanced, the ice plucked and carried along vast quantities of loose stones and debris. Today this jumbled glacial sediment, or "till," lies beneath

Glacial erratics, such as the "Tipping Rock" in Lebanon, New Hampshire, are souvenirs of the glacier's visit to the Connecticut River Valley.

much of our soil at elevations above floodplains. Farmers gathered up these rocks and set them into miles and miles of stone walls. Boulders and stones transported by glaciers to areas of different underlying rock are called glacial erratics. Some of them are startlingly large.

In every part of the Connecticut River Valley between Vermont and New Hampshire, there are landscape features that recall the torrential meltwater that moved and deposited glacial debris for several thousand years. Eroded material held in suspension in raging tributaries eventually settled out, forming winding continuous ridges known as eskers that once filled tunnels in a glacier, and flat kame and delta terraces. Good examples of these occur in Walpole and Westmoreland, New Hampshire.

These land forms are composed of sand and gravel, revealed when the resources are extracted from pits for road and construction projects. Many examples exist along the White River near Royalton, Vermont. Sand banks tower eighty feet above the river in Brunswick, Vermont. When located deep in the ground, these deposits are important storage areas for water supplies, and are known as aquifers.

The quiet bottoms of glacial waters filled up with clay. Some clay deposits are now revealed in slopes high above valley floors. Other clays from Lake Hitchcock are several hundred feet thick underground, presenting a challenge to present-day well drillers who must penetrate this layer fully to reach water below the clay. Some clay deposits were well suited to the local manufacture of bricks.

THE LEGACY OF LAKE HITCHCOCK

Among the most visible fingerprints of glacial Lake Hitchcock are the many level terraces that border the river and its major tributaries. They represent previous elevations of the lake. Many farms along the riverbanks occupy low-elevation floodplain terraces that are flat, fertile, and well-drained. Many settlements—such as Bellows Falls, Springfield and

The river visits floodplain farmlands in this early 1900s view of Orford, New Hampshire, with the village of Fairlee, Vermont, in the foreground.

places as Haverhill, New Hampshire, and Newbury, Vermont, were employed for agriculture first by Native Americans and then by European settlers. As development pressure, market competition, tax woes, and other challenges buffet farmers today, agriculture is retreating to its home range on the finest soils. Especially in New Hampshire, this is the fertile floodplain of the Connecticut River.

St. Johnsbury, Vermont, and Orford, New Hampshire—are squeezed onto terraces of differing elevations, their neighborhoods linked by steep, winding roads.

Prodigious quantities of fast-moving glacial meltwater, coursing for thousands of years, sculpted riverbed outcrops into sinuous shapes and drilled round holes in soft bedrock with harder stones. These "potholes" are visible all over the watershed at waterfalls and cascades.

A large and dramatic relic of Lake Hitchcock is Quechee Gorge, in Hartford, Vermont. The last glacier and lake waters filled the Ottauquechee River's pre-glacial channel with sediment. When Lake Hitchcock drained, the Ottauquechee cut a new channel and carved the present gorge down through some 150 feet of rock in a relatively short period of time.

Floodplain Soils

When the climate stabilized after the glacial period, decayed vegetation slowly improved soil quality. Periodic flooding built up deep deposits of fertile loam in low-lying areas of the river valley. Particularly abundant and rich floodplain soils in such

❀ Threats ❀

Although the northern valley appears environmentally healthy, the Connecticut River and its tributaries are threatened by:

Water Pollution

Our water supplies, both in surface waterways and in the underground aquifers we tap for our drinking water, can be too easily compromised by pollution.

Fuel storage in the floodplain has long been a threat to water quality. Wells River, Vermont, 1927.

It comes from solid waste landfills, illegal trash dumps, industrial sources, leaking underground fuel tanks, failed or poorly sited septic systems, insufficiently treated sewage effluent, storm sewer runoff containing petrochemicals from roadways and parking lots, and farm and residential runoff containing animal wastes, herbicides, and pesticides. Some pollutants still present in the river's sediments are the consequence of long-gone industries and land uses.

AIR POLLUTION

While some of our air pollution is brought by prevailing winds from sources in the Midwest, we also create our own in New England with automobile and truck exhausts, incinerators, and smokestack industries. Reaching even the pristine headwater ponds and streams of our watershed are particles which create sulfuric and nitric acids, and deliver poisonous mercury and lead.

EROSION

Erosion is a natural river process, but poor forestry and farming practices, stream bank clearing, and establishment of lawns to the water's edge result in diminished soils and silted waterways, and exaggerate the process.

Riverbanks that have lost their natural vegetation are especially vulnerable to erosion.

In March, 1927, more buildings were within reach of the river than the citizens of Wells River, Vermont, had previously realized.

DEVELOPMENT

Ill-considered development unnecessarily destroys riparian areas and wetlands that are important for both human and wildlife habitat and contributes to water quality problems for us all. Construction of impervious surfaces changes drainage patterns and rushes the movement of water through the basin, raising the specter of flooding and erosion. The market value of fieldstone for home landscaping leads to disappearance of the stone walls that record more than two centuries of agricultural history.

COMPETITION FOR WATER SUPPLIES

Amazing as it might seem in a part of the country known for its moist climate, the day may come when there are too many competing demands on the natural supply of water flowing through the basin. Municipal water suppliers, farm irrigation systems, industry, domestic wells, golf courses, and the home lawn sprinkler all require water that is drawn directly from rivers, aquifers, or associated reservoirs. Elsewhere in New England, this thirsty combination has at times been enough to drain a riverbed dry. Droughts associated with global warming threaten to bring this problem into sharper focus in the future.

✾ Actions & Activities ✾

The natural landscape we inherit includes the resources essential to human life—air, water, forests, and soil. The natural landscape is the foundation of our economy, providing the physical basis for manufacturing and food production, and an environment whose quality-of-life values sustain liveable communities and employment opportunities.

It is important for communities to take inventory of their natural resources and to develop plans on the local and regional level that balance resource protection with farming, logging, and residential and commercial development.

Look into Local and Regional Planning

A great deal of information already gathered may serve as the foundation or model for local resource protection.

• The Connecticut River Joint Commissions (CRJC) worked with more than 100 citizens over five years to create the *Connecticut River Corridor Management Plan* in 1997. The *Plan* identifies important resources, problems and threats, and offers many solutions. Obtain a copy of the *Plan* and hold a discussion in conjunction with the local river subcommittee in your area.

• Consult your regional planning commission and your town office to learn if and how waterways are protected by zoning in your town. Does your town allow building in a floodplain? How far must buildings be set back from a river's edge to protect them from erosion?

Explore

• Climb to a high mountain top or scenic overlook—or charter a flight in a small plane!—and survey our physical landscape from a high elevation.

• Visit natural history museums such as the Montshire Museum of Natural Science, Norwich, Vermont; the Fairbanks Museum, St. Johnsbury, Vermont; and the Nature Museum at Grafton, Vermont.

• Explore a stone wall in your town. Find out when the property it bounds was settled, who cared for it, and how they might have used the land. Who might have built the wall, and when? Read Robert Frost's "Mending Wall."

• Visit a quarry or mine. Compare different rocks and soils exposed in embankments cut away for highways and roads.

• Check out the visitor centers at hydropower dams at Moore Station in Littleton, New Hampshire, and Wilder, Bellows Falls, and Vernon, Vermont.

• Embark on one of the many adventures detailed in *Valley Quest: Adventures in the Upper Valley.* Contact Vital Communities of the Upper Valley for a copy of its guide to these educational treasure hunts. Among them is the Ely Copper Mine Quest.

The river at work in Vernon, Vermont.

Participate

• Join or lead a clean-up effort for your waterway.

• Attend meetings of your local conservation commission, or help your town create one if it doesn't exist.

• Join the Connecticut River Watershed Council, a membership advocacy organization active in all four states of the river's watershed.

• Get involved with a grassroots organization for the tributary nearest you. If one does not exist, consider starting one with the help of your regional planning commission and CRJC.

• Contact a land trust in your region to find out what it's doing to preserve natural resources and prime agricultural soils by purchasing development rights from willing private property owners.

• Learn about easements, which are legal agreements with willing private property owners that protect land or historic buildings while permitting continued use and some kinds of development.

Make a Map

• Compare road maps and U.S. Geologic Survey maps of the area where you live, to see how water and roads both move in relation to topography. Build a papier-mache relief map of your area.

• Map the ancient shoreline of Lake Hitchcock and imagine how the setting of your community might have looked during its time.

Wonder about Water

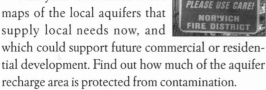

• Talk with well drillers about where and how deep they find water aquifers.

• Visit your town office to see maps of the local aquifers that supply local needs now, and which could support future commercial or residential development. Find out how much of the aquifer recharge area is protected from contamination.

• Talk with your town officials to see if they have considered a well-head protection program. State grants may be available to help.

• Invite a weather historian or meteorologist to speak to your local group.

• Learn how to monitor for water quality, and start a monitoring effort if there isn't one already underway on your nearby stream.

• Help keep storm drainage clean—seek your town's approval to stencil storm drains to show that they lead to waterways.

Volunteers remind others not to discard pollutants down storm drains, which lead to waterways.

Take Care of Your Home Property

• Be sure your home septic system is regularly maintained.

• Manage the movement of water over your land, to slow it down and soak it up. Keep paved areas to a minimum.

• Avoid mowing your lawn to the water's edge. Allow riparian buffers of native vegetation to remain along waterways.

• Consider naturalized landscaping, which often needs less water than exotic plants.

Vegetation on the riverbank (far left and right) keeps lawn chemicals and sediment from reaching the river.

❀ Q & A ❀

• What is your watershed address? Is your community located directly on the Connecticut River or do you live near one of its tributaries? Can you identify all the tributaries between your home and the Connecticut? If they're not all named, imagine appropriate names.

• How many miles are you—by water—from Long Island Sound? How far are you from the headwaters of the Connecticut? How many feet above sea level is the Connecticut River or tributary nearest you?

• What is the average daily volume of the river or tributary where you live? Consult the web page www.crjc.org/riverflow.htm for links to monitoring gauges on the river nearest you.

• Each tributary, down to the smallest brook, has its own watershed. Map the sub-watershed you live in, and those where you work or go to school. How many different watersheds do you move through in a typical day?

• Explore your home landscape to see how water moves through it on a rainy summer day. Compare this to how meltwater moves during the spring thaw, when the ground is still frozen. Does the water leaving your property end up in a stream or in a storm sewer? Where does the storm sewer lead?

• How many signs of glacial activity can you see where you live? Do you live where sediments built up, or where they were eroded?

❀ FYI ❀

GENERAL INTEREST READING

Dinosaurs, Dunes and Drifting Continents: the Geology of the Connecticut River Valley by Richard D. Little, Earth View Publications, Easthampton, MA., 2003. (Amply illustrated with over 100 pictures, maps, and diagrams; interesting descriptions of continental drift, glacial features, and Lake Hitchcock.)

The Granite Landscape: A Natural History of America's Mountain Domes, from Acadia to Yosemite by Tom Wessels, Brian D. Cohen, The Countrymen Press, Woodstock, VT, 2001.

A Guide to New England's Landscape by Neil Jorgensen, Globe Pequot Press, Chester, CT, 1977. (Good general overview of New England geology.)

Roadside Geology of Vermont and New Hampshire by Bradford B. Van Diver, Montana Mountain Press Publishing Co., Missoula, MT, 1987. (Relates landscape development through roadside evidence.)

Vermont's Land and Resources by Harold A. Meeks, The New England Press, Shelburne, VT, 1986. (A basic geography demonstrating the impact of natural resources on culture.)

WATER QUALITY

The Challenge of Erosion in the Connecticut River Watershed, Connecticut River Joint Commissions, Charlestown, NH, 1998. (Series of illustrated fact sheets covering river

Land clearing and water withdrawals upstream can deepen the effects of a drought

dynamics, bank stabilization methods, and how to get a permit for work on the riverbank.)

A Citizen's Guide to River Monitoring in the Connecticut River Valley by Geoff Dates, Connecticut River Joint Commissions, Charlestown, NH, 1995. (User-friendly guide to help people establish long-term, community-based, and scientifically credible river monitoring programs in the valley.)

A Homeowner's Guide to Nonpoint Source Pollution, Connecticut River Joint Commissions, Charlestown, NH, 1998. (Illustrated, easy to read booklet covering a variety of pollution prevention actions for the homeowner.)

The Watershed Guide to Cleaner Rivers, Lakes and Streams: Actions You Can Take to Control Nonpoint Source Pollution by Brian Kent, Connecticut River Joint Commissions, Charlestown, NH, 1995. (Illustrated booklet for town officials, developers, and landowners.)

Technicians take samples of sediments from the Connecticut River at Haverhill, NH, for an EPA study.

INVENTORY & MANAGEMENT

Along the Northern Connecticut River: An Inventory of Significant In-Stream Features, Connecticut River Joint Commissions, Charlestown, NH, 1994. (Copies of this limited printing have been provided to each regional planning commission and riverfront town.)

Best Management Practices to Control Nonpoint Source Pollution: A Guide for Citizens and Town Officials, NH Department of Environmental Services, Concord, NH, 1997.

Connecticut River Corridor Management Plan edited by Sharon F. Francis, Adair D. Mulligan, Connecticut River Joint Commissions, Charlestown, NH, 1997. (Prepared under the auspices of the New Hampshire Rivers Management and Protection Act, RSA 483, following five years of citizen-based planning along the river in NH and VT. Copies available for review in local libraries and town offices. *Volume I*: Riverwide Overview covers river issues and CRJC recommendations based on the findings of the five local river subcommittees. Includes summaries of each of the five subcommittees' plans. *Volumes II-VI*: Complete plans prepared by the five local river subcommittees.)

Instream Flow Uses, Values, and Policies in the Upper Connecticut River Watershed by Kathy Fallon Lambert, Connecticut River Joint Commissions, Charlestown, NH, 1998. (Analysis of federal and state policies and river uses includes recommendations for river management. Oriented toward a professional audience.)

Vermont Rivers Study, Vermont Agency of Environmental Conservation, with the assistance of the National Park Service, Waterbury, VT, 1986.

GOOD LINKS

American Rivers Toolkits for River Conservation: www.Americanrivers.org/toolkits/default.htm

Connecticut River Education Initiative: www.wgby.org/edu/crei/index.html *(A broad spectrum of educational resources inspired by the study of the four-state Connecticut River watershed.)*

The Connecticut River Homepage: www.bio.umass.edu/biology/conn.river/ *(An interesting web site with information about geology and natural history.)*

Connecticut River Joint Commissions page on river flow: www.crjc.org/riverflow.htm

CHAPTER TWO

Natural Communities

The Wild Things

Draped over the bedrock bones of the Connecticut River valley is a rich and many-textured blanket of life. From the summits and slopes of our tallest mountains, through the sheltered creases of their shoulders, to the deeper soils of their valley floors, this layer of life has many moods and many manifestations. It is the natural heritage of the humans who later came to occupy a place within this valley.

❊ The Basic Story ❊

WE can speak of "natural communities" as well as we can of human ones. Picture a scene in a northern hardwoods forest, a community we know well for its maple, beech, and birch, its deer, bear, and perhaps, if we remember to look up, a broad-winged hawk. Beechnuts feed the bear, deer browse the birch, and the hawk hunts from high in the forest canopy. With our limited vision, we often miss equally vital members of the community—the voles and mice that feed the hawk, the insects that feed the voles, the tiny plants and animals that feed the insects, and, perhaps most important and least noticed, the bacteria and fungi which recycle remains of the rest into raw material for another round of life. Each is a community, because the lives of its mem-

A ribbon of water in Whitefield, New Hampshire, mirrors the snow-covered firs beside it.

Pink Ladyslippers—more than meets the eye. These native orchids depend upon the presence of a particular fungus in the soil.

bers are interwoven with each other, as surely as a human community depends upon its parents, children, teachers, farmers, workers, leaders, and those filling countless other roles.

Unlike human communities, natural communities are closely shaped by factors beyond their control. Soil—how deep, how fertile, how sweet or sour, how stony. Temperature—how high and how low it hovers above or below that magical degree, the freezing point of water which fills the cells of all living things. Moisture—how much, what form, when and how it arrives, how long it lingers, and, these days, what it brings with it from the sky. All life forms have adapted over millennia to specific roles or niches within this environment. The assemblage of creatures we encounter in this northern hardwood forest, or at a calcium-rich riverside seep, or in a cold, acid bog, are those best adapted for life in that particular place.

The richest, most biologically diverse of these communities centers on the edge between water and land. The riparian environment provides elements of home, or habitat, for both land and water based creatures, from mink to great blue heron, newt to minnow. A turtle may spend most of its life in water, but must travel over land far enough to prepare a nest to provide for the next generation. Nutrients sustaining aquatic insects which feed frogs come from decomposing leaves falling into the water from trees on the streambank. Plant life is most diverse here at the water's edge, from those rooted or free-floating in the shallows to plants anchoring the soil above.

The Connecticut River watershed is the home of spectacular diversity in these assemblages of life, these natural communities. From the summits of the Green and White Mountains, to the wetlands, ponds, forests, streams, and ultimately to the great river itself, the watershed supports a depth and breadth of life that prompted its designation as a singular national fish and wildlife refuge. In 1991, Congress authorized the U.S. Fish and Wildlife Service to initiate a study of the entire watershed. This effort resulted in the creation of the Silvio O. Conte National Fish and Wildlife Refuge, a step into a new age of landscape scale conservation that encourages private stewardship as well as judicious conservation measures by state and federal agencies.

Ecology is a science that seems to have no end. Research into the private lives of species as familiar as a toad or a maple continues to reveal connections and inter-dependencies that make the phrase "web of life" seem woefully inadequate. A century ago, we might have guessed that deep green

Boreal forest surrounds Second Connecticut Lake.

Heading home.

foliage on a spruce might mean it enjoyed enough sun and liked the soil around its feet. Now we know that it also means the spruce budworm hasn't been by for some time, and suspect that the soil is well buffered or rainfall has not been acid enough here to leach much calcium out of the soil.

Contributing to the diversity of life in the northern Connecticut River Valley is its seasonal role as international flyway, host to visiting birds who breed in our forests and fields, and flee south to escape the challenging winters. Following the great river back north, spring migrants rest and feed in riverside forests more welcoming than surrounding uplands, while winter holds tight for a few more weeks. As spring proceeds, birds disperse to establish breeding territories and raise their young. In fall, they retreat once more, draining down the valley like an ebb tide, announced most boldly by the skeins of Canada geese using the Connecticut as their compass.

Beneath the surface of the waters, a similar migration occurs, as fish returning from the sea move up the river and into its tributaries to spawn. The Connecticut River was once home to a run of American shad, blueback herring, shortnose sturgeon, and especially Atlantic salmon that fed the Abenaki and their European successors. In 1790, the first of many dams blocked this migration at Turner's Falls and initiated a series of human-induced perils to migrating fish.

European colonization pecked more holes in the fabric of the valley's natural communities, as settlers decided which creatures at the top of the food chain could stay, and which should go. They exterminated the Eastern gray wolf, catamount, and timber rattlesnake from the northern watershed. Lacking the Abenakis' well-honed understanding of habitat needs and wildlife population dynamics, European newcomers and their successors also pursued the beaver, turkey, the Sunapee golden trout, and the continent's most abundant bird, the passenger pigeon, into history, and nearly did in the moose, common loon, Canada lynx, and spruce grouse while they were at it. The effects of these deletions upon less prominent animals and plants went largely unnoticed.

By the 20th century, human communities had spread across the landscape and acquired an arsenal of poisons that turned the Connecticut and many tributaries into a dangerous stew that ran a different color each day. A 1951 study found some parts of the northern river were too polluted even for industrial use. Bald eagles, peregrine falcons, and other raptors disappeared as chemical poisons interfered with their ability to raise

Seven-week-old bald eagle chick in its nest.

young. Hitchhikers from the Old World, such as the parasitic brown-headed cowbird and equally aggressive plants, elbowed aside their native counterparts.

Recent years have seen an astounding shift from the last two-and-a-half centuries, partly the result of better human understanding and decision-making, and partly by pure luck. The Clean Water Act of 1972 began the process of returning rivers and streams to its "fishable, swimmable" goal, improving these waters for human use and also for the thousands of other creatures with equal claim to them. Passage for fish opened around several key dams. Some of the most noxious poisons were outlawed, setting the stage for recovery of birds of prey.

Turkey and beaver returned, more or less with the assistance of wildlife biologists, and a concerted effort at management allowed moose to return from Canada and Maine. Farmers and forest landowners, those working most closely with the land, became more aware of the role they could play in sharing it with other species, and society has begun to place a higher value on intact natural communities. The great tradition of natural resource conservation has strong roots in the northern valley, where it continues to grow, parcel by parcel, landowner by landowner, and town by town.

So here we are, one species among many enfolded within the northern Connecticut River Valley. The traditions of fishing, hunting, and annual deer camp—and mosquitoes and black flies—are part of our cultural landscape, along with the abiding pleasure of wildlife watching, tracking, birding, and discovering a wildflower. Exploration of the natural world is one of the great and endless joys of living here.

❧ Resources & Revelations ❧

ANIMAL LIFE

Beneath the Surface

The upper basin of the Connecticut offers hundreds of miles of aquatic habitat, from steep, stony brooks and fast-falling streams to the wide and often slow-moving sandy- and silty-bottomed mainstem itself. The tiny creatures which support larger life in and near the river are equally diverse. The native brook trout was originally the feature fish of this cold- and

The Connecticut River as it leaves Fourth Lake near the Canadian border.

cool-water river system, with thirty-two others and a handful of species of anadromous, or sea-run fish. At the river's source, the Connecticut Lakes provide fine, deep habitat for a renowned fishery of landlocked salmon and lake trout, while free-flowing stretches of the northern river are prime brook, brown, and rainbow trout water. Today, the river and many of its tributaries harbor many warm-water fish as well, after accidental and intentional introductions delivered the fish to vastly expanded warm-water habitat behind newly created dams. The Connecticut River now offers perhaps the most highly varied habitat of any water body in either state.

Resident Fish

Brook trout, once said to average 22 inches in length, tipped the scales at 15 pounds in Lake Sunapee in the late 1600s, and were historically much more common in our region than they are today. Salmon and sculpin joined trout in mountainous tributary streams. Lake trout, whose distribution had much to do with the vagaries of glacial melting, are native to only eight New Hampshire lakes, including First and Second Connecticut Lakes, and South Pond in Stark. Pickerel, yellow perch, sunfish, and horned pout, denizens of warmer water, were present in at least the southern New Hampshire/Vermont portion of the Connecticut River in early times.

Over-fishing of brook trout during their fall spawning runs led to a decline in the 1800s that prompted fishermen to introduce new fish to supplement the trout population, especially pickerel, which could be easily caught through the ice in winter. The brookie, along with its equally beautiful relative, the Sunapee golden trout, later gave way to introduced Chinook salmon and other fish in Lake Sunapee.

It seems that anyone with an empty creel was a fisheries biologist at the time. At Martin Meadow Pond in Lancaster, pickerel were likely stocked as early as 1828. The yellow perch and horned pout arrived the same way. Similar stories come from Lower Baker Pond in Orford and others, where brook trout gave way to the new competition, eventually forcing the state to resort to raising trout in hatcheries. Brown and rainbow trout were introduced to provide a sport fishery as native trout declined. Brook trout are now the focus of management efforts to protect wild populations where they persist in the north country.

An internationally recognized fish culture business, Cold Spring Trout Ponds, was started in Charlestown, New Hampshire, in 1866 by Livingston Stone, whose branch operation in New Brunswick became the largest salmon breeding operation in the world. He left the Charlestown operation to a well regarded scientist, Frances W. Webber. She and Stone exported shad and other Eastern fish to California, and Stone sent millions of Pacific salmon eggs back to Cold Spring Trout Ponds for rearing and distribution to Atlantic rivers.

Other relative newcomers are the largemouth and smallmouth bass, the largest members of the sunfish family. Both were introduced and now support an active, managed sport fishery. Bass nest in spring in shallow bays and sandy bottomed areas, moving to deeper water as the season progresses.

The first smallmouth bass arrived by mistake when flooding of Cold Spring Trout Ponds in 1867 allowed transplanted Lake Champlain fish to wash into the river. Bass also moved down the Sugar River from Lake Sunapee, where they were introduced by the State of New Hampshire. Northern pike reached the Connecticut River during a flood in 1840, when ponds in Ludlow and Plymouth, harboring fish brought from Lake Champlain, overflowed into the Black River. There are now 142 different species of non-native fish in the watershed.

The streams of yesterday were different waters, not only because they ran free and contained none of the non-native species added by stocking or accidental release over the years. The watershed's old-growth forests were likely much more effective at capturing and slowly releasing both water and nutrients than the smaller, second-growth forests and cleared fields that followed, and maintained a steadier, higher flow than we see today. Streams draining such multi-layered forests and thick blan-

Biologists survey stream habitats to evaluate their suitability for trout and other fish.

kets of decomposing material were much less likely
to flash and wither, or to warm up enough to
threaten trout. Such forests also added large woody
debris to streams, providing better cover.

*Atlantic salmon "parr," with the distinctive markings of
this life stage (2–6 inches in length, less than 1–2 years
old), before it becomes a "smolt" ready to enter saltwater.*

Anadromous Fish

Until 1790, when they finally met an obstacle they
couldn't jump, Atlantic salmon once ran the river for
all but 30 of its 410 miles, from its mouth to Beecher
Falls near Canada and into the Ammonoosuc system almost to Crawford Notch, returning to spawn
in their natal streams after roaming the open ocean.
Spawning salmon at the time ranged from 8 to 12
pounds, with some reported at 35 to 40 pounds. The
crash of the salmon fishery after construction of the
Turner's Falls dam prompted an early but unsuccess-
ful restoration effort in the 1800s.

In the 1960s, federal and state wildlife officials
set out anew to restore anadromous fish to the Connecticut and other Eastern rivers by requiring fish
passages at dams and by cleaning up pollutants.
American and gizzard shad and blueback herring
responded well, with numbers of returning fish increasing ten to fifteen fold, but the recovery has a
long way to go, most especially for salmon.

The Atlantic salmon restoration effort, led by the
Connecticut River Atlantic Salmon Commission,
has been a long and heroic one. It faces challenges

both from the need to genetically recreate a fish tha$
can "remember" the Connecticut River and its hom$
stream while it is at sea, and the unpredictability o$
that ocean environment. Most returning fish are captured at the Holyoke Dam in Massachusetts fo$
breeding, and a few are released to continue upstream, where they have appeared as far as th$
Ammonoosuc River. Spawning runs last from mid-
April to mid-June. This movement of fish from th$
open ocean back to the freshwater stream may be a$
important natural conveyor belt for minerals an$
nutrients from the ocean to the upland ecosystem.

Fish ladders at the dams at Vernon, Bellow$
Falls, and Wilder are part of this attempt to reintroduce salmon to the upper watershed. Fish can now
pass up (and down) stream as far as the foot of th$
Dodge Falls Dam at Ryegate, 270 miles from the sea
although American shad still stop at Bellows Falls
the historic upstream limit of their range. Recogniz-
ing the benefit of providing free run of the river system for resident as well as sea-run fish, bot$
Vermont and New Hampshire are now looking
closely at removing smaller obstacles in the basin
either by demolishing obsolete dams or by restoring fish passage around them.

Other Aquatic Life

Fish, of course, are the most obvious creatures i$
the water food web, but many more often escap$
notice. Some are microscopic, others are small animals without backbones such as crayfish and insects. Aquatic macro invertebrates, "fish food" t$
some, are indicators of water quality to others. Scientists have learned that they can sample the natu-

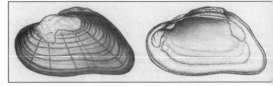

*The Connecticut River hosts one of the largest surviving
populations of the federally endangered dwarf
wedgemussel. Shown approximately life-size.*

ral community of a stream bottom to learn about the quality of the water and sediment in which these animals live.

The dwarf wedgemussel is a tiny mussel which once lived in fifteen major river basins from North Carolina to New Brunswick. Damming and channelization eliminated much of its former habitat and many of the fish, including the Atlantic salmon, upon which it depends for a part of its life cycle. The mussel is now endangered, surviving in a small portion of its former range, including parts of the mainstem and in the Ashuelot River. An important water quality indicator, the mussel is more sensitive to heavy metals and pollutants than commonly tested fish and aquatic insects. Other rare mussels include the brook floater in the West River and the yellow lampmussel in the mainstem.

Insects

At least one town in the northern valley asserts its in-

Above, home of the official Town Beetle of Plainfield.

sect sensitivity and stewardship: Plainfield, New Hampshire has adopted the Cobblestone Tiger Beetle as its official town beetle. This threatened insect, known to exist in only five places in the entire four-state watershed, lives among cobblestones and patches of sand at the upstream end of cobble islands in the river, a lively location which receives the full brunt of ice scour and flooding.

Amphibians and Reptiles

Silent dwellers of mostly moist places throughout the year, the valley's amphibians come audibly to life in spring, when their chorus reassures the rest of the world that summer will indeed return. The most valuable but ephemeral habitat for such creatures is

The marbled salamander, a handsome creature considered endangered in our northern region.

the vernal pool, a forested pond that exists only for this part of the year. Salamanders and frogs breed there, without fear of fish predation.

Some 20 species of salamanders, newts, toads, and frogs round out the northern valley's amphibian roster. Among reptiles, five species of turtles, some more secretive than others, and almost a dozen of snakes frequent shorelines to wooded uplands. Spotted turtles, for example, require loose, sandy soils in open uplands for nesting, but spend most of their time in wetlands. Timber rattlers were last seen in the valley on the sunny ledges of Mt. Wantastiquet.

Birds

A superhighway for birds as well as humans, the Connecticut River provides four hundred miles of north-south migration corridor. Waterfowl find a smorgasbord of resting and feeding habitat in the "setbacks," or marshy shallows, along the mainstem, at the mouths of tributaries, and in nearby ponds and wetlands. Impoundment of the river has created more of this valuable habitat.

Retreat Meadows, at the mouth of the West River in Brattleboro, is good for 400 Canada geese and 60 black ducks in a glance. Across the river in Hinsdale, hooded mergansers appear on their way south, and Sora rail breed at marshes in Westminster. Herrick's Cove, at the mouth of the Williams River, is a Vermont Important Bird Area. This 100-acre site, owned by the hydropower company, has a bird list of 221 species, including waterfowl, black tern, shorebirds, and marsh

Male wood duck, a cavity-nesting bird.

birds such as rails, American bittern, and herons. The company's Great Meadow in Charlestown is another key stop for thousands of birds on the move. The Ompompanoosuc River flats, just upstream from the mainstem, are a fine place to view migrating shorebirds, including dunlin, sandpipers, and snipe.

State and locally protected river setbacks clustered at the Wilder Wildlife Management Area and the mouth of Grant Brook in Lyme, Fairlee Marsh, and Reeds Marsh in Orford provide wonderful waterfowl and wildlife watching. Snow geese gather in riverside fields on their way from their northern breeding grounds. Other key waterfowl areas include the Connecticut Lakes, Moore and Comerford reservoirs, and the Audubon Society of New Hampshire's Pondicherry Refuge in Whitefield.

Thousands of smaller land birds also use the Connecticut as a migration corridor on flights from neo-tropical wintering grounds to breeding territories throughout the valley. Relying upon riverside forests as stopover resting habitat before dispersing into the surrounding uplands, these birds' ultimate destinations range from high elevation spruce forests to alder swamps or even our back yards. The Connecticut River Birding Trail, a series of publicly accessible sites for observing birds and other wildlife, recommends Hurricane Forest in Hartford,

Vermont, Bedell Bridge State Park in Haverhill, New Hampshire, and North Springfield Lake in Springfield, Vermont. Lebanon's Boston Lot Lake is another favorite. Migrating warblers visiting Windsor, Vermont's 220 acres of diverse habitat at Lake Runnymede and Paradise Park, are among 100 species recorded there.

For those declining in population, like warblers that require unbroken expanses of forest for nesting, the protection of some 8,000 forested acres surrounding Moore and Comerford reservoirs is a welcome result of an updated license for the nearby hydroelectric facilities. Farm abandonment means shrinking habitat for some grassland birds such as the bobolink and Eastern meadowlark. The Eastern bluebird may never be as common as it was a century ago, when the more open landscape better suited its nesting habits, but seems to be holding on well in the watershed. The constellation of resident birds has shifted in recent years, as climate moderation and perhaps the popularity of backyard bird feeding have tempted south-

Shallow, marshy "setbacks" on the Connecticut River mainstem and its tributaries, like this one in Thetford, Vermont, welcome migrating waterfowl.

Wild turkeys have something to strut about after such an impressive population rebound.

ern birds such as the tufted titmouse and cardinal to remain over the winter in northern latitudes.

There are few visions as arresting as a flock of wild turkeys haunting a misty field. As recently as 1990, this was a rare sight indeed, and only in Cheshire and Windham counties. Following release of 25 Pennsylvania birds in 1970, turkey populations have grown to 22,000 birds in New Hampshire alone. An excellent place to see wild turkeys and woodcock is Surry Mountain Lake on the Ashuelot River.

The Fairbanks Museum in St. Johnsbury, Vermont, exhibits comprehensive collections of northern New England's birds and wildlife, and Weeks State Park in Lancaster, New Hampshire, has a spectacular Victorian era collection of mounted birds. The Meriden Bird Club in Plainfield is the oldest bird club in the United States with an established sanctuary, offering trails through a forest of sizeable trees, hosting warblers, scarlet tanagers, and orioles.

Birds of Prey

The return of raptors to the Connecticut River Valley is yet another success story. While all owls and hawks suffered in the 1950s and 1960s from pesticide contamination, none were so noticeably diminished as the bald eagle and peregrine falcon, and both were listed as federally endangered. They have recovered enough to warrant changes in this listing, but the states still consider them endangered. The bald eagle, which disappeared entirely from our area half a century ago, now winters near dams where open water promises good fishing, and a pair has begun nesting on the mainstem near Hinsdale.

The peregrine falcon, also long absent, now soars above a dozen cliff-face eyries in the northern valley. Banding studies show that the Connecticut River indeed serves as a dispersal route. Birds hatched at Devil's Slide near the Upper Ammonoosuc River in Stark, New Hampshire, for example, have later appeared tending chicks downriver at Barnet Mountain, Sawyer Mountain in Fairlee, and Holt's Ledge in Lyme. A falcon eyrie at the Palisades is easily viewed from the village of Fairlee.

Adult female peregrine falcon defends her cliff-face nest.

Volunteer climbers partner with wildlife biologists, like Chris Martin of the Audubon Society of New Hampshire, to visit peregrine falcon nests to band the young before they fledge.

Osprey have returned to the Connecticut Lakes, and to encourage nesting near the rest of the river, platforms with "starter homes" of sticks have been erected. Turkey vultures are back, traveling north in corridors that seem to follow interstate highways. Northern harriers, or marsh hawks, once again hunt and nest in

The Project Osprey partnership seeks to restore breeding ospreys to the Connecticut River Valley by installing new nesting platforms, such as this one in Westmoreland, New Hampshire.

riverside meadows, favoring Stewartstown and Colebrook, New Hampshire.

Hawk-watchers anticipate the fall migration each year in mid-September, especially when strong fronts follow periods of bad weather. Thousands of broad-winged hawks and their kin pass over Putney Mountain, a premier roost for hawk-watchers in the Windmill Hill Nature Reserve. Mount Prospect at Weeks State Park in Lancaster, New Hampshire is another good spot to watch hawks, eagles, falcons, and osprey as they head south.

The common loon once again lifts its haunting call from Third Connecticut Lake in the north to Woodward Pond in Roxbury, New Hampshire, near the Massachusetts border. There are active recovery and research efforts with strong volunteer participation in both states, although New Hampshire seems to offer more suitable habitat than Vermont, where the loon nests at Maidstone Lake and several other ponds.

The Vermont Institute of Natural Science has specialized in introducing people to the lives and spectacular abilities of birds of prey, including eagles, falcons, owls, hawks, vultures and ravens, at its Raptor Center and in public programs throughout the valley.

Mammals

In many rural communities, the tradition of hunting for some of a family's food supply is as strong as it was two centuries ago. While the number of hunting licenses sold in both states has declined in recent years, the lure of fall hunting is well rooted in the valley. Women and men don hunter orange, and children are introduced through hunter safety classes to the lore of woodsmanship. Others prefer watching wildlife, and hunters and watchers both develop skills in tracking. One might shiver in a blind all day for the pleasure of seeing the creatures pass by, or pursue the evidence with a good walk in the woods after a snowfall. There is much to discover either way.

Lacking their primary predators, the wolf and the catamount, deer populations have expanded beyond those of colonial times, although coyotes now prey upon them. Deer often retreat to "yards" under hemlocks when the snow exceeds 18 inches. These are important for winter survival.

Both Indians and settlers depended for food and clothing upon the moose which were once numerous

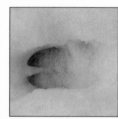

Deer are abundant in woods and field.

in the north. By 1850, unregulated hunting had almost eliminated the half-ton herbivore, and fewer than fifteen moose survived in New Hampshire. The state passed legislation limiting the season in 1875,

but did not enforce it until 1901 for fear of losing tourist dollars. Careful management has brought the population back to 9,600 moose in New Hampshire, where they occasionally stop traffic throughout the watershed, including downtown Lebanon. Legendary among moose-watchers is "Moose Alley," Route 3 north of Second Lake in Pittsburg, New Hampshire.

Habitat protection has also brought back the black bear. This intelligent and social omnivore, which needs room to roam, nevertheless dens near downtown Hanover and has learned to appreciate bird feeders as much as open dumpsters. Increasing numbers of bear interactions have helped their human neighbors to better understand the concept of wildlife travel corridors and the needs of wildlife for space. Interest in high quality bear habitat prompted an ambitious landscape-scale effort in central Vermont, where several towns have been cooperating on the Chateauguay—No Town conservation project. The 1371-acre Rocks Estate in Bethlehem, owned by the Society for Protection of New Hampshire Forests, protects a diverse landscape for bears and other wildlife.

If it could speak, North America's most successful rodent could tell a story of here-one-moment-gone-the-next, and back again. The silky pelt of the beaver was the currency of the northern valley well before settlement. Beaver were trapped out by the time the stockade rose around the Fort at No. 4 in 1743, although their legacy lingered for years in the wetlands they created. Six beaver were released in New Hampshire between 1926 and 1930, and by 1955, the entire region was repopulated. Beavers are back, building luxurious wetlands they share with turtles, herons, and dozens of other species.

Mink were so plentiful in the 1600s that fur traders discarded their skins, and while the population felt the effect of the trap, it persisted, and mink today live near pond and river shores, along with their larger cousin the otter. The fisher, a wide-ranging predator which thrives only in unbroken habitat, declined due to over-trapping, logging, and land conversion but has rebounded. The Audubon Society of New Hampshire's Scotland Brook Wildlife Sanctuary in Sugar Hill is a good place to look for evidence of fisher, bear, and snowshoe hares. The

more secretive pine marten persists in the north country, but is still considered threatened.

In addition to the snowshoe hare of the north, two species of cottontail rabbit live in the valley. The Eastern cottontail, introduced to the Northeast, may be edging out the less common native New England cottontail, which survives in fragmented populations in southwestern New Hampshire near the river.

Of the three cats which once prowled the northern Connecticut River Valley, only the bobcat remains in a strong position. Settlers pursued and presumably extirpated the catamount, or mountain lion, and although reports of sightings or tracks excite people from time to time, clear evidence of a reproducing

Ecologist Susan Morse captured this bear scent-marking a birch tree. The bear has bitten the tree and is now rubbing his scent upon it as a message to other bears.

Beavers—landscape architects with ambition. Here, a series of two dams on the mainstem of a major brook.

population remains to be confirmed. More likely to return from Maine and Canada to its former haunts in the northern valley is the Canada lynx, a superbly adapted predator of the boreal forest.

Also gone but not easily forgotten is the gray wolf. The settlers of southwestern New Hampshire famously set fire to Mount Monadnock to rid their area of remaining wolves, and two centuries later, the discussion over whether to reintroduce this prime predator is swiftly becoming moot, as the animal has recently crossed the St. Lawrence River in Canada and may soon return home. It will take much more than two hundred years for soil and vegetation to return to the summit of Monadnock, if it ever does.

During the wolf's absence, the Eastern coyote moved in to the northern valley. The first verified account of a coyote in New Hampshire was in Grafton County in 1944, and the coyote has been common throughout the watershed since the 1980s. Though coyotes are often mistaken for a domestic dog hybrid, genetic research attributes their larger size and behavioral traits to interbreeding with

Canadian gray wolves. The red fox remains common, the gray fox less so. Dozens of smaller mammals, from shrews to bats and skunks to raccoons, complete the mammal inventory.

Plant Life
Forest History

A deep forest somehow feels timeless, but anyone watching a woodlot over the years knows better. Most of the northern Connecticut River valley forests of today are a shadow of what the Europeans first encountered, but change has always been a constant here.

A hiker descending the slopes of Mount Washington today sees in a single afternoon the parade of plant and animal life she might have witnessed in the valley over the last 11,000 years since the withdrawal of the last glacier, had she been able to sit still that long. At the summit, the land appears bare, until the careful observer notices the lichens, mosses, and tufts of the arctic-adapted grasses and sedges we associate with tundra. Traveling downslope, she encounters tiny wildflowers and small woody plants hugging the ground, which become more diverse as she contin-

A pioneer yellow birch seemingly rooted on rock.

ues through this zone, called krummholz. Stunted spruces and firs appear as she enters the boreal forest, frozen by climate into the territory between 3,000 and 4,800 feet in the White Mountains, although farther north, the boreal forest claims lower elevations. Eventually, she descends to the familiar northern hardwoods forest that occupies the lower slopes of both Mount Washington and much of the northern Connecticut River Valley. This same series of plant communities, and the animals that depended upon them, dispersed north through the valley in the wake of the glacier.

In 18th-century valley forests, venerable two- to four-hundred year old hemlocks, maples, and beeches presided over their progeny. Older openings, particularly old burns, included white and yellow birch. White pines, which cannot tolerate much shade, were especially prominent on sites of past disturbance, and on old floodplain terraces. On warm, south-facing slopes, red oak joined the others, and on cooler, north-facing sites, hemlock abounded, replaced by spruce and balsam fir farther north or at higher elevations. A wild diversity of understory plants, from the sometimes homely yet highly evolved orchids to the brilliant cardinal flower, bloomed where their seeds found a suitable bed.

The woods greeting the European were anything but an unbroken "forest primeval." Openings occurred through the work of wind and weather, and centuries of human activity. Hurricanes and windstorms visited the valley for many thousands of Septembers, uprooting trees and cutting swaths later resown by those left standing, and creating a patchwork of different-aged forests. Ice storms bent and broke the brittle birches. Lightning touched the trees, and so did native insects such as the spruce budworm. Native Americans used fire to open the understory and encourage berry-bearing shrubs, birch and other young browse that would attract deer, grouse, turkeys, and other game.

Nevertheless, the forests encountered by European settlers were impressive by any standard. White pines

up to five feet through and two hundred feet tall were ships' masts with roots, in the eyes of the Crown, and the valley's forests were a naval gold mine. His Majesty had the Abenaki to thank, since the pine often grew in openings made by their fires or on sites of Indian villages abandoned a few centuries before.

In 1770, the site of the Dartmouth College green in Hanover was heavily wooded with enormous white pines, including one felled tree measuring 270 feet. By comparison, Baker Library, which currently towers nearby, is a mere 210 feet to the tip of its pine-decorated weathervane. These old-growth pines did not last long, and the only one on the Green today is that pictured on the college flag. The lone survivor fell in 1895, its stump preserved on the hilltop near the observatory. Timothy Dwight, Yale chronicler of 18th-century New England, lamented, "There is reason to fear that this noblest of all vegetable productions will be unknown in its proper size and splendor to the future inhabitants of New England."

No one was talking about "globalization" a century ago, but its effects were already creeping into our woods. The American chestnut, tall and sturdy, was once a centerpiece of the forest as far north as Lebanon, its wood prized for its durability and its

A tall tree on its way to join the river drive.

seeds sought by both wildlife and people. In 1904 trees in Brooklyn, New York, began to succumb to a fungus arriving on nursery plants imported from Asia. By 1920 the chestnut blight had toppled this species from its former prominence, and only rare stump sprouts struggle to remain.

The American elm, its distinctive vase-like shape once common along streams, fell in a similar story. Farmers sought its rot-resistant wood for fenceposts, although its twisted grain made it difficult to split. In the 1800s elms were widely planted along main streets and commons. The elm bark beetle and a fungus known as Dutch elm disease arrived from Europe around 1930, finding the aging elms an easy mark. Today their standing skeletons still guard some wetlands and host cavity-nesting wildlife. The Dartmouth campus boasts what may be the finest remaining collection of graceful American elms anywhere in the United States, carefully protected by the College.

Plant Communities of Today

Although today some parts of the valley feel wilder and more remote than others, it's been many generations since any large part was truly "wilderness." Few stands of trees have escaped cutting, some many times over. Still, forested land makes up well over 80 percent of the watershed in each state. Today's forests see less of fire and more of the saw than in days past, but they still experience hurricanes, like

the 1938 storm whose evidence still lies in the woods, and ice storms. The 1998 ice storm, which affected 700,000 acres of Vermont forests (18 percent) and 800,000 acres in New Hamp-

Effects of the 1998 ice storm.

shire, may have been the worst on record, but it is neither the first nor the last.

Several thousand species of plants grow in our region, sorting themselves based on growing conditions, disturbance history, and succession. Should our patient imaginary hiker stop to rest in a meadow on the day of its last cutting, she would witness another parade of plants over a lifetime of sitting there. The next few summers, sun-loving goldenrod and asters would bloom in the abandoned field, buzzing with finches while foxes hunted meadow voles. In a few years, she would notice sprouting poplars, pines, birches, or fir, depending upon how far north she was, and these pioneers would be head-high before she'd been there a decade. Deer, or moose farther north, and hare would nibble their buds. In another decade, a tall thicket would confine her view, and little would grow on the forest floor, until a few years later, when she'd notice seedling maples and ferns.

Competition would thin out the pioneer trees, leaving more light for those waiting their chance to leap up from the understory. Sixty years later, our observer would enjoy more wildflowers blooming on the forest floor, more varied birdsong, and glimpses of bear, hawks, and bobcat. By her eightieth anniversary, knee-high hemlocks might be growing on the fallen trunks of birches, ovenbirds and warblers would flit through the woods, and the carpet would include ferns and mosses. At one hundred, our hardy hiker might enjoy

American elms once graced Claremont's Broad Street, as they did many a main street in New England between 1850 and 1960.

the fall-flaming canopy of a maple-birch-beech forest, a barred owl at night for company, and if the beechnuts were especially good, a neighborhood bear sow and cubs. Yet, she would have to live to five hundred or a thousand years more to see the forest fully grown, after the day the hay was last cut.

Forest Communities

Forest types include deciduous, coniferous, boreal, and more, of many descriptions and with varying casts of characters. Vermont biologists recognize twenty-five different kinds of forest types, with almost as many variations, naming them with the few plants whose presence hint that conditions might be right for scores of others to share their stage, such as the Sugar Maple-White Ash-Jack-in-the-pulpit Northern Hardwood Forest.

On south-facing slopes which catch the sun, forests such as at Fort Dummer State Park in the southern Vermont foothills are more like those of Massachusetts and Connecticut than the central or northern parts of the valley. Southern trees such as white, red, and chestnut oaks dominate the woods here, providing food and shelter for gray squirrels, turkeys, and deer. The open understory attracts ruffed grouse.

On the cold northern slopes in Vermont's Northeast Kingdom, spruce-fir forest, with its moist understory of lichens and mosses, dominates the 72,000-acre Nulhegan River basin and its bogs and freshwater wetlands. At least thirteen rare plant and animal species have been recorded here. The Nulhegan basin hosts nesting spruce grouse, loons, hooded mergansers, black, ring-necked and wood ducks, and birds of the deep woods. The Conte Refuge manages this exceptional wildlife habitat in its 26,000 acre Nulhegan Basin Division, and collaborates with owners of adjacent conserved land. Vermont's West Mountain Wildlife Management Area,

where alkaline soils provide buffering for waters in a region assaulted by acid rain, protects high quality black bear feeding areas, vernal pools, and deer wintering habitat.

The spruce grouse of the boreal forest, rarer than its more southern cousin, the ruffed grouse.

In the high elevation home of the Connecticut River, New Hampshire's natural areas around Third and Fourth Lakes, Scotts Bog, and South Bay Bog surround some of the most prized wetlands in the state, habitat for at least a dozen known rare species and natural community types. Pine marten and three-toed woodpecker, which prefer mature spruce-fir forests, are found in few other places.

Between the boreal spruce-fir forests and the southern oak-pine forests lie the northern hardwood forests of sugar maple, white ash, beech, birch, oak, cherry, and others, the particular assemblage depending upon exposure, moisture, and soil. For example, the Fifteen Mile Falls region is right in the transition zone between northern and southern

Thousands of acres of largely unfragmented forested habitat surround Moore Reservoir in Waterford and Littleton, where Moore Dam (lower left) impounds the Connecticut River.

types. Red oak, musclewood, and ironwood are common here but drop out farther north. The glacial till-covered hillsides around Moore Reservoir are northern hardwood forest, leaning heavily to oak on steep slopes along the Vermont shoreline. The influence of the local bedrock results in "rich" forests, or assemblages of plants which require ample nutrients and the soils which supply them. Some unusual forest types grow below Moore Dam on sediments left over from glacial Lake Hitchcock, where the old lake bed was never converted to agriculture or development. Seeps are common along the steep river terrace slopes, especially close to the dam at McIndoe Falls.

Wetland Communities

The northern valley still has a wealth of wetlands, from high elevation mountain tarns to bogs, fens, marshes, wet meadows, and shrub or forested swamps of red maple, black gum, or Atlantic white cedar. Pine Mountain Wildlife Management Area in Groton, Newbury, Ryegate, and Topsham, Vermont protects a white cedar swamp and habitat for black bear, moose, bobcat, coyote, fisher, ruffed grouse, woodcock, white-tailed deer, and brook trout. The Black Gum Swamp, in Vernon, Vermont, features 400-year-old trees thousands of miles north of the center of their range in the southern United States.

The most revered high elevation wetland is the source of the Connecticut River itself—tiny Fourth Lake, just 300 yards from the Canadian border in Pittsburg, New Hampshire, protected by The Nature Conservancy. Other complex wetlands in the river's headwaters, on lands formerly owned by the International Paper Company, are being studied and protected through a landmark conservation project that involved the State of New Hampshire, local officials, and organizations with expertise in natural resources.

Marshes often form in old river oxbows, where they begin the process of reclaiming the old river bed

The Connecticut River bypasses an old oxbow in the north country. Without the river's active flow, natural succession returns open water to marsh and eventually to forest.

and returning it to floodplain forest. An example is an old Ammonoosuc River oxbow near Route 302 north of Woodsville, New Hampshire. Bogs are poorly drained acidic wetlands with an unusual assemblage of plants, many of them insectivorous, an effective way of getting by on a poor nutrient supply. Cranberry, sheep laurel, and rhodora are other distinctive bog shrubs.

Dominated by sphagnum moss, bogs are very sensitive to disturbance. Excellent examples are the Philbrick-Cricenti Bog in New London, New Hampshire, and the Victory Bog in Victory, Vermont. This state-owned wildlife management area is a complex of ponds, bogs, wooded swamps, and sedge meadows forested with red, white and black spruce, balsam fir, red and sugar maple, yellow birch, and beech. The Moose River and several small streams flow through the area, which provides good birding for boreal species such as gray jay and black-backed woodpeckers. The wildlife list includes black bear, moose, beaver, mink, otter, coyote, bobcat, snowshoe hare, woodcock, ruffed grouse, wood ducks, hooded merganser, and brook and brown trout.

Riparian Habitat and Floodplain Forests

Down by the river exist habitats unlike any other in the valley. Blanketed against killing cold by shrouds of fog, it is the last to freeze in fall and the first to green up in spring. Soils fertilized by spring freshets are deep and fertile, sometimes punctuated by steep high ledge, always drinking in the moisture that hovers above the river. There is a rich combination of water, land, and weather here that supports an equally rich constellation of plant and animal life.

The Connecticut River was once lined with magnificent floodplain forests, dominated by enormous silver maple and black willow, often with an understory of ostrich fern. These forests are well adapted to changing flows, and don't mind wet feet. They provide habitat for migrating birds while their roots anchor the soil against the river's pull. Many of them fell as settlers sought out the fertile floodplain soils for their crops. The remains of ancient floodplain forests are visible at the so-called Nine Islands, where the Passumpsic and Connecticut Rivers mingle at Barnet. Other remnants can be explored at New Hampshire's Hubbard Wildlife Management Area in Walpole, and behind a shopping center in West Lebanon, north of the interstate bridge.

Only remnants of the once grand silver maple floodplain forest remain, seen here on a farm in Windsor.

The fruit of silky dogwood, a common native riverbank plant, is a favorite of birds and mammals.

Rare Communities

Nowhere is the northern valley's biodiversity more apparent than in the stretch of the Connecticut River from the Ompompanoosuc to Weathersfield Bow, a section biologists call the "Connecticut River Rapids Macrosite." It is home to 84 rare species and natural community types, and three globally endangered species which have disappeared from other places. While they vary in their ability to excite our imagination, from the homely dwarf wedgemussel to the magnificent bald eagle, they are all rightful occupants of the river valley.

Each species of plant and animal has evolved to succeed under a different menu of conditions, and the task of the biologist is to puzzle out what they are. Some, like the crow, are generalists, and others are specialists like the Northeastern bulrush, a federally endangered plant known in only a handful of river meadows and small ponds in the southern part of the valley. Dependent upon disturbance, it grows only where water levels fluctuate.

Some natural communities are rare because they require conditions which are rare within the valley. For example, limestone occurs for the most part only on the western edges, and plants requiring the soils it produces are thus relatively rare. The White River Wildlife Management Area in Sharon, Vermont, protects such a calcareous riverside seep community.

Alpine conditions occur only on the peaks of the Green and White Mountains, and so the plants adapted to such life are also rare. The alpine azalea and mountain heath form low mats to avoid cold, drying winds. While relatively common in the alpine zone in New

The tiny alpine Robbins' cinque-foil, no longer endangered.

England, in New Hampshire these two are found only within our watershed. Because harsh conditions allow only very slow growth, they have difficulty recovering from trampling.

Ledge communities are especially interesting, their hardy plant colonists differing with exposure and type of rock. Mt. Wantastiquet State Forest in Chesterfield and Hinsdale, New Hampshire, is a thousand acre natural area featuring intriguing older woodlands and prominent ledges, where the northern New England acidic rocky summit community meets the southern New England acidic talus forest. Its sycamores and mountain laurels are rare north of this area.

Along the Connecticut River mainstem and larger tributaries are sand bars and "scour communities" whose plants and animals not only tolerate flooding and abrasion by ice floes and debris each spring, but require it. Flood control and damming can actually destroy these communities. The world's only known population of Jesup's milk-vetch lives on three calcareous bedrock outcrops which are ice-scoured annually.

Old Growth Forests

Old growth forests, to modern eyes rarely calibrated to recognize them, are much more than just big trees. Over the many generations (tree, not human) it takes to create such a community, a complex understory develops of the smaller trees, shrubs, herbs, mosses and lichens which are precisely adapted to the local growing conditions. Together they accumulate a deeper, richer layer of duff or "retired" plant material from above, and a microclimate all their own.

The Town of Windsor, Vermont has protected a fragment of old growth forest at Paradise Park. New Hampshire's Mount Sunapee State Park protects another remnant, recognized nearly a century ago, and rediscovered in 1997. In a sheltered bowl high on the mountain's east side, immense yellow birches, sugar maples, and beeches tower over a forest floor littered with their fallen forebears, now nursing the next generation of trees. A spur of the Sunapee-Ragged-Kearsarge Greenway makes this old growth forest easy to explore. One of the first privately sponsored conservation efforts in the valley is Pine Park,

Granite boulders in an old growth forest wear a thick mantle of lichens and mosses, a nursery for larger plants.

The black-throated blue warbler is an interior forest nesting bird, which preys upon the spruce budworm and other defoliating insects.

on the Connecticut River in Hanover, protected by college alumni who recognized both the value of old growth white pines and the threat to their future posed by the thriving community nearby.

Conserving Natural Communities
Valley Pioneers

The northern Connecticut River Valley has long been home to leaders in natural resource conservation. One of the foremost sites in America for interpreting the history of conservation stewardship is Marsh-Billings-Rockefeller National Historic Park, in Woodstock, Vermont. The park honors three men and their families who were owners, developers and stewards of the land for two centuries. George Perkins Marsh, who spent his formative years here, published *Man and Nature* in 1864, a volume which became the foundation of American ecological thought and the conservation movement. His successor, Frederick Billings, developed the property as a model for farming and forestry practices. Laurance S. Rockefeller, a leader and shaper of 20th century American conservation efforts, preserved it for the public.

The destruction resulting from the sale of all public lands in New Hampshire to logging interests by 1876 led to an investigation in 1881, and to the 1901

founding of the Society for the Protection of New Hampshire Forests. U.S. Senator John Wingate Weeks of Massachusetts, a native of Lancaster, New Hampshire, could see the stripped mountainsides from his home on Mount Prospect. In 1911, he sponsored the Weeks Act, which enabled private land to be purchased for a public purpose, clearing the way for the White Mountain National Forest. The Green Mountain National Forest in Vermont followed in 1932. Both protect cold headwater streams feeding the Connecticut River. The Weeks-McLean Act in 1913 provided the first protection for migratory birds.

In the mid-19th century, when the wilderness of central and southern New England was little more than a memory, the concept of natural resource conservation and appreciation for a natural landscape had already taken hold in the American Transcendentalist movement, centered in the literary community of Concord, Massachusetts. Visiting the northern valley in Chesterfield, New Hampshire,

The Nature Conservancy protects the forest surrounding the source of the Connecticut River, tiny Fourth Lake.

in the fall of 1856, Henry David Thoreau set out with friends to climb Mount Wantastiquet and observed, "This town will be convicted of a folly if they ever permit this mountain to be laid bare."

Landscape Scale Conservation

It makes sense that the best way to protect individual plants or animals is to protect their homes. Conservation of the property itself, however, is sometimes not enough, since influences from surrounding areas—pollutants entering a bog from adjacent parcels, for example—can render the place a poor home.

Because no natural community can survive in complete isolation, conservationists understand that for the effort to be worthwhile, good conservation efforts connect conserved community types. It does a spotted turtle little good to have her forested wetland home protected, only to face the prospect of crossing a busy road, even in all the hurry a turtle can muster, to get to her upland nesting grounds. This is what is meant by landscape scale conservation, the state of the conservation art. This is also why those seeking a healthy Connecticut River need to look upstream, deep into the watershed, to understand its hundreds of headwaters.

Public Lands

The national forests are John Wingate Weeks's legacy to the high elevation habitats and headwaters of the northern valley. Since his time, each state has also endeavored to care for the natural resources in their public trust, through state forests, parks, and wildlife management areas. At the turn of the 21st century, both states rose to the challenge posed by large-scale divestment of industrial timberlands. Working closely and creatively with the timber industry, the private conservation community, and local officials, Vermont succeeded in conserving the former Champion lands in the Northeast Kingdom, and New Hampshire the former International Paper Company lands in the North Country.

Northern valley communities have also created their own constellations of town forests, local parks and pocket sanctuaries. Such places may be small in acreage, but large in impact, simply because they are close to home. You can take a lunch break at the Ashuelot riverside park in downtown Keene or see if the ladyslippers are blooming on your way home from the store.

Silvio O. Conte National Fish and Wildlife Refuge

In 1991 the U.S. Congress directed the U.S. Fish and Wildlife Service to establish the Silvio O. Conte National Fish and Wildlife Refuge in the 7.2 million acre watershed of the Connecticut River in Connecticut, Massachusetts, Vermont, and New Hampshire. A new concept of refuge was clearly required, since over two million people already occupy this same space. The Conte Refuge has emerged as a combination of education, voluntary habitat restoration on private lands, partnerships with other conservation groups, research, and acquisition of critical threatened habitat, including the basin of the Nulhegan River in Vermont.

View from The Nature Conservancy's Bunnell Tract in Stratford, NH.

The Vermont Youth Conservation Corps assists with restoration of a Fairlee farm's river bank. Several federal agencies came together to support the project.

The Refuge sponsors education centers at the Montshire Museum in Norwich, Vermont, Colebrook, New Hampshire, and Turner's Falls, Massachusetts.

Conservation Programs

Both states maintain natural heritage programs to locate, track, and provide information about rare plant species and ecosystems. They work with landowners, land managers, and natural resource professionals to help them understand and protect the state's natural heritage and meet their land use needs. New Hampshire's Natural Heritage Bureau, for example, maintains a database of more than 4,700 rare plant, animal, and ecosystem occurrences. The U.S. Fish and Wildlife Service and the U.S. Department of Agriculture's Natural Resources Conservation Service provide expertise and support for landowners, including farmers, who want to improve wildlife habitat on their property.

The remarkable growth of one local non-profit organization demonstrates the enthusiasm of northern valley residents for conservation of natural communities and open space. The Upper Valley Land Trust has worked with forward-thinking landowners in forty towns on both sides of the river, to permanently protect over 250 parcels and more than 24,000 acres in its first 17 years.

The valley's rich natural heritage, and residents eager to protect it, have launched a number of other local land trusts, while state-wide organizations, like the Society for Protection of New Hampshire Forests and the Vermont Land Trust, continue to thrive, along with state chapters of well-respected national and global organizations, such as The Nature Conservancy.

Economics of Conservation

Attempts to understand the value of natural communities are now maturing as our understanding of our own place within them expands. While once the value of a clean stream might have been measured simply in terms of the trout filling a down-country sport's creel, or the value of a forest by the number of board feet it might contain, we now can add the value the forest provides as home to warblers dining upon defoliating insects. Birds, bats, bees, and other insects pollinate orchards and other crops without sending a bill. Wetlands previously thought worthless are now valued for their ability to absorb flood waters and purify drinking water.

Economic analyses consistently show that open space costs a community less in services and tax dol-

Healthy streams mean fine fishing.

lars than does residential development, and the concept of "best and highest use" for a piece of land is getting a hard new look. Outdoor recreation, wildlife watching, fishing and hunting are a major source of dollars which come home to stay, whether spent on transportation, guide services, binoculars, dues, a fishing license or lunch. Exploring the intricacies of climate change, we are realizing that the massive amounts of carbon sequestered in the northern valley's forests play a role in the planet's thermal budget, although we have yet to agree upon a dollar figure for its value in society's fiscal budget. In the end, it is sharing the valley with those creatures, large and small, that makes us proud to live here.

❊ Threats ❊

CLIMATE CHANGE

Whether natural, man-made, or both, the shift in global climate we are beginning to experience will profoundly affect the distribution of plants and animals in the valley. Those that are specialists of colder habitats now prevailing over much of the region may find themselves with nowhere to go when this kind of habitat shrinks. Others adapted to more southern climatic conditions may invade habitat previously too cold for them. Some may not get the climatic cue to drop their leaves at the right time, or to head for hibernation. One creature's rhythms might no longer be matched to those of another on which it depends, like a mis-firing ignition system.

LOSS OF HABITAT

Human population growth, and the development pressure that goes with it, threaten loss of habitat, or fragment larger habitats into smaller ones which become disconnected and uninhabitable. In New Hampshire, 13,000 acres are converted each year to development, an area about half the size of an average town. Loss of riparian forests, that red carpet for migratory birds, puts them and shorelines at risk.

Telecommunications towers, especially in the path of bird migration, are a well-known cause of bird kill.

DISPLACEMENT BY EXOTIC SPECIES

The rest of the world is knocking on our door, in the forms of plants and animals, on land and in the water, which push aside native life or kill it outright. The Asian long-horned beetle has potential to wipe out the sugar maple, and is started on the same path as the chestnut blight. First detected in New York City's Central Park

A colony of hemlock wooly adelgid on the underside of a branchlet.

in the 1990s, it arrived from China in pallet wood. The hemlock wooly adelgid threatens to kill the trees that provide deer yards and stabilize cool mountain streambanks. Purple loosestrife, Japanese knotweed, Eurasian milfoil, barberry, and others crowd out native plants more valuable to wildlife. Zebra mussels have not yet invaded the watershed but are not far away, and could devastate aquatic life. Introduction of non-native fish is still a problem.

Phragmites, the giant reed, invades wetlands and overwhelms cattails and other native plants with more value to wildlife. Seen here at Mink Brook in Hanover.

Beauty and the beast—sometimes trash in our waterways is visible, sometimes it's not.

CONTAMINATION

Invisible contaminants, the leavings of human society scattered in the air, on the waters, and in the soil, are taken up by plant and animal life. We are learning more about the effects of mercury and heavy metals, but no one really knows how pharmaceuticals in the waste stream might affect wildlife.

COMPETITION FOR CLEAN WATER

Streams and rivers, and the underground storage areas known as aquifers, do not carry an infinite supply of clean water, yet society seems to have a boundless thirst, and governments are sometimes reluctant to impose protection for instream flow or underground supplies. Wetland communities which purify this water are too often rationalized away, and lost through development.

❧ Actions & Activities ❧

EXPLORE

• Visit Conte Refuge education centers at the Montshire Museum, Colebrook, and the Great Falls Discovery Center in Turner's Falls, MA.

• Check out the power company's visitors centers at hydropower dams at Moore Station, Littleton, NH, and Wilder, Bellows Falls, and Vernon, VT. The last three are equipped with fish ladders which operate during fish migration season.

• Take your family or school group on a Valley Quest. Better yet, help create one in your community.

• Adopt a local trail and experience it throughout the seasons.

• Virtually visit the underwater world—follow the temperature of the river as measured in real time at various gages (www.crjc.org/riverflow.htm).

• Tour your yard after a light snow to search for evidence of wildlife travelers.

PARTICIPATE IN LOCAL PROTECTION EFFORTS

• Organize a cleanup of a neighborhood stream.

• Hold a green-up day in your community.

A group of home-school families picked up an entire truckload of trash at Herrick's Cove, with the help of US Gen New England, on the Connecticut River Watershed Council's annual Source to the Sea Clean-up Day.

• Establish a conservation commission if your town does not already have one.

• Take an inventory of your town's "green infrastructure."

• Start a column on conservation issues in your community's newsletter.

• Contact the Audubon Society of NH or Vermont Institute of Natural Science to find out how you can help monitor a raptor or loon nesting site near you.

• Offer to help develop interpretive trail guides and management plans and provide signage for town-owned conservation lands.

• Encourage low impact recreation and enjoyment of local conservation lands.

• Encourage riparian buffers along streams and rivers.

• Search your community for signs of invasive exotics and organize a group to eradicate a patch of invasive plants.

• Volunteer to breed beetles for control of purple loosestrife and release them at infested sites.

• Help your community map potential habitat for species of concern to your town. See links below.

• Help your town's conservation commission to prioritize local natural resource lands for conservation.

Volunteers plant willow stakes to replant a riparian buffer for erosion control.

Participant in a Keeping Track workshop imitates the bear which left claw marks on this red pine. Black bears prefer red pines and white birches to communicate with other bears, according to data collected by Susan Morse.

• Establish a Keeping Track monitoring program in your community and become more effective at planning for and conserving necessary wildlife habitat.

• Help your school get involved in community mapping using geographic information systems technology. Contact the Vermont Institute of Natural Science to learn more.

PARTICIPATE

• Participate in farm and forest field days and tours sponsored by your county conservation district.

• Take a kid fishing.

• Sign up for walks and public programs offered by local conservation groups, including RiverFest and WinterFest.

• Join a conservation organization and participate in their activities.

• Volunteer to help with Atlantic salmon stocking

• Consider purchasing a conservation license plate, whose proceeds go to support conservation projects.

• Attend naturalist programs at a state park near you, such as Weeks State Park, or Saint-Gaudens National Historic Site, the Fells, the Rocks Estate, and other conserved properties, or evening programs such as those offered by local bird clubs.

• Participate in the Seasons on the Land programs offered by the Upper Valley Land Trust.

TAKE CARE OF YOUR HOME PROPERTY

• Purchase shrubs and trees for wildlife plantings or riparian buffer restoration from your county conservation district's annual sale.

• Consider the collective impacts of your personal choices with respect to pesticides, herbicides, automobiles, and solid waste disposal. Select the least toxic substance, keep it away from surface waters, and dispose of it properly.

The Montshire Museum in Norwich, Vermont, is a Conte Fish and Wildlife Refuge Education Center.

• Recycle mercury-containing products and other household hazardous waste.

• Learn about and use best management practices for your property.

• Enlist the Environmental Quality Incentives Program or Wildlife Habitat Incentives Program to help make effective use of land while safeguarding water quality.

• Explore cost-sharing grants, conservation easements, and cooperation with the USFWS to enhance the wildlife value of your property.

LOOK INTO LOCAL AND REGIONAL PLANNING

• Read your town and regional plans to see if they list and protect local natural resources. Compare these documents to the Conte Refuge Action Plan and the *Connecticut River Corridor Management Plan* for your town and region.

School kids help rear and stock Atlantic salmon.

• Does your town's zoning ordinance have protection for floodplains, aquifers, wetlands, and riparian areas?

• Encourage your town to conduct a cost of community services and open space study.

❧ Q & A ❧

• What percentage of your town's land use change tax is dedicated to conservation purposes?

• What kinds of plants and animals do you think inhabited your property 300 years ago?

• How many different kinds of birds can you tally on your home property in one day?

• What are the environmental extremes outside your home, compared to those indoors in your own habitat? The coldest and warmest temperatures? Strongest winds? Driest and wettest conditions? Brightest light, deepest shade? What kinds of adaptations allow wildlife to survive this range?

Hemlocks anchor streambanks and shelter deer from deep snow.

❧ FYI ❧

GENERAL INTEREST

Among the Bears, by Ben Kilham and Ed Gray, Henry Holt Publishers, New York, 2002. (Chronicles the experience of a wildlife rehabilitator raising orphaned bears and returning them to the forests of the Upper Valley, the lessons he has taught the bears, and those they have taught him.)

Fishing in New Hampshire, A History, by Jack Noon, Moose Country Press, Warner, NH, 2003.

W. D. Wetherell's trilogy in celebration of fly fishing, the northern Connecticut River Valley, and the life within it: *Upland Stream*, Lyons Press, 1991; *Vermont River*, Globe Pequot Press, 1993; *One River More*, Lyons Press, 1998.

GUIDES & INTERPRETIVE LITERATURE

Birdwatching in Vermont by Ted Murin and Bryan Pfeiffer, University Press of New England, 2002. (Guide to watching birds in Vermont, with a special section for beginners. Includes a chapter on the Connecticut River Valley.)

"Map and Guide to the Connecticut River Birding Trail Sites" by Bill Shepard, CT River Birding Trail, 2002.

New Hampshire Wildlife Viewing Guide by Judy K. Silverberg, Falcon Press, 1997. (Where, when and how to see wildlife all across the state. Descriptions of 73 sites include details on the species likely to be present.)

Reading the Forested Landscape: A Natural History of New England by Tom Wessels, etching and illustrations by Brian D. Cohen; The Countrymen Press, Woodstock, VT, 1997. (Illustrates how to "read" the woods to learn its history and includes a time line of events that shape our present forests.)

The "Wet Sneaker Trilogy" by David M. Carroll: *The Year of the Turtle*, Camden House Publishing, 1991; *Trout Reflections: A Natural History of the Trout and Its World*, St. Martin's Press, 1993; *Swampwalker's Journal: A Wetlands Year*, Houghton Mifflin, 2001. (A New Hampshire naturalist guides the reader through the wetland and underwater worlds of the trout, the turtle, and others with his own elegant illustrations.)

Wetland, Woodland, Wildland: A Guide to the Natural Communities of Vermont by Elizabeth H. Thompson and Eric R. Sorenson, University Press of New England, 2000. (A field guide to Vermont's natural communities and their assemblages of plants and animals. For the serious reader.)

CONSERVATION PLANNING

Connecticut River Corridor Management Plan edited by Sharon F. Francis, Adair D. Mulligan, Connecticut River Joint Commissions, Charlestown, NH, 1997.

Final Action Plan and Environmental Impact Statement, The Silvio O. Conte National Fish and Wildlife Refuge; U.S. Fish and Wildlife Service, Turners Falls, MA, 1995.

A Fishway for Your Stream, Connecticut River Watershed Council, Greenfield, MA, 2000. ("How-to" manual for river conservationists and communities interested in restoring access for migratory fish to spawning habitats that have been blocked by small dams.)

Growing Greener—Putting Conservation into Local Plans and Ordinances by Randall Arendt, Washington, D.C., Island Press, 1999.

Natural Resources: An Inventory Guide for New Hampshire Communities by Phil Auger and Jeanie McIntyre, Upper Valley Land Trust & UNH Cooperative Extension, 1992.

Open Space Lands: A Community Resource by Jeanie McIntyre and Phil Auger, The Upper Valley Land Trust, Lebanon, NH, 1989. (How-to hand book on identifying and evaluating open space and agricultural lands.)

Riparian Buffers for the Connecticut River Watershed, Connecticut River Joint Commissions, Charlestown, NH, 2000. (Illustrated fact sheets for various land uses, including buffers for habitat, plant lists, and sources of aid.)

GOOD LINKS

The University of Vermont's Spatial Analysis Lab is developing a web page for each of 306 land animals, with range maps and predicted distribution: www.snr.uvm.edu/sal

Bear Pond Natural Area, Canaan, NH. Assisted by the Upper Valley Land Trust, the Mascoma Watershed Conservation Council purchased and conserved this 923 acre tract at the headwaters of the Mascoma River, with funding from the NH Land & Community Heritage Investment Program, CRJC, and many others.

The University of New Hampshire is developing web pages for land cover maps and conservation lands in the state: www.granit.sr.unh.edu

Keeping Track: www.keepingtrackinc.org

The Wilderness Society's Ecology and Economics Research Department is developing a map-based tool for discovering economic trends: www.eco2eco.net. Point-and-click creation of custom economic profiles for use in conservation, sustainable development and other planning.

Project Learning Tree:
NH: www.nhplt.org
VT: www.state.vt.us/anr/fpr/coned/plt.htm

Project Wild:
NH: www.wildlife.state.nh.us/Education project_WILD.htm
VT: www.anr.state.vt.us/fw/fwhome/index.htm

Project Wet:
NH: www.des.state.nh.us/wet
VT: www.anr.state.vt.us/dec/waterq/lakespwet.htm

NH Natural Heritage Bureau: www.nhdfl.org/formgt/nhiweb

Vermont sites: Non-Game and Natural Heritage Inventory: www.anr.state.vt.us/fw/fwhome/nnhp/index.html
For Vermont educators: www.anr.state.vt.us/students.htm
Wildlife management area descriptions and maps: www.anr.state.vt.us/wmamaps/index.html
Wildlife management unit maps:
interactive www.anr.state.vt.us/gismaps/wmuindex.html

Important Bird Areas: www.audubon.org/bird/iba/index.html

CHAPTER THREE

Amerindians

Early Life on the Long River

"We walk around on the bones of our ancestors." In this expression, contemporary American Indians living in our region convey both spiritual and literal meanings. The statement asserts lineal descent from indigenous people, and it's a reminder that for thousands of years humans have lived and died in the places we occupy today. Archeological sites document the life of indigenous people, European settlers, and early industries of our own culture. It is important to protect known archeological sites, to investigate potential sites before development, and to honor these places and artifacts as an inheritance from many cultural ancestors.

❈ The Basic Story ❈

SOMETIMES, early on summer mornings along the Connecticut River, a ghostly fog hovers in horizontal planes above the water. When the first rays of the sun warm the air, the fog lifts. Small columns of mist stand on the water, then rise up in spirals even as they disappear. It's not hard to imagine these mists as human spirits of the place, of those who came before us here along the river.

Fortunately, we don't have to rely on our imaginations alone. Archeological sites document the presence of humans here for at least 11,000 years. Artifacts and their associated contexts make it possible to know a great deal about these peoples' lives and times. Contemporary ethnohistories and Western Abenaki oral traditions provide more perspectives on how people probably lived here before

Prehistoric petroglyphs at Bellows Falls, later altered.

Archeological site at Fort at No. 4, Charlestown, exposed on the river bank. Trowel points to charcoal feature.

Europeans arrived. That arrival—called Contact—marks a divide between "history" and "pre-history." The scientific quest for pre-historic information through archeology recently has been tempered by a greater awareness that contemporary American Indians consider many such sites particularly sacred.

While *Homo sapiens* appears to have been around for about 200,000 years on the planet, our species is a relative newcomer to the Connecticut River Valley. As the last glaciers were receding, about 12,500 years ago, humans walked here in the arctic tundra of frigid lakes and wooly mammoths. According to evidence they left in the ground, people evolved a way of life here that parallels similar human cultural developments in other parts of the world.

After the climate stabilized, about 8,000 years ago, their populations began to grow. They traveled on and fished the Connecticut River and its tributaries. They traded as far south as Long Island Sound, and moved between the Connecticut and Lake Champlain watersheds over the White and Black rivers. The Connecticut River and its tributaries were a means of transportation, a focus of settlement, a source of food, and a unifying presence in the landscape. Over time, native inhabitants changed the land. They burned off trees and brush to facilitate travel and to manage wildlife habitat and fruit such as blueberries. They built settlements and cleared fields on the floodplains to grow crops. A map of Indian trails in New Hampshire appears on page 103.

Based on cultural and technological distinctions, archeologists divide pre-history into three periods, dated approximately as follows: Paleo-Indian (before 8000 BC), Archaic (8000-1200 BC), and Woodland (1200 BC-1600 AD). The Archaic Period is subdivided into Early (8000-6000 BC), Middle (6000-4000 BC), and Late (4000-1200 BC).

PALEO-INDIAN PERIOD

Evidence of early human occupation, which exists in much of North America, has been discovered at more than 138 sites near the Connecticut River in Vermont and New Hampshire. About 70 of these can be identified as to their approximate age. Given the number of inhabitants and a long period of time, it is certain that more pre-historic material is yet to be discovered.

Native American sites documented by archeology generally have been found on lower terraces of the floodplains of the river and its tributaries, and particularly where waterways join. The earliest known Paleo-Indian sites in the Connecticut River Valley, which date from 9-10,000 years ago, occur on sandy terraces above the river or its major tributaries. The upper Connecticut valley at that time was just emerging from the glacial ice. It was open country covered by grasses, herbs, sedges, and stunted trees such as spruce, fir, larch, birch, willows and alder.

While Paleo-Indians were food foragers, they also hunted caribou. They used a distinctive fluted

Fluted point. This Paleo-Indian tool, dating to 11,000 years ago, was found in the valley of Israel's River in Jefferson, New Hampshire, some ten miles east of the Connecticut.

spear point, named for the groove on each side. Kill sites have been found at the edges of wetlands and rivers. Campsites were on high ground overlooking places to which animals came for water, and in river valleys, which were travel corridors for both humans and wildlife. It's conjectured that Paleo-Indians lived in small family bands, with population densities probably less than 10 per 100 square kilometers, resembling the density of present Inuit in interior Alaska.

Archaic Period

The beginning of the Archaic Period was marked by a dramatic warming trend that lasted for several thousand years. The region was completely forested by about 6500 BC. Climate change, and the extinction of more than a hundred species of large animals, required humans to adapt to different sources of food and clothing. Mammoths and mastodons, the Pleistocene denizens of tundra environments, were replaced by the bear, deer, and small game better adapted to the newly returned mixed northern hardwood forests. Plant foods and fish were diverse and abundant.

Over time, spear and dart points having a variety of shapes succeeded the fluted point. A stone-weighted wooden spear thrower (atlatl) increased the speed and distance of the thrown weapon. Other stone tools were used for hammering, cutting, skinning, and carving wood. Around this time, people moved seasonally to take advantage of different food sources, such as migratory fish and mammals. Cook-

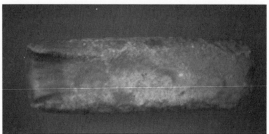

The gouge, a carpentry tool used over many time periods.

ing was accomplished by heating stones in a fire and then placing them in birchbark, woven, or wooden containers.

Woodland Period

By the beginning of the Woodland Period, about 3,000 years ago, the residents of the northern valley carved bowls out of soapstone, and made clay cooking pots which they placed directly in the fire. They hunted with bows and arrows. Some thousand years ago, they began to grow corn, beans, and squash in the fertile floodplains, and established villages along waterways. With cultivated foods supplementing harvests from hunting and fishing, the population of indigenous people increased. Bands living in the northern valley traded with others who lived near the mouth of the river at Long Island Sound.

When Europeans arrived in the Connecticut River Valley in the early 1600s, they encountered Late Woodland inhabitants, who called themselves the Alnôbak and their land Wôbanakik. They are also called the Western Abenaki, who inhabited most of Vermont, western New Hampshire, northwestern Massachusetts and lower Canada east into the Maritimes. Primary Abenaki settlements were located in northwestern Vermont near Lake Champlain and in St. Francis, Quebec, known as Odanak. Among Abenaki bands inhabiting the Connecticut River were the Sokoki and Cowasuck. The Alnôbak today say they have lived in Wôbanakik "since the beginning of time."

Contact Period

The transition between pre-history and history, known to historians as the Contact Period, took place during the first decades of the 17th century. In northern Vermont and New Hampshire, Samuel de Champlain and other French explorers met the Abenaki about 1605. By 1612, far downriver, Dutch sailors were interacting with other tribes in Long Island Sound and southern Connecticut and Massachusetts, and word of those interactions probably

A French illustration of an Abenaki couple of the 18th century.

Massachusetts and Connecticut, Abenaki from the northern valley fought and died alongside Wampanoags, Nipmucks, and Narrangansetts.

English settlers, migrating northward up the Connecticut River, resorted to a series of forts to provide protection for their manifest destiny. The northernmost of these outposts was Fort at No. 4 in Charlestown, which sustained numerous raids and ambushes, until Robert Rogers and his Rangers attacked the Abenaki settlement at St. Francis in 1759. The French signed a treaty with England in 1763, leaving the Abenaki without European allies. It marked the end of armed conflict and opened the Connecticut River Valley to a flood of settlers from Massachusetts and Connecticut. Surviving Abenaki went into exile, or continued to live quietly among whites or in remote areas, or were assimilated into European cultures.

Abenaki descendants still live in the upper river valley. The strongest contemporary Abenaki identity centers in the northern Lake Champlain community of Swanton, Vermont, where the Abenaki Tribal Council occupies the Mississquoi River region.

traveled swiftly to Native American tribes and clans throughout the watershed.

Over the next 150 years of conflict and strained co-existence, the consequences of invasion by Europeans decimated the Abenaki population. By the 1630s, the Abenaki experienced a mortality rate of about 98 percent from European diseases such as smallpox to which they had no natural immunity. By the 1650s, those populations that had survived the epidemics were further reduced by warfare with Mohawk Iroquois from New York. Settlers farmed the Indians' cleared fields, and adopted Native American practices such as hunting and fishing.

Despite their reduced numbers, Abenaki allied with the French conducted sporadic warfare with English settlements in Massachusetts, Vermont and New Hampshire from about 1670 to 1780. The most intense conflict occurred from 1675-1676, during what is known as King Philip's War. While most of the actual warfare occurred south of our region, in

Post mold outline of one side of a long house, circa 650 A.D. (Near the Souhegan River, Milford, New Hampshire.) Evidence of similar structures has been discovered in the Connecticut River Valley.

Sieving for artifacts at the Fort at No. 4, Charlestown, New Hampshire, 2001.

❋ Resources and Revelations ❋

Archeological Sites

Projectile stone points and tooled tips—"arrow heads" in the common phrase—still turn up in the plow zone of fields all over the Connecticut River Valley. But it's through professional, methodical excavation of sites that information has been gathered about earlier peoples' diet, food preparation methods, shelter, and burial practices.

Among the earliest, best-documented Paleo-Indian sites in our region is the Whipple site, on a sandy terrace above the Ashuelot River in Swanzey, New Hampshire, which dates from about 9000 BC. Among the findings were fluted points, stone tools and caribou bones. Further north is the Colebrook

site, discovered in 1997 on a terrace above the Connecticut River, and carbon-dated to about 10,300 years ago. The Israel's River complex, now including five sites on a tributary to the Connecticut in Jefferson, New Hampshire, is still under active investigation.

One of the best-documented Archaic-Woodland sites is the Hunter Site in Claremont, New Hampshire. There, seven strata in eleven vertical feet of depositions suggest occupation over a period of 4,000 years prior to AD 1300. In the great oxbow of the river, in Newbury, Vermont, and Haverhill, New Hampshire, there was a large village of Cowasuck and Sokoki bands in the late 1600s. In the oxbow floodplains, test pits have uncovered evidence of occupation going back 2,500 years.

At Sumner's Falls, in Hartland, Vermont, a number of hearths and workshop areas have been found, dating to about 750 BC, along with points associated with the Orient culture, which was centered on Long Island. This and other discoveries of Orient points in other portions of the river valley suggest that travel and trade among Native Americans flourished from the mouth of the river to its northern reaches.

One of the most dramatic discoveries about prehistoric culture was made at the Skitchewaug site in Springfield, Vermont. Stored maize, beans and squash

Excavation at the Hunter site in Claremont yielded fragments of the bowl seen in the color insert.

vere found associated with a radiocarbon date of AD
ı120. It's the earliest evidence of farming in a settlement anywhere in New England. Other artifacts were
'ound suggesting occupation of the site for some
2,000 years previous to the farming.

*Contemporary bent-sapling frame for a traditional
Abenaki shelter at Brunswick, Vermont.*

More recently occupied was the Fort Hill Site,
in Hinsdale, New Hampshire. It was a fortified
settlement built and occupied in 1663 by
Squakheags, also known as Sokokis, who were allied with the French, to protect themselves against
raiding Mohawks.

Mineral springs in the present town of
Brunswick, Vermont, were valued by Native Americans for their healing qualities. Immigrant Europeans drove out the Abenaki and beginning in 1869
constructed three resort hotels, each of which
burned down, the last in 1933. In 1992, Wobanaki,
Inc., a non-profit Abenaki corporation, purchased
the land.

In 1993, archeologists discovered evidence of
Contact Period wigwams when they conducted a dig
on the bank above the Connecticut River at the site
of the Fort at No. 4 reconstruction in Charlestown.
The site has not been fully explored, but archeologists deem it to be of unusual significance since so
little evidence from that period has been found.

PETROGLYPHS

Petroglyphs chiseled into bedrock near the Great
Falls at Rockingham, Vermont are compelling
reminders of Native American culture. Although
they cannot be dated accurately and have been
modified in the recent past, these rock carvings of
ornamented heads may date from 300 to 2,000
years ago or more.

According to contemporary Abenaki, the carvings have existed there "since the beginning of time,"
and have spiritual meanings which no one today may
interpret. Native Americans gathered on the river
between Rockingham and Walpole, probably for
thousands of years, to catch anadromous fish such
as shad and Atlantic salmon that were migrating upstream and paused at turbulent cascades in the river
there. The Indians likely cured their catch in nearby
settlements.

In the 1930s, in a misguided effort to "preserve"
the carvings, the local chapter of the Daughters of
the American Revolution hired a mason to deepen
them. They have since been accented with yellow
and red paint. Unaltered petroglyphs are believed
buried nearby under stone rubble created in the 19th
century. Another set of petroglyphs once seen in
Brattleboro, at the confluence of the Connecticut
and West Rivers, was inundated after the dam at
Vernon-Hinsdale was constructed early in the 20th
century.

HISTORIC MARKERS

In Haverhill, New Hampshire, a site marker commemorates the pre-arranged rendezvous for Rogers'
Rangers after their destruction of St. Francis, Quebec in 1759. After pursuing Indians and starvation
threatened their retreat, the Rangers found that the
expected rescue party with food had come and gone.
"Many Rangers perished and early settlers found
their bones along these intervales," reads the marker.

A marker in Royalton, Vermont, commemorates
a 1780 attack of settlements from Tunbridge to
Royalton, by three hundred Native Americans led

by a British officer. Four residents were killed, 26 were taken prisoner, and Royalton was burned to the ground. Carved into a granite arch in the park is a tribute to Hannah Handy, who rescued a number of children from their Indian captors.

CULTURAL BORROWINGS

The word "Connecticut" is said to derive from a Native American word meaning "long tidal river," or "long estuary" (variously rendered by the English as Quinnetukut, Quonehtacut, Quinatucquet or Quenticut). Other Native American words survive in names such as Quechee, Ottauquechee, Ammonoosuc, Passumpsic, and Ompompanoosuc.

European settlers adopted many Native American practices and customs that survive today, among them camping, hunting, fishing, maple sugaring, and the use of canoes, snow shoes and moccasins.

❧ Threats ❧

Archeological sites come to light through chance discoveries, as part of environmental review for road and bridge projects, exposure by riverbank erosion, or through investigations of the historical record. There are a number of threats to archeological sites:

EROSION

When river and stream banks erode in areas of prehistoric use, they may spill the contents of graves and habitation sites.

LOOTING

Individuals who believe in "finder's keepers," even on someone else's land, remove human remains and artifacts from the ground for their personal "collections." This looting is considered theft and is against the law. It violates human decency in the case of burials, insults contemporary Native Americans, and deprives everyone of the knowledge that could be gained from the artifacts within their context in the soil.

SOIL DISTURBANCE

Public works and private development projects sometimes inadvertently or intentionally destroy archeological sites.

LACK OF PUBLIC SUPPORT

Archeological issues, and archeologists themselves, are sometimes viewed by the public as presenting last-minute obstructions to development. (Some of this is due to the scheduling of archeological and environmental review toward the end of the development sequence.)

❧ Actions & Activities ❧

Archeology is important as a means of discovering and protecting information about those who came before us, including Paleo Indians, Native Americans, early European settlers, and others of the more recent past. Whether physical objects are found in a cooking hearth thousands of years old or an industrial site from the previous century, they have a story to tell of an evolving material culture from which we have emerged ourselves.

Just as important as an artifact itself is the matrix in which it is found in the ground. Considering its physical association with other artifacts and soil characteristics, archeologists may more accurately date the materials and identify their historic context.

VISIT

• Visit the Indian Museum in Warner, NH.

• Attend the annual PowWow at Dartmouth College.

• Visit fish ladders at dams where Native Americans formerly harvested migrating species.

• Explore the Fort at No. 4, Charlestown, NH, and its Abenaki village down by the river.

• Visit the Sargent Museum and its Connecticut River collection.

Excavations in 2001 on a former island adjacent to the reconstructed Fort at No. 4 in Charlestown. The site was occupied by Native Americans before and during the Contact Period.

ports generally gather dust on agency shelves. Advocate for wider distribution and public interpretation of these reports.

• Make sure town and regional plans acknowledge the significance of archeological sites and establish policies for their protection. Advocate for archeological reviews to be carried out early during development planning phases.

• Support shoreline protection and riparian buffers to prevent erosion.

• Travel to the Mashantucket Pequot Museum and Research Center, a state-of-the-art Native American museum, in Ledyard, Connecticut. Its exhibits of traditional Indian life and pre-Colonial New England convey a sense of pre-history in the upper valley, too.

Advocate

• Support sound archeological practices. If you find portions of skeletons or bones, notify the State Police. If you find arrowheads or other artifacts, get in touch with the historic preservation agency in your state for advice about what to do.

• Advocate for stiff penalties for archeological looting, and help enforce the laws.

• Support Native American "repatriation" efforts to rebury human remains unearthed by erosion and development.

• Advocate for a systematic survey of the region's archeological resources.

• State and federal transportation agencies have documented many archeological sites, but their re-

Learn

• Get involved in an archeological dig, learn the right way to do it, and make discoveries with your own hands. Participate in the Vermont program "Archeology in the Schools" and the New Hampshire program called S.C.R.A.P. Study early hilltop settlements and cellar holes.

• Invite Native American story tellers and crafts producers to your school or organization to learn about their culture and the oral tradition.

• Become knowledgeable about gathering and storing natural herbs and medicines.

Participate

• Canoe the Connecticut River and its tributaries; hike and camp out in the woods.

• Engage in safe hunting, fishing, or trapping.

• Join in at the annual fall game dinners like the one held in Bradford, Vermont, where the entire menu is prepared with the meat of wild animals obtained by hunters.

❧ Q & A ❧

• Assume that the past 200,000 years of human history occurred during one 24-hour day. What time was it when the last glaciers melted and Paleo-Indians arrived in our region? What time was it when the Contact Period occurred and "pre-history" became "history" in the Connecticut River Valley? What time was your town settled or chartered?

• If you were set down in a wilderness, where would you look for food, clothing, and shelter? What would you use for tools?

• Without telling someone why, ask them to select any household object. Then consider it an artifact from a culture that you know nothing about, and discuss what conclusions you might draw about that culture from the object alone. What information about the artifact's context would be helpful in drawing your conclusions?

• If you were a European colonist and were told that "savage" Indians visited land where you wanted to live, how do you think you would react? Are there modern parallels to this collision of cultures?

❧ FYI ❧

RECOMMENDED READING

After King Philip's War: Presence and Persistence in Indian New England edited by Colin G. Calloway, University Press of New England, Hanover, NH, 1997. (Native American culture in New England in the 18th and 19th centuries.)

Aunt Sarah, Woman of the Dawn Land by Trudy Ann Parker, Dawnland Publications, Lancaster, NH, 1994. (The life of an Abenaki healer, who lived from 1823-1931 in the upper valley, written by a descendent, a local writer.)

Changes in the Land: Indians, Colonists, and the Ecology of New England by William Cronin, Hill and Wang, New York, 1983. (The collective impact of cultural behavior on the environment.)

Keepers of the Earth: Native American Stories and Environmental Activities for Children by Michael J. Caduto and Joseph Bruchac, Fulcrum, Inc., 1988. (A work by two excellent story tellers.)

The Original Vermonters: Native Inhabitants, Past and Present by William A. Haviland and Marjory W. Power, University Press of New England, Hanover, NH, 1994. (A good general text on Native American people of the Connecticut River Valley.)

The Voice of the Dawn: An Autohistory of the Abenaki Nation by Frederick Matthew Wiseman, University Press of New England, Hanover, NH, 2001. (A compelling narration from the point of view of Abenaki political and spiritual sovereignty.)

The Western Abenakis of Vermont, 1600-1800 by Colin Calloway, University of Oklahoma Press, 1990 (A detailed ethnographic and cultural history of Connecticut River Valley Native Americans.)

"Early Evidence of Maize Agriculture in the Connecticut River Valley of Vermont," by M. Heckenberger, J. Petersen, N. Sidell; published in *Archaeology of Eastern North America*, 1992

"The Peopling of the Upper Connecticut River Valley," by Andrea Ohl; published in *The New Hampshire Archeologist*, 1994

"A Prehistoric Inventory of the Upper Connecticut River Valley," by Daniel F. Cassedy; Raleigh, NC: Garrow & Associates, Inc., 1991

GOOD LINKS

The Sargent Museum of Archeology and Anthropology: www.sargentmuseum.org

Westford, VT, Elementary School's "History in Our Back Yard" program: www.vetc.vsc.edu/ws/archeology/arch.htm

Online newsletter of the Society for Industrial Archeology: http://141.219.41.56/IA/sian/siancurr.html

OTHER RESOURCES

"A Rich and Ancient Heritage: Vermont's Archeological Sites," a 27-minute video in the Vermont Heritage Series is available from many public libraries as well as the Vermont Historical Society.

For teaching materials and information about Western Abenaki culture and language: New Dawn publications, Franklin Northwest Supervisory Union Title IX Indian Education Program, 14 First Street, Swanton, VT 05488

"Historic Indian Trails of New Hampshire" by Chester B. Price in *The New Hampshire Archeologist*, Vol. 14, June 1967. (An 11x17-inch map and pamphlet with detailed annotations on each trail are available from the New Hampshire Archeological Society [see Appendix B].)

CHAPTER FOUR

Settlement

The Shape of Community in Town & Countryside

When people who have never lived in New Hampshire or Vermont visit here, they often say they feel like they've come home. Our urban centers, commercial districts, small villages and industrial enterprises are set amid farmlands and forests. This is a landscape in which the natural and built environments are balanced on a human scale. This delicate balance is the nature of our "community character." It's important to strengthen our distinctive, traditional settlement patterns to counteract the commercial and residential sprawl that upsets this balance and destroys our economic and social stability.

❈ The Basic Story ❈

"CAN a Town have two centers?" The question was posed in a newspaper headline over an article about a developer who wanted to name his new strip mall "Town Center." The new mall was located on a highway bypass far from the crossroads where the town's original commercial center had grown up around a typical New England green.

Local residents knew the difference between authenticity and marketing. At a well-attended public meeting, they spoke out against the bogus name, arguing that it would confuse people and devalue the real Main Street that had been the physical and economic heart of their community for 200 years. They didn't want to lose the sense of place and continuity their real town center provides.

High in the Waits River watershed, Corinth Center, Vermont (seen here c. 1910) was typical of hill villages clustered around a meetinghouse and surrounded by stone wall-lined lanes and open fields.

Most families settling in the northern valley came from communities down river in Massachusetts and Connecticut.

The northern valley's 18th-century settlers hoped to achieve a similar sense of familiarity by recreating here the physical shape of the towns in southern and eastern New England from which they had come. Beginning in the first two decades of the 1600s, the English (in eastern Massachusetts) and the Dutch (along the Hudson River in New York) established towns that quickly multiplied along the Atlantic coast, from Long Island Sound to Maine. By the 1630s, the Dutch had pushed as far north as present-day Hartford, Connecticut, where they established a trading post. But slow population growth, challenging topography, and warfare with French and Native Americans all impeded the northward spread of immigrants for another century.

When the migration took place, the Connecticut River was the primary corridor by which early Americans first launched themselves deep into a wilderness. It was here in our region that a settlement model evolved that was later applied in the Ohio Valley, the Mississippi Valley, and the West.

The earliest outposts in the northern valley were fortified stockades built near the river, the travel route of both immigrants and indigenous people. The first (but not permanent) outpost was Fort Dummer, built in Vernon, Vermont, in 1724. It was the most northerly of a string of six forts scattered across northern Massachusetts intended to protect anticipated immigrants from the south. The first permanent settlement in our region was in Charlestown, New Hampshire, where a fort was constructed in 1743.

For the first half of the 18th century, Native Americans attacked these fortified outposts and scattered homesteads, for the intrusion these represented upon their ancestral lands. The Indians were supported by French military in the field, and by the French government in Montreal, which awarded bounties for captured English settlers. The early histories of many Connecticut River towns include stories of surprise and bloody fights, of captives being marched to Canada for ransom, and sometimes of their eventual return.

The Treaty of Paris in 1763 ended the long period of warfare between England and France. The French withdrew their support of Native Americans in the French and Indian wars in New England. Surviving Abenaki withdrew to Canada or remained quietly in the region.

Their safety thus more sure, settlers poured up the river valley from Massachusetts and Connecticut, and around the White Mountains from coastal New Hampshire. (In the far north, French-Canadian settlements near the border persisted or took root.) Some newcomers sought homes, while others pursued business and investment opportunities. Many were adventurers and Indian wars veterans who had tramped throughout the upper Connecticut River valley over its early military routes such as the Crown Point Road and Bayley-Hazen Road in Vermont, or who traveled over early turnpikes in New Hampshire. Remote hilltop villages sprouted along these overland routes and more dense settlements took shape along waterways.

These were no primitive pioneers or backwoods bumpkins. They transplanted a society into a wil-

derness. They gave new places the old names of the
towns they had left—Chester, Hartford, Lebanon,
Windsor, Enfield, Ludlow, Lyme, and Springfield.
They brought animals, wagons, tools, household
goods and a trove of personal possessions. They also
brought habits of society-making that included ideas
about town planning, spatial relationships, and architecture developed in the southern and eastern
New England towns they left behind.

Within a remarkably short time, the towns of the
upper river valley achieved a population balance
with those of the lower. From the mouth to the
source, there was a single, contiguous, homogenous
culture whose lifeline of commerce and communi-
cation was the Connecticut River.

In 1760, the entire state of Vermont contained
less than 1,000 soldiers and settlers. Just fifty years
later, in 1810, a census found 129,000 people fairly
evenly distributed in the riverfront towns of the
four states, in Connecticut (48,000), Massachusetts (17,000), New Hampshire (25,000), and Vermont (39,000). A comparison of the larger towns
in 1810 shows a similarly equal distribution. In
Connecticut, while Hartford had the most residents (6,003), Windsor (2,868) was not much
larger than Windsor, Vermont (2,757). Springfield,
Massachusetts (2,767), was comparable to Springfield, Vermont (2,115). Other large population centers in the upper valley at that time were Claremont
(2,094) and Hanover (2,135) in New
Hampshire.

Among the tributaries, some of the
earliest towns were built on hilltops,
above the thickly forested, marshy
lands along the brooks and rivers.
Within a generation, many hill town
centers were picked up and moved to
valley locations, and toward mill sites
and improved roads.

Many early settlements clustered
around waterfalls and river crossings,
shaping themselves to the contours of

*The Wyoming Valley Dam later built on the site of
Guildhall Falls has since been breached.*

the land and waterways. Available water power offered opportunities for a variety of mills and the
villages which then arose around them. Crossroad
villages on level ground took axial and linear form,
dense in the centers and thin at the edges. Settlements established by loggers and foresters tended
to be random and haphazard, and many were
ephemeral, disappearing when nearby lumber
sources were depleted. Those established by farmers tended to be more orderly, with village commons
adjacent to churches and schools. Even the shape
and size of pasture and crop lands were a fingerprint
of the ethnic or geographic traditions settlers
brought from elsewhere.

In the early 19th century, town greens took shape
and served as parade grounds and public gathering
places. Photographs of such places fill the pages of

*Soldiers of the 16th New Hampshire Regiment in parade formation
on the Lyme Common during the Civil War.*

our regional magazines and live in our imaginations as symbols of small town life. However romanticized, these images are based on the reality of how many of our communities still look today. Urban commercial districts and residential neighborhoods cluster around these greens, forming compact settlements dispersed throughout a working landscape of farms and forests.

All of these elements combine to create our physical "community character." They are the sum of what we have made of our places since the 1750s. The details of this history and its importance are covered in following chapters on Agriculture, Industry and Commerce, Transportation, and Architecture. For an exercise in determining the significant parts of your own community's character, turn to the Community Profile.

Over the past two-and-a-half centuries, our communities have gone through periods of rapid physical change, slow change, and little change at all. Today we're experiencing quick and dramatic alterations to our historic settlement patterns and traditional local economies. They are changing the character of the physical settings that have given generations of us the sense of living in a special place and being members of real communities.

The reconstructed Fort at No. 4 at Charlestown, New Hampshire.

❊ Resources & Revelations ❊

FRONTIER FORTS

Fort Dummer—the site of the first European outpost in our region—is now under the waters of the Connecticut River, inundated by a hydroelectric dam in the early 20th century at Vernon, Vermont. Built in 1724, the fort was dismantled in 1763. Artifacts from the fort are displayed at Brooks Memorial Library, Brattleboro.

The second outpost—the Fort at No. 4—was located along present-day Main Street in Charlestown, New Hampshire. Constructed in 1743, it was a log enclosure surrounding a number of dwellings. The town and fort were known as Number Four, because Charlestown was so numbered among towns in the region chartered by the province of Massachusetts. The Fort at No. 4 is now represented by a reconstructed log fort museum that stands on the banks of the river. The museum's structures and programs interpret the Colonial period in the northern valley. Charlestown's Main Street is a National Register historic district.

INDIAN RAIDS & CAPTIVES

In 1704, in one of the bloodiest raids in Connecticut River history, native Americans attacked an English settlement at Deerfield, Massachusetts, and escaped north with a group of captives. Near the mouth of a river that later was named for him, in present Rockingham, Vermont, Rev. John Williams persuaded their captors to let him conduct a Sunday worship service. There, on March 5, 1704, Rev. Williams preached the first Protestant sermon in the territory that later became the state of Vermont. This story was published as the novel, *The Unredeemed Captive.*

The Norwich Congregational Church presides over the town green, scene of community gatherings and celebrations throughout the year.

Among the notable confrontations between Native Americans and settlers were several incidents in Charlestown, New Hampshire. In 1747, the Fort at No. 4 was besieged by a band of several hundred Indians who gave up after several days. However, in 1754, a smaller band of Abenaki returned and took captive five adults and three children, and set off with them toward Lake Champlain. Among the captives was Susannah Johnson, who gave birth on the second day to a child she named Elizabeth Captive Johnson. With one exception, all of the captives were sold in Montreal to French residents, and all came back to New England by 1760.

In 1799, after returning and determining the location of her daughter's birth, Susannah Johnson gained support to raise two slate markers to com-memorate the event. The slate markers are now displayed in a pull-off on Route 106 in Reading, Vermont. They are the oldest historic site markers in the state, among the oldest in the United States, and are listed on the National Register of Historic Places.

TOWN COMMONS & GREENS

The town greens of our region are reminiscent of their predecessors in southern New England towns, but they did not originate in the same way. The towns to the south had been settled by religiously cohesive, like-minded people who set aside common space for grazing cattle and arrayed their homes and fields around the center.

In our region, individualism and business practices generally produced different results. Mid-18th-century proprietors obtained charters and then tried to maximize their profits by selling off as many parcels as possible. Those who purchased land largely did so as individuals or small family groups. Proprietors sometimes drew up parcels without any plan in mind or much knowledge of the land, resulting in property lines and town boundaries that are awkwardly at odds with topography and waterways. Some

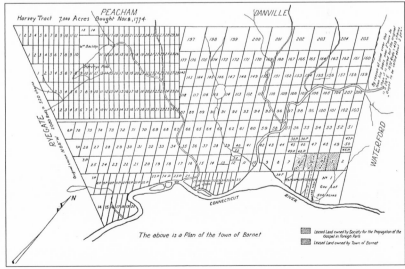

1785 plan of Barnet, showing a layout of lots more appropriate for Iowa than the rugged hills of the northern valley.

Lebanon's Colburn Park and its canopy of American elms, c. 1910.

lands were designated for common use by churches and schools. Some parcels were donated by philanthropists. In time, these plots were improved to become our town commons and greens of today. They are typically grassy lawns that may include ornamental trees, bandstands, cast iron furniture, flag poles, statues, monuments and memorials.

Each town green in our region is the product of unique origins, and these commons vary widely in character and setting. In Lebanon, New Hampshire, busy traffic follows a rectangular pattern around Colburn Park, a somewhat formal common, now a grassy island in an urban grid. Not far away, in rural Lyme, the green is set to one side of the main through street and remains a tranquil refuge. Walpole's commercial main street took shape one block away from its earlier green. Similarly, in Brattleboro, Vermont, the town common stands removed from the commercial district that formed closer to the river and its bridge crossing. Elsewhere in Vermont, in Thetford Center, the green abuts a church, a library, and residences, and offers a vista of New Hampshire hills to the east. Chelsea has two commons.

The village of Westminster, Vermont, was set out on an elevated, terrace alongside the river. Civic buildings and residences are well set back on each side of a wide, straight thoroughfare. Fields extend behind the houses and their associated barns. This setting survives as a remnant of a layout dating to 1736, which apparently was conceived in the tradition of Baroque city planning, unusual in New England. An 18th-century courthouse once stood in the center of the road, which divided to pass around it on both sides.

Canaan Street in Canaan, New Hampshire, is a good example of early town planning. Laid out as "Broad Street" in 1788, it is about a mile in length and beautifully situated. Its orderly arrangement includes a restored meeting house and a variety of late 18th- and early 19th-century buildings and settings, both modest and monumental.

HILL TOWNS

Early turnpikes in New Hampshire and military roads in Vermont followed higher ground to avoid muddy bogs and wide water crossings, stimulating hilltop settlements at travel intervals and crossroads. *(For more, see Transportation.)* Many settlers in the late 1700s were drawn to the hilltops. Damp, tree-tangled floodplains were thought to be unhealthy compared to drier, breezier elevations. Oxen were equal to the task of hauling wagons over steep, stony ground. In the first half of the 1800s, however, many

By 1910, when his family posed in front of their new home in Lyme Center, the village surrounding Charles Sanborn's sawmill had drawn homesteaders from the hills above, but town affairs centered in Lyme Plain, in the valley below.

Industry in Lyme Center included a tannery (no longer standing) at a falls on Grant Brook.

of these hamlets were moved, building by building, to lower ground, to take advantage of mill locations, fertile farmland, new roads, and later, railroads.

Newfane and Grafton, Vermont, are among the former hill towns relocated to lower ground. In 1787, Newfane was a hilltop county seat consisting of about twenty houses and two hotels. In 1825, the hilltop village was dismantled and carried two miles downhill. By 1860, only the old cemetery remained on the hill. Grafton's first settlement is visible only by its cellar holes. In Randolph, Vermont, a hilltop village was established in 1783 and thrived as the town's primary settlement for about 70 years until a railroad line was located two miles away in Randolph Village.

Lyme, New Hampshire, experienced a similar shift of population from a higher to a lower elevation, swelling two early hamlets known as Lyme Center (formerly "Cook City") and Lyme Plain. A Dartmouth College professor's article about this trend was entitled simply "A Town That Has Gone Downhill."

CELLAR HOLES & STONE WALLS

To build their houses, early settlers dug cellars in the ground and lined their sides with large stones to build up a foundation upon which to set their timber framed structures. Today, little remains of some house sites except the hole and the stones. They stand deep in the woods throughout our region like reminders of a past civilization, which indeed they are. Along with miles of stone walls, they are living archeological evidence of our period of settlement, when settlers subsisted on little more than what they could grow themselves. The abandonment of these house sites is also a reminder that woodland and hilltop soils could rarely support even a marginal agricultural life.

Stone walls which now run on through deep woods record the most intense and widespread period of agricultural activity in our history. *(For more, see Agriculture.)*

AGRICULTURAL VILLAGES

The rich alluvial floodplains of our river valleys attracted farmers who formed communities based on agricultural activities, products, and exchange. Among the first settlements established north of the forts in Brattleboro and Charlestown were those of Haverhill, New Hampshire, and Newbury, Vermont (1763), located on fertile oxbows of the Connecticut River. Guildhall is the oldest community

The classic New England town green of Guildhall is ringed by the Community Church (l), Essex County Courthouse (r), and a former schoolhouse, several homes, the Public Library, the Village Store, and the Guild Hall (not pictured).

Calvin Coolidge, 30th President of the United States, at work behind his horses in Plymouth.

in northeastern Vermont, settled in 1764. It remains a quiet example of a rural county seat.

The forested hills and mountains in the upper reaches of the northern valley, also sparsely settled, invited logging—a kind of farming on a longer, larger scale—which produced another kind of community. Pittsburg, New Hampshire, is a small, linear settlement at the southern end of a town nearly 300 square miles in area, the largest township east of the Mississippi River.

Many of our smaller towns and villages have not grown much beyond their origins as settlements based on agriculture. Even where they have, earlier generations of agriculture-related buildings survive here and there among modern structures. Rural life—as distinct from what is known today as a rural "lifestyle"—produced a certain collection of building types and functions gathered together in a particular way.

For example, houses may face each othe around a village green or across a thoroughfare while behind each house is arrayed its associated outbuildings, orchards, and fields. In addition t the general store (with post office), town hall and churches, there may be—or may have been—a gris mill, saw mill, wool mill, blacksmith shop, leathe shop, Grange hall, cheese factory, cooperative creamery, farm equipment manufacturer and farn supply store. The presence or absence of a rail lin and depot is a clue to whether the community wa thriving before or after the railroads arrived around 1850-1860.

The Connecticut River Valley's most outstand ing example of a preserved agricultural communit is the Plymouth Notch Historic District in Plymouth, Vermont. A National Historic Landmark and a state historic site, it includes the 1872 birthplace and boyhood home of Calvin Coolidge, 30th President of the United States. The rural village i virtually unchanged since the turn of the 19th century.

Among the buildings preserved is the modes house with the kitchen where Vice-President Coolidge was sworn in to the presidency by his father by the light of a kerosene lamp early on Augus

The Connecticut River broadens where it links Brattleboro (r), and Hinsdale. The island in the center, once the scene of fairs hosting thousands, a pavilion, and grandstand, largely washed away during the 1936 flood.

3, 1923. The c. 1875 barn built for the President's maternal grandfather contains a museum rich in vernacular agricultural artifacts. The community church, cheese factory, one-room schoolhouse and general store have also been preserved.

RIVER & CONFLUENCE TOWNS

Many early settlers arrived via water or found social and economic reasons to locate near waterways. Commercial and industrial centers took shape around waterfalls, dams, transportation canals, bridges, and riverbank crossroads. These became some of our largest population centers: Brattleboro, Bellows Falls, Springfield, Windsor, White River Junction, and St. Johnsbury, Vermont, and Keene, Claremont, Lebanon, Hanover, Littleton, and Lancaster, New Hampshire.

St. Johnsbury illustrates the 19th-century concept of a town center divided according to topography and function. It has an "upper Main Street" of mansions, schools and churches, and a lower commercial district organized around the railroad. Lyndonville, Vermont, is an example of a community planned and established by a railroad company. *(For more, see Industry & Commerce.)*

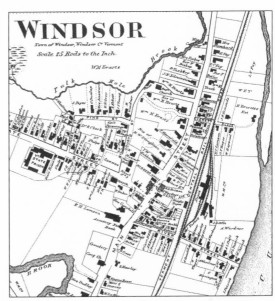

Windsor, Vermont, depicted in 1869, still boasts an arresting array of homes and commercial buildings dating from its glorious mid-19th century.

Brattleboro's historic downtown speaks of a vibrant economy over a century old.

HISTORIC DISTRICTS

Throughout the northern valley, as elsewhere in New England, stand hundreds of buildings that are remarkable for their individual historic and architectural qualities. But what sets the northern valley apart from many other places in America is the number of our communities that retain great numbers of such buildings. This is reflected in the many historic districts documented by the states of New Hampshire and Vermont and listed on the National Register of Historic Places.

Our communities have reason to be proud that these historic districts are unaltered enough to qualify for listing on the National Register. The written nominations for these districts are treasure troves of information about how our commercial and residential and rural areas were established and have evolved over time. Although the histories are based on buildings, they really tell the stories of the many individuals who established the traditions upon which our communities depend today.

COMMUNITY CHARACTER

More than two centuries of settlement and growth produced communities that have a particular look and feel that we cherish. Our places have become materially layered over time just as our local histories are layered by stories from different eras. Maintaining and enhancing the historic physical character of our special places strengthens community identity, civic continuity, and opportunities for economic development. This requires us to work on two fronts at once: revitalizing our traditional commercial centers and reducing the impact of sprawl in agricultural and natural areas.

✻ Threats ✻

Traditional settlement patterns are undermined by a wide variety of economic and social trends and by a myriad of individual and public policy choices. Commercial and residential sprawl diminishes our farmlands and forests at the same time it weakens our longtime commercial centers in villages and downtowns and diminishes our quality of life.

Main Street in Jaffrey, New Hampshire, viewed in two centuries. Change is inevitable, but can be guided constructively by interested citizens with their heritage at heart.

AUTOMOBILES

Since the 1950s, federal investments in the construction of interstate and state highways have promoted the use of automobiles and created an impetus for construction of shopping malls, strip developments, and far-flung housing subdivisions. Dispersing economic activity throughout the landscape saps the commercial vitality of downtowns. Dispersing residences throughout rural areas fragments agricultural and forest lands and wildlife habitat, and contributes to fuel consumption, pollution, and increased costs in municipal services.

LACK OF VIABLE PUBLIC TRANSPORTATION

Many of our historic downtowns were shaped by the golden ages of interstate railroad travel and urban light rail "trolley" systems. Lack of public investment in "pedestrian-friendly" design and alternatives to automobile use inhibits downtown revitalization.

SPRAWL

Sprawl is everywhere around us. Many parts of the northern valley still feel remote or "unspoiled," and retain a distinctive regional character. Other areas are undergoing the same changes that are homogenizing the rest of the country.

As Walt Kelly's comic strip character Pogo declared, "We have met the enemy and he is us." Sprawl is the sum of what we all do. It has many appearances, and can be difficult to perceive. Unless we know what to look for, it may even be invisible.

The commercial strip, pictured here in 1975, had been creeping up on the cornfields of West Lebanon, New Hampshire, even before Interstate 89 and its Exit 20 arrived in the 1960s.

The following summary was developed by the Vermont Forum on Sprawl, sponsored by the Orton Family Foundation. It has been modified slightly for application to the northern valley.

Sprawl is dispersed development outside of compact urban and village centers along highways and in rural countryside.

Sprawl is typically characterized by:

Unnecessary land consumption

Low average densities compared to older centers

Auto dependence

Fragmented open space, wide gaps between development, and a scattered appearance

Separation of uses into distinct areas

Repetitive one story commercial buildings surrounded by acres of parking

Lack of public spaces and community centers

Sprawl is distinct from traditional compact urban centers and villages that are:

- Higher density than surrounding areas
- Mixed use
- Pedestrian oriented
- Served by public facilities, services and spaces
- Diverse in type and scale of housing, business and industry
- Centers for community activities
- Surrounded by open spaces, including productive farm and forest land
- Exemplify a unique cultural heritage

Among the causes of sprawl are:

- Public investments in roads, public buildings, water, sewer and other infrastructure in peripheral areas; faltering investment in existing centers
- Lower land prices in peripheral areas
- Higher costs of development associated with existing centers
- Land regulations that promote suburban-style development
- Concern about financial liability in redeveloping urban brownfields sites
- Other public policies, including tax policies and utility rate policies

- Low cost fuel
- Consumer desire for a rural lifestyle with large homes and large yards, safe environment and less traffic congestion
- Preference of business and industry for easy highway access, plenty of free parking and opportunity for display of corporate identity
- Demands of commercial tenants for particular locations and building or site design
- Telecommunications advances
- Commercial lending practices that favor suburban development

Among the effects of sprawl are:

Increased public costs
- Unnecessary public costs for redundant infrastructure outside existing centers
- Excessive public costs for roads and utility line extensions and service delivery to dispersed development
- Unutilized and underutilized infrastructure in existing centers
- Reduced opportunity for public transportation services

Loss of sense of place and community decline
- Fragmented and dispersed communities and a decline in social interaction
- Isolation of some populations, such as poor and elderly, in urban areas
- Decline in vitality and economic and fiscal viability of existing urban and village centers

Decline in environmental quality and natural resource production
- Fragmented open space and wildlife habitat
- Loss of productive farmland and forestland
- Increase in auto dependency and increased fuel consumption
- Decline in water quality and groundwater supply from increased urban runoff, shoreline development and loss of wetlands

Sprawl can cut off public access to public waterways.

Decline in economic opportunity
- Premature disinvestment in existing buildings, facilities and services in urban and village centers
- Relocation of jobs to peripheral areas at a distance from population centers
- Increased commuting time and cost
- Decline in number of jobs in some sectors, such as retail
- Isolation of employees from activity centers, homes, day care and schools
- Reduced ability to finance public services in urban centers
- Inability to capitalize on unique cultural, historic and public space resources (such as waterfronts) in urban and village centers

REGULATIONS & POLICIES

Many regulations and policies reward the paving of pastures and cornfields, discourage investment in downtowns, and inhibit the redevelopment of mixed commercial and residential uses in commercial centers. These include government and land use regulations and banking and insurance policies.

LACK OF AWARENESS

Neglect and indifference often contribute to the loss of historic and natural resources that are significant to local history and community identity.

❧ Actions & Activities ❧

It deepens our "sense of place" to know how our communities were established, settled, and have changed over time. It's important to reinforce traditional settlement patterns for the sake of social stability, economic vitality, and environmental quality.

In both New Hampshire and Vermont, state agencies and non-profit organizations are working to revitalize downtowns and encourage economic alternatives to sprawl.

EXPLORE

• Look at the grave markers in your local cemeteries and find the oldest dates. From the names on the stones, identify the ethnic groups that are part of your local history. Look for clusters of dates that may be associated with lean farming years, wars, or epidemics (like influenza, 1917).

Students investigate the history told by a quiet corner of their town, while preparing a Valley Quest.

• Visit historical interpretive sites such as Fort at No. 4 and others along the Connecticut River Byway.

• Explore the agricultural village of Plymouth Notch State Park.

• Follow a "Valley Quest" treasure hunt in your area or create one of your own. *(For more about Valley Quest, see FYI below.)*

TRACE LOCAL HISTORY

• Look into regional and local histories for stories about your community's settlement, including contacts with, and attitudes about, Native Americans.

• Find out what date your town was chartered and compare it to the time-line of regional settlement. Look for the first survey to see how the grid of property lots was set out and compare its lines to the natural topography.

• Learn about local history by reading the National Register of Historic Places nomination forms for historic districts and significant properties. The portions labeled "Statement of Significance" describe the growth of towns, neighborhoods, and rural and commercial districts. The forms may be available from your library, town clerk, regional planning commission, or state historic preservation office. (See Appendix D for a list of National Register historic districts in the northern valley.) A significant database of National Register nomination documents in our region can be found at www.crjc.org/heritage.htm.

• If your town has a National Register historic district, share the nomination document with your planning board and compare it with your town's zoning ordinance and site plan review regulations to see if they adequately protect the values it describes.

FATHOM THE FUTURE

• Read the portions of your town and regional plans that pertain to housing, economic development, and natural resources to see how well they articulate policies and goals that guard against the many forms of sprawl. These plans ought to encourage development of traditional commercial centers and discourage development of agricultural and natural areas.

• Find out if there are local plans and zoning regulations that preserve architectural, historic, and natural aspects of your community that are important to its character. Your town office and regional planning commission can guide you. Evaluate these policies and their application to see how well they are functioning.

• Contact the state agencies and non-profit organizations listed in Appendix B and obtain information about tools and activities to maintain and enhance community character.

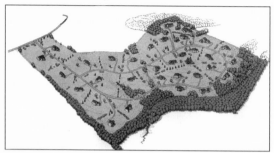

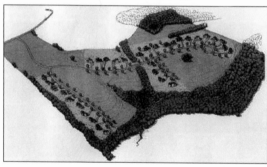

Compare the open space resulting from a conventional subdivision (above) and a conservation subdivision plan (below). After Randall Arendt, 1996.

PARTICIPATE

• Participate in workshops and round table discussions to learn about and share techniques for community and downtown revitalization.

• Attend meetings of your town's planning board or commission.

❊ Q & A ❊

• Take a walk or drive through your town in search of five features that are unique to your home place, and five more which could be found just about anywhere in America.

• Is your corner store a one-of-a-kind family-run business with uneven wooden floors and its own distinctive inventory, or is it part of a national chain with predictable items sold from the same brightly lit shelves you'd find in New Jersey or Ohio?

• Crossing the local stream, do you travel through a wooden covered bridge or over a steel span so common in design you don't even notice it? Which one would you miss if it were gone?

• See the Community Profile chapter for a group of questions whose answers will sketch the history and character of your town by identifying your community's special places.

❊ FYI ❊

HISTORICAL PROFILES

Hands on the Land: A History of the Vermont Landscape by Jan Albers, published for the Orton Family Foundation, MIT Press, Boston, MA, 2000. (Details the interaction of agriculture, settlement, and the natural environment.)

Jaffrey Then and Now, Changes in Community Character by Robert B. Stephenson and Catherine L. Seiberling, Jaffrey Historic District Commission, Jaffrey, NH, 1994. (An engaging and instructive photographic comparison of changes in community character over time, in a village on the edge of the Connecticut River watershed.)

The Last Yankees: Folkways in Eastern Vermont and the Border Country by Scott E. Hastings, Jr., University Press of New England, Hanover, NH, 1990. (Photographs, interviews, and stories about the lives of rural people of the northern valley in the decades before 1950.)

New Hampshire: Crosscurrents in its Development by Nancy Coffey Hefferman, Ann Page Stecker, University Press of New England, Hanover, NH, 1986, 1996.

North Country Captives: Selected Narratives of Indian Captivity from Vermont and New Hampshire compiled by Colin G. Calloway, University Press of New England, Hanover, NH, 1992. (First-person accounts, with historical context explained.)

Over the River and Through the Years: Books One and Two by Katharine Blaisdell, The Courier Printing Co., Littleton, NH, 1980 and 1982.

The Story of Vermont: A Natural and Cultural History by Christopher McGrory Klyza and Stephen C. Trumbulak

Middlebury College Press, University Press of New England, Hanover, NH, 1999.

This American River: Five Centuries of Writing on the Connecticut; an Anthology, edited and selected by W. D. Wetherell, University Press of New England, Hanover, NH, 2002.

Time and Change in Vermont: A Human Geography by Harold A. Meeks, Globe Pequot Press, Chester, CT, 1986. (History and inventory of settlement and industry.)

The Unredeemed Captive: A Family Story from Early America, John Demos, Knopf, 1994. (A novel which tells the story of settlers captured in the 1704 raid on Deerfield, MA.)

Sprawl and Community Planning

Changing Places: Rebuilding Community in the Age of Sprawl by Richard Moe and Carter Wilkie, Henry Holt, New York, 1997. (Two books by the president of the National Trust on the theme: "Communities can be shaped by choice or they can be shaped by chance. We can keep on accepting the kind of communities we get or we can insist on getting the kind of communities we want.")

Conservation Design for Subdivisions by Randall Arendt, Island Press, 1996.

Dealing with Change in the Connecticut River Valley: A Design Manual for Conservation and Development by Robert Yaro, Randall Arendt, Harry Dodson, and Elisabeth Brabec, Lincoln Institute of Land Policy, Cambridge, MA, 1988. (One of the nation's earliest books on preserving the cultural landscape; its Massachusetts examples are applicable to the northern valley.)

Community character is a reflection of who we are, who we were, and who we will be.

The Geography of Nowhere: The Rise and Decline of America's Man-Made Landscape by James Howard Kuntsler, Simon and Schuster, New York, 1993. (A history and critique of how suburbia and sprawl sapped Main Street, civic optimism, and the public realm.)

Growing Smarter: Fighting Sprawl and Restoring Community in America by Richard Moe, National Trust for Historic Preservation, Washington, DC, 1997.

Home from Nowhere: Remaking Our Everyday World for the Twenty-First Century by James Howard Kunstler, Touchstone Books, 1998. (The follow-up to *Geography of Nowhere* proposes antidotes.)

How Superstore Sprawl Can Harm Communities—And What Citizens Can Do About It (1994), "Alternatives to Sprawl" in *Smart States, Better Communities* (1996), and *Better Models for Superstores, Alternatives to Big Box Sprawl* (1997). (By Constance E. Beaumont and published by the National Trust for Historic Preservation, these are rich in case studies, best practices, and recommendations culled from national experience.)

Rebuilding Community: A Best Practices Toolkit for Historic Preservation and Redevelopment, Northeast Office of the National Trust for Historic Preservation, 2002. (A collection of success stories with historic preservation as the driving force behind revitalization. Public policies, financing partnerships, design and adaptive use approaches.)

Rural by Design: Maintaining Town Character by Randall Arendt, American Planning Association, 1994. (A comprehensive manual offering a toolbox of policies and practices.)

Saving Place: A Guide and Report Card for Protecting Community Character by Philip B. Herr, National Trust for Historic Preservation, Boston, MA, 1991. (A groundbreaking workbook.)

Resources

North of Now: A Celebration of Country and the Soon to Be Gone by W. D. Wetherell. The Lyons Press, 1998. (A heartfelt memoir of life, nature, family, and fishing, centered in the northern Connecticut River Valley.)

Valley Quest: Discover Our Special Places (89 Treasure Hunts in the Upper Valley), published by Vital Communities, White River Junction, VT. (Quests are treasure hunts, written by children, that lead us to explore our communities by following clues imbedded in rhymes.)

"The River That Connects Us" poster, Connecticut River Watershed Council, Greenfield, MA, 1998. (Depicts and lists the special historic & cultural resources of the Connecticut River Valley.)

Good Links

http://memory.loc.gov/ammem/pmhtml/panhome.html *Panoramic maps collection from the Library of Congress. The panoramic map, also known as a bird's-eye view, was a popular cartographic form used to depict cities and towns during the late nineteenth and early twentieth centuries. Although not generally drawn to scale, they show street patterns, individual buildings, and major landscape features in perspective. A number of Connecticut River Valley communities may be "visited" on this site.*

www.newurbanism.org *New Urbanism has been described as the revival of the lost art of place-making which promotes the creation and restoration of compact, walkable, mixed-use neighborhoods, towns, and cities.*

www.smartgrowth.org *The Smart Growth Network was formed to look at new ways to grow that boost the economy, protect the environment, and enhance community vitality.*

www.sustainable.doe.gov. *The Sustainable Development Center at the US Department of Energy site offers a variety of useful information.*

Greener Prospects: www.greenerprospects.com *Access to expertise in conservation planning*

Brattleboro Historical Society: www.brattleborohistoricalsociety.org *(This local historical society has posted an extensive, searchable archive of 2500 professionally scanned historical glass plate photos, from which copies can be ordered, and voice recordings of first-person narratives of local luminaries.)*

Windows on Hollis Past: www.hollis.nh.us/windowsonhollispast *(A model for Connecticut River Valley communities. This southeastern NH town has posted old and new maps, photos and stories, and links for conservation and preservation, presenting views of the town's "rural character.")*

CHAPTER FIVE

Agriculture

Our Roots in the Soil

The physical and iconic landscape of the northern valley is firmly grounded in "agri-culture"—as food source, family livelihood, signature land use, economic force, scenic tourist attraction, mythic link to the past, and seasonal reminder of life cycles. Barns and silos stand tall on the land and in our imaginations, and harvests feed our bodies and sense of well being. It is important to support agriculture in its traditional sense as well as its contemporary diversified forms as a contributor to a sustainable economy, civic stability, open space, and sense of place.

❈ The Basic Story ❈

FOR the past two-and-a-half centuries, farming life has shaped and re-shaped the physical character of our cultural landscape and the outlook of generations of residents. Farming provided the means for settlers to gain a foothold in a wilderness. Farming stamped its imprint on our traditional settlement pattern of towns and villages dispersed in a patchwork of fields and forests. In a region now

approximately 85 percent forested, crop lands and pastures are open, patterned lands that form the principal breaks in a virtually continuous canopy of trees. These all form the northern Connecticut River Valley's "working landscape."

More than two centuries of diversified farming produced the relatively small-scale farmstead, a home workplace composed of a variety of agricul-

---

Round barn in Barnet, Vermont.

Sky Farm in Charlestown, a hill farm with connected construction to allow a dry trip from hearth to barn and back.

tural structures linked to a residence. This abundant, evocative, picturesque and still-useful architecture is the emblem of the Connecticut River Valley. Over time, the region's farmers helped to generate periods of growth in our urban centers that served as hubs for the agricultural economy. Those commercial centers today are the downtowns that hold the potential for community vitality.

Although farmers make up an increasingly small minority of our population today, they contribute immeasurably to our physical health and quality of life. Crops like maple syrup, apples, corn, and pumpkins have central places in our public tradi-

Cattle graze in Vernon, Vermont.

tions and family rituals. Most non-farmers are aware that commercial farming is hard and dirty work, and also that most of us know practically nothing about it. Yet most of us are, only somewhat irrationally, convinced by the sight of cows or sheep grazing on a hillside that something is very right with the world.

The history of farming in the region has been one of constant change, and adjustment to weather, technology, economics and market conditions. Archeological evidence shows that humans have farmed in the northern valley since at least AD 1120, when Native Americans grew corn, beans and squash next to the river in present-day Springfield, Vermont. That discovery suggests that agriculture likely was widespread in the river valley. Six-and-a-half centuries later, European immigrants moved onto land cleared by Western Abenaki and planted the seeds they'd carried in from eastern and coastal New England.

Settlers poured into the region beginning in the 1760s, after the conclusion of the French and Indian Wars. Sons and daughters of farmers in Massachusetts, Connecticut, and eastern New Hampshire were stirred to move by rumors of rich soils. Veterans of the Indian wars convinced the New Hampshire legislature in 1773 to build a road from Concord to Haverhill, to access the rich alluvial floodplains known as the Coös or Cohass Meadows. Settlers brought with them the knowledge and skills of subsistence and semi-self-sufficient farming and animal husbandry. They introduced foreign animal and plant species and adapted crops and practices to a new climate and terrain. By necessity, as well as by tradition, some 90 percent of the early population engaged in farming.

Before the 1770s, the first noteworthy crop produced in the Connecticut River Valley in New Hampshire and Vermont was timber, principally tall pines for Royal Navy masts. Later, trees were cut down to clear land for farming and burned to produce charcoal or potash. Potash, one of the first cash crops, was valued as fertilizer, as an ingredient of soap, and for softening wool. Softwood trees in the north still are harvested and ground into pulp to make paper, an industry that blossomed in the 1870s. *(For more about forest products, see Industry & Commerce.)*

The landscape of Vermont and New Hampshire was as open in the mid-19th century as it is forested today. This view of Springfield, Vermont, shows the influence of a century of agricultural activity.

After 1800, many of the mostly self-sufficient farms of the valley began specializing in one thing or another, and began trading and exporting cash crops such as butter, cheese, wool, potatoes, corn, grain, wheat, hops, maple sugar, cattle, horses, and livestock for meat. Farmers carried products by ox- or horse-drawn wagons to local markets and sent them by flatboat down the Connecticut River to more distant customers.

New England was transformed in 1811 when Merino sheep from Spain were introduced to the Connecticut River Valley. Their superior wool prompted farmers to rush into the new market, and by the 1840s, more than two million Merino sheep grazed in both states, most of them in Vermont. The need for sheep pastures stimulated the clearing of nearly three-quarters of the land in the region. Some of the earliest photographs made in the Connecticut River Valley are shocking to modern eyes for the absence of trees in places where forests now stand.

After 1850, the arrival of railroads profoundly influenced agriculture in the region, first generally for the better, then for the worse. Railroads made it possible for northern valley farmers to ship perishable products like cheese, butter and eggs rapidly to new, distant urban markets. New rail depots rewarded farmers who lived nearby but put at a disadvantage more distant hill farmers, who moved to the valleys for both better soils and links to markets. But the railroad companies soon extended lines into the Midwest, and to gain new business, offered western farmers such discounts that it cost less to ship wool from Ohio to Boston than from Grafton, Vermont, or Lancaster, New Hampshire. Farmers responded to these monopolized market forces in the 1870s by forming the national Grange to lobby for their interests.

Hay moves toward home in this undated postcard image created to represent White River Junction, Vermont.

As the sheep industry collapsed in New England, it rose in the West. In the second half of the 19th century, dairy business—first butter and cheese, and then milk—gradually emerged to dominate farming in the northern valley. The Civil War and the prospects of better soils and cheaper land to the west depleted the region's population and resulted in the abandonment of many farms in the second half of the 19th century. Much open land returned to forest. Both states made efforts to resettle abandoned hill farms, and encouraged farmers to seek new business opportunities such as tourism.

In the early 20th century, the number of farmers and farms in the region continued to fall due to continued emigration and economic hardships of the Depression. Gasoline-powered tractors gradually eroded the role of the horse in farming. At mid-century, many long-time farmers retired rather than put away their five-gallon milk containers and invest in bulk tanks, milking machines, and pasteurizing equipment.

Today, the number of farms and farmers continues to shrink, as the price of milk remains low, the cost of producing it increases, and real estate prices entice farmers to sell the land for development. While milk, cheese, and egg production continues,

Greenhouse culture of ornamentals is the fastest growing area of agricultural activity in northern New England today, joining more traditional crops.

diversification has become the trend in regional agriculture which now includes apples, vegetables, cheese made from sheep and goat milk, flowers, herbs, Christmas trees, seeds, farm-raised game animals, and a variety of specialty products. Organic produce has become an increasing part of the market. Greenhouse culture is said to be the fastest expanding area in New Hampshire agriculture, and the interest in heirloom orchard and plant varieties is growing in both states. All these agricultural enterprises, along with farm stands and farmers' markets are significant contributors to the current economy and cultural flavor of the region.

❧ Resources & Revelations ❧

GLACIAL AND FLOODPLAIN SOILS

As the glaciers melted, Lake Hitchcock and thousands of smaller bodies of water acted as settling basins for small-particle soils and terrace deposits of sand and gravel. After the lake drained, humus from generations of decaying plants and the delivery of fresh soil from periodic flooding have built up deep deposits of fertile loam near the Connecticut and its many tributaries. These well-drained soils in glacial terraces form our prized prime agricultural soils. Not only does the Connecticut River Valley boast some of the finest agricultural soil in

Sheep grazing at a conserved Westminster farm produce milk for award-winning cheese.

The Cohass Meadows in Newbury and Haverhill, shown here in high water, owe their fertility to the river. Much of this valuable land is now conserved.

New England, but the extended growing season—sometimes weeks longer next to the river than in nearby uplands—makes for doubly productive conditions.

Stone Walls

When New Hampshire-Vermont poet Robert Frost quotes a neighbor that "good fences make good neighbors," it is in the poem "Mending Wall" and the two are resetting rocks in the wall that marks their common property line.

Stone walls made by human hands in the northern valley were built of rocks broken free of bedrock at higher elevations, by erosion and action of glaciers. Later tillers of the land removed these glacial leavings from fields cleared for farming and set them into walls as boundaries for crop fields, orchards, animal pens, pastures, and wood lots. These walls still stand as a testimony to their backbreaking labor.

You can tell something about both the character of the farmer and how he used the land by checking the size of stones in the wall. The smaller the stone, the more careful the farmer or the more intensive his use. Small stones, for example, suggest the adjacent ground was cleared for crops. Sometimes the stones were simply dumped in a pile at the edge of a field.

Stone walls which now run on through deep woods record the most intense and widespread period of agricultural activity in our history. Along abandoned hill roads, stone road abutments and walls are integrated into building foundations and cellar holes.

Morgan Horse

In the 1790s, schoolmaster Justin Morgan brought into Vermont the colt that was to bear his name and become the progenitor of the Morgan breed of the animal that provided the "horse power" of the regional farming community in the 19th century. The Morgan horse, now Vermont's official "state animal," was strong and versatile enough to drag logs or pull a plow through the week and also prance a carriage to church on Sunday. Justin Morgan is buried in the Randolph, Vermont, village cemetery.

Merino Sheep & Animal Breeding

In 1811, William Jarvis, U.S. consul at Lisbon, Spain and resident of Weathersfield, Vermont, imported some 500 Merino sheep from Spain, including 200 rams from the royal Spanish flocks. The Merino were much larger and their wool longer and thicker than the American sheep breeds of the period. On his floodplain farm in the river road hamlet of Weathersfield Bow, Jarvis raised these sheep and sold their purebred offspring to neighbors and farmers in the region.

Stone walls built long ago now fence in trees, not sheep.

Orford, New Hampshire's celebrated Tullando Royal Maxima set a world record for milk production in 1995.

The introduction of this breed to the upper Connecticut River Valley turned New England into a national center of sheep raising and woolen manufacture. The Connecticut River ferry at the eastern edge of Jarvis's pastures led directly to Claremont, New Hampshire, where a member of his family was among the incorporators of its first textile mill.

This agricultural boom economy in the first half of the 19th century produced what we might fancifully describe as houses and towns built by sheep. On many back roads in still-rural areas there are surprisingly imposing brick or clapboarded houses in the Federal Style, built not by subsistence farmers but by enterprising agricultural innovators who cashed in on the Merino boom. Another example are the scores of water's-edge wool-processing mills that survive from the period when newly-sheared local fleece had to be cleaned, softened, carded, and prepared for shipment to industrial centers for manufacture into clothing and blankets.

Animal breeding remains a part of the agricultural economy. Hubbard Farms, in Walpole, New Hampshire, hatches and raises chickens. The Holstein-Friesian Association, headquartered in Brattleboro, Vermont, maintains records and research on cow breeding. Scottish Highland cattle are also now bred in the valley, particularly in Northumberland, as is the beautiful and powerful Suffolk Punch draft horse, in Cornish.

Dairy Farming

The black-and-white Holstein cow—now a visual icon of tourism promotions and the public imagination—is a relative newcomer. Nineteenth century diversified homesteads relied on generally smaller breeds whose milk was higher in butterfat, such brown-and-white Jerseys. The 20th-century development of milk as a commercial enterprise stimulated a movement toward bigness—both in the size of individual cows and the size of herds. The economics of dairy farming in the 21st century has encouraged further consolidation, resulting in fewer but larger herds. Thus, the traditional "family farm" with a maximum of 75-100 cows is now facing competition from industrial farms milking 1,000 head. The consequences of this "industrialization" of producing milk and cheese using cows, among others, have included the environmental impact of handling and disposing of enormous quantities of manure.

Even as cow-based dairy farming has trended toward the large, a resurgence of small, family-based dairy farming is occurring based on sheep and goats.

Each of these sheep's milk cheeses is handled many times in the Major Farm's cheese cave in Westminster, on its way from the dairy parlor to the dinner table.

University Grange in Norwich, Vermont, one of the valley's unusually large collection of surviving grange buildings.

as well as cows. Milk from all three animals is now used to produce a rich variety of artisan, prize-winning cheeses. These operations are closer in scale to traditional farming in our region in the 19th century, except that their production methods integrate modern equipment and their marketing taps the potential of the Internet.

Farmstead Architecture

Farmhouses, barns, and silos are also architectural icons of the northern valley. Historic agricultural structures are some of the most difficult buildings for which to find new uses once they no longer serve their original purpose. However, as an important part of our working landscape and our sense of who and where we are, their survival depends on more than the limited resources often available to their owners. *(For more on historic agricultural buildings, see Architecture).*

The Grange

Surviving in many small villages and some larger ones, including Hanover, New Hampshire, Grange

halls are another example of "agricultural architecture." The national Grange was organized in the 1870s as a means for farmers to lobby for their interests in state and federal legislatures. Grange halls, built approximately from the 1870s to around 1900, were quasi-public meeting places that served as political and social centers for agricultural life. The Grange is said to be the first national organization to offer leadership positions to women.

Working Farms Open to the Public

A number of working farms in the northern valley are open to the public in a variety of ways, from bed & breakfasts to "petting zoos" to farm museums. One of the most notable is Billings Farm and Museum, in Woodstock, Vermont. It is closely associated with Marsh-Billings-Rockefeller National Historic Park, which interprets two centuries of farming and conservation through the three owners and their families who lived on the property, developed it, and conserved it. The farm museum, named for Frederick Billings, interprets and demonstrates farming history and practices with its herd of big-eyed Jerseys.

Maple Sugar

Before European immigrants arrived in the upper Connecticut River Valley, Western Abenaki boiled

Sugaring has as much to do with love of the tradition as it does with the sweetness of the maple.

maple sap to make sugar. Maple has long been a cash crop for the region's farmers, first as sugar and then as syrup.

Like most farmers, sugar makers have followed trends toward mechanization and centralization. Sap-gathering has passed from ox teams to trucks, from wooden buckets to galvanized buckets to plastic tubing, and wood-fueled evaporators have given way to gas-fired. Some employ reverse-osmosis filtering machines to remove water from sap before boiling. Despite such changes, maple still plays a central role in the agricultural economy, rural iconography and seasonal rituals.

ROADSIDE STANDS, FARMERS' MARKETS & CSAs

When American travelers in the 1920s and 1930s jumped in their cars and took to the region's back roads, they created an expanded seasonal market for the region's fruit, vegetable, and maple syrup producers, who erected simple sales sheds by the sides of the roads. Some new farm stands offer the usual farm produce as well as items common to urban and suburban "convenience stores."

Many communities have revived local traditions that used to give over streets and sidewalks a day or two each week to farmers who brought their produce into town. Some contemporary farmers' markets offer produce, flowers, baked goods and crafts in a festival atmosphere with musical accompaniment. The revival of this link between downtowns and farms renews the role that many of our current commercial centers played as regional market towns for agricultural products.

Community Supported Agriculture (CSA) refers to vegetable farms which provide fresh produce on a regular basis to subscribers throughout the growing season. Growers achieve some financial security

through membership deposits, members receive fresh local produce, and the community benefits through the maintenance of open space. Several CSAs thrive in the Connecticut River Valley, and at least one provides fresh food to nearby low income families.

❋ Threats ❋

Agriculture and our traditional rural landscape are threatened by pressures from real estate and food markets, tax and land use policies, changing cultural values, and lack of public awareness.

DEVELOPMENT PRESSURES

The potential development value of flat, cleared ground encourages the conversion of agricultural land to commercial and residential uses, resulting in unconnected parcels of farmland. Such fragmentation increases the time and energy required to move equipment between various parcels, with the result that an isolated piece, however fertile, might no longer be worth the travel and effort to cultivate.

Communities should plan carefully for the future of their best agricultural lands.

LOSS OF PRIME AGRICULTURAL LAND

Much of our best agricultural land has been—and is being—converted to commercial and residential purposes. This conversion is most regrettable when

the lost farmland includes the region's fertile flood-plain soils best suited to producing crops.

Loss of the Farming Tradition

Continuing a trend of the past two-and-a-half centuries, members of the recent generation continue to leave the family farm, unwilling to take on the lifestyle and face the prospect of long hours of labor, little vacation, and meager income. Soon no one is left to run the farm, and sale of the land is the only option left to older farmers who never could afford to save for retirement. At the same time, land grant colleges have been cutting back on the portion of the curriculum devoted to the education of farmers.

Erosion & Soil Depletion

Rich soils that took thousands of years to accumulate are subject to erosion and depletion, especially along riverbanks where erosive forces of flooding, ice scour, boat wakes and the raising and lowering of water levels behind hydro dams take their toll.

Lack of Public Awareness

Even in our rural region, many children believe that milk originates at the supermarket. The globalization of agribusiness now stocks store shelves with apples from China and lamb from New Zealand. Consumers are largely unaware of local producers

or of the relationship between their purchasing habits and the quality of life they associate with the traditional rural landscape. Some new residents eager to take up a "country lifestyle" sometimes don't bargain on the sensory accompaniments to being farm neighbors, and find it difficult to share the road with slow-moving farm equipment or accept the sounds, odor, truck traffic, or other activity that is part of a farm business.

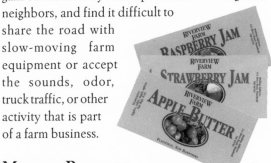

Market Policies

Small producers find it difficult to gain shelf space in chain supermarkets due to the cost of "slotting fees" more easily absorbed by agribusiness conglomerates.

In some places today, diversified agriculture means being able to purchase a flavored coffee at a farm stand along with a chrysanthemum.

Farm Economics

The high cost of doing business (fuel, labor, and equipment) is hard to control and the farmer cannot pass on those costs to the consumer as other businesses do. The weather remains an unpredictable factor in crop success or failure.

❧ Actions & Activities ❧

Our cultural landscape is literally grounded in a diversified agriculture that contributes to a sustainable economy, civic stability, open space, locally-produced food, and sense of place. Farms need friends in their communities, people who appreciate the numerous contributions of agriculture, and who will stand up for agriculture in local zoning decisions, and will make the connection between the views they enjoy and the food they eat by buying locally at every opportunity.

Experience Agricultural Life

• Attend the Upper Valley Land Trust's "First Cutting" event, held every few years in June.

• Cultivate your own gardens. Test your soil, fertilize and control pests organically, and develop your sense of the growing season.

• Visit Stonewall Farm in Keene to experience historic and modern methods of farming.

• Visit Billings Farm Museum in Woodstock and the President Calvin Coolidge Historic Site in Plymouth Notch to learn about historic agriculture.

• Attend Open Barn Day at a local farm.

• Attend farm tours sponsored by the county conservation district.

• Encourage events or fairs to help the public recognize the value of having farms in town such as an apple festival, Old Home Day parade, county fair.

• Attend a county agricultural fair; listen to the conversation, talk with the 4H kids caring for their animals, and enjoy the displays of farm bounty.

• Participate in a farm-related Quest (Valley Quest).

Purchase Locally Grown Products

• Request that your local grocer carry local produce and identify it clearly, perhaps with a sign carrying the farm's name and location.

• Explore the world of tastes past by purchasing heirloom fruits and berries.

• Support your local farmers' markets.

• Visit a farm to pick your own apples or berries in season.

• Join a CSA.

• Find nearby farmers markets, farm stands, and farms where you can pick your own fruits and vegetables at www.ctrivertravel.net.

The First Cutting has introduced hundreds to the ways of farm life in the past.

Look at Local Policies

Read your regional and town plans to evaluate their policies and goals for agriculture. Does your town:

• Have a detailed section on agriculture in your town master plan?

• Allow agricultural uses in more than one zoning district?

• Make allowance for seasonal agricultural businesses such as farm stands in your zoning and site plan review regulations?

• Allow simpler design standards for site plan review regulations on agricultural businesses limited to seasonal use?

• Allow flexibility in regulations to accommodate the unusual needs of some agricultural businesses, such as horse arenas, landscape nurseries, or greenhouses?

• Require buffer zones between farmland and residential uses?

• Provide for the agricultural use of open space land created by innovative residential subdivisions?

• Allow off-site signs to attract and direct farm stand customers? Provide flexibility in local rules, fees, and parking for farmer's markets?

• Allow accessory uses to agriculture?

• Allow farm stands to sell produce purchased elsewhere?

• Allow non-traditional or retail-based farm businesses in an agricultural zoning district?

• Address agricultural structures in building and safety codes?

• Consider farmland a natural resource and encourage conservation easements and purchase of farmland?

• Respect the state Right to Farm law, which has specific exemptions for odor and noise?

• Have farmers serving on the local planning, zoning, conservation, and heritage board or commission?

• Have farmers serving on the local economic development committee?

• Advocate for your town to encourage development in places other than on prime agricultural lands near rivers and streams. Direct development onto low quality soils or sites, in a clustered village pattern, to retain as much contiguous agricultural land as possible.

Gather Information

• Advocate for your town to identify, map, and protect prime agricultural lands.

• Conduct a citizen-led, town-wide agricultural profile to identify current farming activities in town, as well as potential future activities.

• Compile oral histories (with photographs, or videotape) from farmers of various ages, particularly elders with knowledge of previous eras in farm history. Compile and publish them, or create exhibits or videos that tell the story of farming in your area or region.

Support Conservation of Agricultural Land

• Join or support your local land trust and learn how farm land is protected through the purchase of development rights.

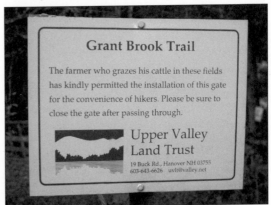

It is essential for farms to have sympathetic neighbors.

Nearly half of the town of Orford turned out to celebrate Tullando Royal Maxima's world record at a festival in her honor.

• Support the current use assessment programs in both states, which tax land based on its use and not on its potential for development.

• Support the assignment of all or some of your town's land use change tax (the tax paid when land which has been enrolled in the current use program is taken out for development) for conservation purposes.

• Encourage listing of suitable local land in the current use program.

• Encourage owners of historic barns to consult the town about tax relief based on a discretionary preservation easement.

• Encourage your town to place conservation easements on farmland which becomes town property before it is resold.

• Encourage your town to consider a cost of community services study to explore the relative tax impact of conserved farmland and other open space.

SUPPORT TRAINING AND ASSISTANCE PROGRAMS FOR FARMERS

• Learn about and support farm programs operated by the U.S. Department of Agriculture's Natural Resources Conservation Service and the University of Vermont and University of New Hampshire's Cooperative Extension. Such programs help farmers pay for control of non-point source pollution, improve business skills, explore new products, and plan for estate taxation issues, among many kinds of useful help.

• Learn about and support state programs that help farmers market their products, adapt their farms for agri-tourism, and find new uses for old barns and outbuildings.

❊ Q & A ❊

• How long is the average growing season in your community? How long is it in the Massachusetts border towns of Brattleboro and Hinsdale? In the Canadian border towns of Pittsburg and Canaan?

• What percentage of your family's food is produced locally or regionally? What would you do if present food distribution systems suddenly collapsed? How long would your present stock of food sustain your family?

• What vegetables, dairy products, and meats are produced by farmers in your area?

• Is there an active grange or 4-H group in your town? Who are the members and what are their activities?

Home-grown marketing at work.

• Are there old cellar holes and stone walls running through the woods in your community?

• Look up the agricultural census information for your town, and match them up with historic maps of your town to identify 19th-century owners of those house sites and stone walls. From the agricultural census information, make an educated guess about what crops or animals occupied the fields enclosed by the walls.

• From the size of trees growing in and around the cellar holes, surmise an approximate date when the house site was abandoned.

"The girls" at the state-of-the-art milking parlor at Tullando Farm in Orford, New Hampshire.

❋ FYI ❋

RECOMMENDED READING

A Long, Deep Furrow: Three Centuries of Farming in New England by Howard S. Russell, University Press of New England, Hanover, NH, 1976 and 1982. (Comprehensive history of people, crops, markets, and farming technology.)

Over the River and Through the Years: Book Three, Farming and Logging by Katharine Blaisdell, The Journal Opinion, Bradford, VT, 1981.

Stone Walls & Cellarholes: A Guide for Landowners on Historic Features and Landscapes in Vermont's Forests by Robert Sanford, et. al., Vermont Agency of Natural Resources, Waterbury, VT, 1994. (This illustrated guide describes the origins, context, and importance of these remnants of an antique agricultural society.)

Stone by Stone: The Magnificent History in New England's Stone Walls by Robert M. Thorson, Walker & Company, 2002. (A view of stone walls, from their geologic origins to their contemporary dismantlement, including the citation of an 1871 census that found 240,000 miles of stone walls in New England.)

LAND USE, PLANNING, ECONOMICS

Preserving Rural Character Through Agriculture: A Resource Kit for Planners, NH Coalition on Sustainable Agriculture, UNH Cooperative Extension, 2000. (http://coopext1.unh.edu)

Conserving the Family Farm by Annette Lorraine, UNH Cooperative Extension and NH Coalition for Sustaining Agriculture, 2002. (Explores the business and personal issues involved in farmland conservation, and recommends a process for developing farm friendly easements. Also available on-line: http://ceinfo.unh.edu/agpubs.htm)

Connecticut River Valley: Opening New Markets for Agriculture, Conference Proceedings and Recommendations, Connecticut River Joint Commissions, Charlestown, NH, 1994. (Ideas specific to strengthening the regional agricultural economy, dealing with financing, market regulations, government support, processing and distribution, agri-tourism, cooperatives and contract marketing, and community supported agriculture.)

HISTORIC BARNS & AGRICULTURAL BUILDINGS

Field Guide to New England Barns and Farm Buildings by Thomas Durant Visser, University Press of New England, Hanover, NH, 1997. (Clear, concise history and guide to agricultural architecture.)

The Granite Kiss by Kevin Gardner, Countryman Press, Woodstock, VT, 2001. (A complete guide to the construction and lore of stonewalls. Its premise is that stonewall building is one of the only rural crafts a layperson can tackle without extensive training and tools.)

Preserving Old Barns: Preventing the Loss of a Valuable Resource by John C. Porter and Francis E. Gilman, 2001. UNH Cooperative Extension, 2001.

"Taking Care of Your Old Barn: Ten Tips for Preserving and Reusing Vermont's Historic Agricultural Buildings," by Curtis B. Johnson and Thomas D. Visser, Vermont Division for Historic Preservation, Montpelier, VT, 1995. (Booklet of practical information; also available on-line at www.uvm.edu/ffvhnet/hpres/publ/barnb/bbtit.html)

HISTORICAL MAPS & CENSUS DATA

Agricultural and Industrial Schedules. United States Bureau of the Census (New Hampshire and Vermont) Washington, DC. 1850, 1860, 1870, 1880.

Town and City Atlas of the State of New Hampshire. Hurd, D. Hamilton. Boston 1892.

GOOD LINKS
Federal
US Department of Agriculture: www.usda.gov

USDA New England Agricultural Statistics Service: www.nass.usda.gov/sub-form.htm

NH offices USDA Natural Resources Conservation Service: www.nh.nrcs.usda.gov

VT offices USDA Natural Resources Conservation Service: www.vt.nrcs.usda.gov

National Association of Conservation Districts: www.nacdnet.org

State—New Hampshire
NH Dept. of Agriculture, Markets & Food: www.state.nh.us/agric/aghome.html

UNH Cooperative Extension: Agricultural Resources: http://ceinfo.unh.edu/aghome.htm

NH Coalition for Sustainable Agriculture: http://ceinfo.unh.edu/agsustbl.htm

New Hampshire 4-H/Youth Development: www.ceinfo.unh.edu/4hyouth/documents/4hyouth.htm

NH Farm Bureau: www.nhfarmbureau.org

New Hampshire Stories, Inc. (farm product marketing): www.nhstories.org

Experience Rural New Hampshire: www.state.nh.us/agric/rural.html

State—Vermont
VT Dept. of Agriculture, Food & Markets: www.state.vt.us/agric/index.htm

UVM Extension Service: www.uvm.edu/extension

Center for Sustainable Agriculture (at University of Vermont): www.uvm.edu/ffsusagctr/

Agriculture in the Classroom Program: www.state.vt.us/agric/AITC/index.htm

Vermont 4-H/Youth Development: www.uvm.edu/extension/4h

VT Farm Bureau: www.vtfb.org

Women's Agricultural Network: www.uvm.edu/ffwagn

Northeast Organic Farming Association—VT: www.nofavt.org

Vermont Farms Association: www.vermontfarms.org

Historic Farm Architecture
Barn Again! www.agriculture.com/ba/ba!home.html

Association for Living History, Farm and Agricultural Museums: www.alhfam.org

NH Farm Museum: www.farmmuseum.org

NH Preservation Alliance: www.nhpreservation.org

The Preservation Institute, Vermont: www.historicwindsor.com

Agri-Tourism
Stonewall Farm, Keene NH: www.stonewallfarm.org

Billings Farm Museum, Woodstock VT: www.billingsfarm.org

President Calvin Coolidge State Historic Site, Plymouth VT: www.dhca.state.vt.us/HistoricSites/html/coolidge.html

Marketing Connecticut River Valley Farm Products
The web site of the Connecticut River Byway (www.ctrivertravel.net) includes listings of farmers' markets, stands, and pick-your-owns in the northern valley.

Vermont Fresh Network creates connections between Vermont farmers and restaurants: www.vermontfresh.net

Vital Communities has focused attention on agriculture and the Food Web in the Upper Valley: www.vitalcommunities.org

CHAPTER SIX

Industry & Commerce

Taking Care of Business

From the days of barter to our cash-and-credit economy, the marketplaces of the northern valley have energized villages and urban commercial centers. These centers first took shape around small, water-powered sawmills and gristmills at waterfalls and cascades. Steam and electricity powered the rise of factories that manufactured machine tools, guns, paper, textiles, and farm equipment. These industries spawned nearby Main Streets whose thriving heydays are being rekindled by a new generation. It is important to strengthen local businesses and traditional commercial centers for the sake of our regional economy and sense of belonging.

❦ The Basic Story ❦

EARLY European immigrants to the upper Connecticut River Valley weren't exactly looking for a "job" the way we think of it today, but most were motivated by the same desires as ours. They sought to earn a living, own and develop property, sell a product, get ahead, be a member of a community, leave something for the children.

Since then, more than two centuries of doing business—certain kinds of businesses, conducted in

a certain way—have shaped our communities. *(For related information, see chapters on Agriculture and Architecture.)* The character of our cultural landscape is itself a product of the work of generations of entrepreneurs, business barons, bankers, investors, production managers, factory workers and laborers, shop keepers, clerks, and customers, too.

They left their mark. There are old stone foundations of early hilltop settlements in southern

Sullivan Machinery Company, Claremont, NH, c. 1907.

The thundering Waits River has powered industry since 1847 at this mill in Bradford, Vermont.

Beginning thousands of years ago with the min ing and fashioning of tools by indigenous people residents of the upper Connecticut River Valle have drawn on its natural resources for manufactur ing. Early subsistence settlers scratched out a livin through agriculture and extraction industries, whic are a response to place and natural resources. Set tlers located mills to take advantage of hydro powe opportunities presented by waterfalls, cascades an gorges, and used their power to cut wood and pro cess food. Later, water supplies were instrumenta in developing large industries based on wool an paper, as they were for local industries based on suc operations as tanning and soapstone cutting.

Products of the forest formed the valley's firs industry. Before 1800, the only crop harvested i appreciable amounts in the Connecticut River Val ley in New Hampshire and Vermont was timbe Logs were sent to sawmills in England and south ern New England, including tall pines for Roya Navy masts.

The British Royal Navy claimed for masts th tallest and straightest pines found in the wilder ness—all trees greater than 24 inches in width—an floated them down the Connecticut as early as th 1730s. The King's arrow-shaped blaze on the bes trees was a source of insult and irritation to settlers The region's forests offered the basis for logging, it first major industry. Waterways provided the mean to float logs to mills, as well as the hydro power t saw the logs. Abundant local wood products wer utilized in building construction, firewood, furni ture and farm machinery, and a variety of househol and commercial goods. In the second half of the 19t century, as erosion and deteriorating soil and wate quality made clear the consequences of indiscrimi nate clear-cutting, new concepts and practice evolved for the conservation of natural resources.

Logging boomed in the last quarter of the 19t century when wood pulp replaced cotton fibers i the making of paper. From 1880 on, steam-drive and gasoline-powered portable sawmills replace

Vermont, and similar traces left by ephemeral log ging camps in remote northern New Hampshire. All over the watershed there are small villages gathered at water-powered mill sites, and a few larger urban centers that coalesced around industries that rode successive waves of invention and technical innova tion. Connecticut River communities excelled at "precision manufacturing" in the machine tool in dustry, at making paper and textiles, and at forging a variety of equipment essential to farming. Commer cial centers grew, first based on river locations and then railroad lines. They took shape during the years when the consumer economy came into being and the classic American Main Street was invented.

A number of modern tools and trends—automo biles, trucks, interstate highways, international free trade, the Internet—have now dispersed commer cial activity throughout the countryside. Industrial "parks" and the occasional shopping mall are sym bolic of the evolution of doing business in the north ern valley.

Log drives on the Connecticut provided a considerable source of excitement.

he small water-powered mills that had straddled streams for a hundred years. Logs were floated down he river and its tributaries to saw and pulp mills. The men who lived in remote logging camps and felled the trees, and then took on the job of running them down the rivers, left a host of colorful, true-life stories and tall tales. The last large log run on the Connecticut, 65 million board feet, mostly spruce, took place in 1915, and provided an occasion for a reunion of old-time log drivers.

Early builders hewed and sawed trees for building frames, quarried stone for foundations and walls, made bricks from deposits of clay, and mixed mortar with local sand. Trees felled to clear land for farming were burned to produce potash and char-

coal. Potash was employed in making glass, fertilizer, mortar, bleaches, dyes and soap.

Mineral resources throughout the region are scattered and small in volume, typically enough to provide only brief boom periods for local economies. Among the region's many small mining industries, the one which attained the greatest stature was copper. Small communities grew up around deposits of granite, limestone, marble, iron, talc, soapstone, and asbestos. A few lime kilns survive as archeological sites. Today the region's most important extraction industries are the mining of sand and the production of gravel by crushing stone and aggregate.

The arrival of railroads in the valley about 1850 improved the transportation of raw materials and finished goods. The new network was much faster than previous flat boats on waterways or wagons over primitive roads. It spurred the growth of industries tied to the region's agricultural economy such as farm equipment makers, cooperative creameries and cheese manufacturers, and wool processing and textile mills. Railroads provided the region with access to iron products previously unavailable due to a lack of ore deposits in the region. The creation of electricity distribution systems—and the construction of major hydro power dams on the Connecticut River in the first half of the 20th century—liberated manufacturers from riverside locations, and dispersed manufacturing throughout the region.

Another advance around 1850 expanded the valley's industries beyond what was local and small in scale—the revolutionary invention and development of "precision manufacturing" of interchangeable parts for weapons and later, machine tools. Precision manufacturing brought economic success and international renown to Windsor and Springfield, Vermont, just as it did to Springfield, Massachusetts, and Windsor, Connecticut.

Many industries were responsible for the growth of small villages and large towns that became residential and commercial centers. Industry owners and managers provided leadership and financial resources

Precision manufacturing, invented in Windsor, Vermont, brought international fame to the valley.

for political, civic, religious, and cultural institutions of their communities, and workers—many of them recent immigrants from other countries—contributed their labor and lively participation in the activities and institutions of their day.

These population centers in the northern valley participated in the evolution of a nationwide consumer economy and the creation of "Main Street" commercial centers in the late 19th and early 20th centuries. Dozens of these are now historic districts listed on the National Register of Historic Places. The narrative histories compiled during the registration process describe how residential and commercial areas of towns grew in relationship to the industries that spawned their creation.

The economic vigor of many of our communities now turns on the revitalization of these traditional commercial centers in the face of modern sprawl development that invites investment and business activity elsewhere. Today communities are adapting to a changing world, not by adopting the generic face of the commercial strip that scars much of America, but by rebuilding their identities and economies around their historic downtowns with the distinctive flavor of northern New England.

❊ Resources & Revelations ❊

EARLY INDUSTRIES

Scattered archeological sites throughout the north ern valley attest to widespread, small-scale min eral extraction during the settlement period. Clue to their existence survive in place names such a Lime Kiln Road in Haverhill, New Hampshire One of the largest concentrations of early indus tries may be found in Tyson village, in the town o Plymouth, Vermont. The village grew up aroun an early iron foundry as well as small mining op erations of gold, iron, talc, soapstone, marble, as bestos and granite. In another part of Plymout there are nine lime kilns, one adjacent to the Crow Point Military Road.

While the center of granite quarrying in Vermon remains outside the Connecticut watershed in Barre

Men and women put their hands to whatever needed doing at Smith & Son in White River Junction, Vermont.

Vermont, at one time many small granite quarries were active. These enterprises produced building stone for local projects and, after the railroads improved transportation, then shipped all over the nation and world. Among these small communities was South Ryegate, Vermont, whose small historic district embodies the history of Scottish immigrant families who provided skilled labor for the mining and shaping of stone.

Above, the industrial complex at Appalachian Sulphides, in South Strafford Vermont. Below, one of the tailing piles at the Elizabeth Mine, a half-century after copper mining operations ceased.

Soapstone quarries were active about 1800-1835 on Cottonstone Mountain in Orford, New Hampshire, and in Grafton, Vermont. Soapstone and talc are still mined in Chester, Vermont. Lisbon, New Hampshire's Old Coal Kiln produced coal around 1860 for use in nearby iron smelters.

MINING

Abandoned gold and silver mines and prospects survive in Littleton, Monroe, Lyman, Bath, and Pittsburg, New Hampshire. Prospectors there tapped the Gardner Mountain mineral belt that runs generally perpendicular to the Connecticut River.

A vein of copper running through Vershire, Strafford and Corinth, Vermont, was the basis for the most significant mineral businesses in the northern valley. These mines helped make Vermont one of the nation's largest producers of copper for a short period of time in the late 19th century, second only to operations around Lake Superior.

Vershire witnessed a boom-and-bust cycle in operations at a village called Copperfield. The Vermont Copper Mining Company, begun in 1853, was later taken over by the Ely family and culminated in an 1883 shut-down accompanied by a miner revolt that drew the intervention of the Vermont National Guard. What remains today is a virtual ghost town where one can still find substantial remains, including flues, mining shafts, refuse piles, and former roasting beds. The mansion of owner Ely Goddard

still stands at the north end of Lake Fairlee. The small rail depot in Ely once hummed with activity from the mines.

Copper mines in South Strafford yielded more minerals over a longer period of time. Operations were focused on what became known as the Elizabeth Mine. This, the oldest copper mine in the United States, opened in the Ompompanoosuc River watershed in Strafford and Thetford, Vermont in 1809, after copper was discovered there in 1793. The site quickly became so important that President James Monroe paid a visit during his 1817 tour of

New England. First a source of copperas, an iron-sulfur substance used in making dyes and inks, a wood preservative, and disinfectant for privies, in the 1830s the mine added smelting for copper in eight furnaces. Eventually, miners worked in shafts 1,000 feet below the surface.

Activity peaked in the 1950s when the mine employed 250 workers and used a ton of dynamite a day. After producing 90 million tons of copper in 15 years, the mine closed in 1958. The century and a half of mining left their mark in the moonscape of mountainous tailings piles left behind, where copper, other heavy metals, and acid leached into tiny Copperas Brook and then into the West Branch of the Ompompanoosuc, a major tributary of the Connecticut. By the late 1990s, it became clear that the result was the near biological death of the nearby waterway, and concerned citizens decided to take action. In 2001, EPA added the Elizabeth Mine to the Superfund List, after carefully developed cooperation between the federal, state, and local governments and citizens.

WATER-POWERED MILLS

The earliest power source employed for industrial work in the northern valley was falling water. Water impounded into millponds above falls and cascades dropped through mills to generate power for turning machinery to saw wood, process wool, and grind grain. Stone-walled and timber-framed mills constructed in the first half of the 19th century survive throughout the northern Connecticut River Valley. An 1828 woolen mill in Bridgewater, Vermont, has been rehabilitated for retail use, as was an 1847 mill in Bradford, Vermont, just downstream from falls on the Waits River. The 1830 Adams Grist Mill in Bellows Falls, Vermont, constructed adjacent to the Bellows Falls Canal, drew its waters to grind food for people and farm animals. Ben Thresher's mill in Barnet, Vermont, that once made sled runners, ox yokes, wagons and other custom wood items for the surrounding agricultural community, was the sub-

ject of a documentary film and is now a local preservation effort.

The forests of northern New Hampshire once supported many water-powered saw mills in the 19th century. Ironically, many were washed out by freshets made more catastrophic by the clear-cutting of forests in the watersheds above. By the 1850s, when three-quarters of the landscape stood deforested, the resulting hydrology forced the focus of manufacturing to shift from small streams which tended to flood and then dry up between storms, to rivers with larger watersheds which could provide a more dependable supply of water power.

Ben Thresher's Mill in Barnet, Vermont, built 1872, pictured in the 1980s (above) and in 2002 during its restoration as a working museum. The cider end and blacksmith shop were added in the early 1900s. The mill made wagon wheels, sleds and water tubs, and repaired farm and logging equipment.

Such a mill that survives is the Garland Mill on Garland Brook in Lancaster, listed on the National Register of Historic Places. First built about 1860 and reconstructed in 1877 after a fire, it was at the time one of five water-powered sawmills in Lancaster and about two hundred in Coös and Grafton Counties. When a logging railroad reached the headwaters of Garland Brook and quickly depleted the area's timber supply, this and many such mills were abandoned. Today the Garland Mill is back in operation.

Many of the mill ponds on our rivers and streams are picturesque but now often functionally obsolete and full of sediments. Their dams impede the passage of fish, and reduce water quality by capturing and storing pollutants and allowing water to warm up and become more inhospitable to native fish. In both states there is support for removing or breaching some of these "deadbeat dams" while preserving historically significant portions of early mills and their stone foundations. In a number of communities, dams may have outlived their usefulness, yet the millpond is a much loved and scenic fixture of the village center. In those cases, it may be preferable to add a fish ladder and restore the dam rather than remove it.

Hydroelectric Power

A hydro dam built at Lyman Falls between Bloomfield, Vermont, and Stratford, New Hampshire, in 1903 (breached in the early 1960s) may have been small, but it played a big role in local history, bringing the first electric power to Bloomfield and the rural hamlets on both sides of the river. Log drives moved through this stretch using a boom which caught the timber just upstream from the dam, holding the wood until it could be funneled through a narrow path of booms leading to a sluiceway on top of the dam.

New England's largest river naturally attracted the attention of those who would capture its power. "Speed bumps" in the river, in place as early as 1792 at Turner's Falls, Massachusetts, have proliferated over the last two centuries, with eleven dams now harnessing its power on the mainstem in New Hampshire and Vermont and impounding 144 miles, or slightly over half the river between the two states.

Several, such as the Wyoming Valley Dam between Guildhall and Northumberland, have evolved full circle from an early timber crib structure, later reinforced with concrete and a powerhouse, reverting once more to a falls as the river crushed the dam in the 1980s and slowly rediscovered its old riverbed. Others, such as the massive 178-foot Moore Dam between Waterford and Littleton, have barred the river only since 1957. The impoundment behind it amounts to the fourth largest lake in New Hampshire. Beyond these behemoths, many of their smaller brethren are at work on tributaries large and small, some directly powering industry, others producing electricity to run one household or a hundred.

Some dams are "run of river," and simply pass water through a turbine as it moves downstream, and others are "peaking" facilities, which capture and store water to generate power at a later time. Unlike other power sources, which need a spark or other

The Wyoming Valley Dam between Guildhall and Northumberland, before the river breached the dam in the 1980s.

electrical stimulus to initiate generation, a running river is ready to deliver power whether the switches are on or off. A hydroelectric dam is able to supply power instantaneously at times of high demand, and even to provide a "cold start" to a dead electrical grid. During the widespread blackout in the Northeastern U.S. in 1965, Wilder Dam started the process that turned the lights back on throughout this darkened corner of the nation.

Fifteen Mile Falls, which consists of the Moore, Comerford, and McIndoe Falls hydroelectric generating stations on the Connecticut River between Littleton/Monroe, New Hampshire and Waterford/Barnet, Vermont, is the site of a former series of powerful and legendary waterfalls. Now buried beneath towering dams and miles of captured river, the biggest hydroelectric site in all of New England is a critical source of power for the region.

The federal government issues long-term licenses for such dams which control their operation. Understanding the need to balance the competing values and uses of the river, the owner of Fifteen Mile Falls worked with the governors, state and federal agencies, local interests, and non-governmental organizations to negotiate a Settlement

Agreement for the license issued by the Federal Energy Regulatory Commission in 2002. The Agreement set out general standards for the protection of the public values of water quality, fisheries, wildlife, recreation, land use, and aesthetic and cultural resources.

Peaking power plants such as Vernon Dam result in changing water levels.

LOGGING & PAPER MANUFACTURING

Logging in the northern forests of Vermont and New Hampshire in the 19th and early 20th centuries is the stuff of legends. The men who spent the winter months felling and gathering trees, and the spring season running logs down the rivers, were larger than life. And the companies they worked for were larger in influence than the governments that failed to anticipate the consequences of their practices.

Downstream from vast forest tracts, the village of Bellows Falls, in Rockingham, Vermont, was the primary destination of logs first floated down the Connecticut and later carried on railroad cars. In 1869, William A. Russell, born upriver in Wells River, Vermont, established a company that became one of the first to manufacture paper from wood pulp on a commercial basis.

By the 1890s, his company and several others made Bellows Falls one of the world's leading paper manufacturers. In 1898, Russell was an early president of the International Paper Company whose consolidated holdings included pulp and

The massive Comerford Dam was the largest hydro project of its kind when it started operating between Barnet, Vermont, and Monroe, New Hampshire, in 1930.

paper mills in Bellows Falls and Wilder, Vermont, sawmills in Hinsdale and Lancaster, New Hampshire, and a paper and pulp mill in Montague, Massachusetts, all in the Connecticut River watershed. International Paper pulled out of Bellows Falls in the mid-1920s, and paper manufacturing there lasted only into the 1950s. Only a few of Bellows Falls' paper mill buildings have survived. While some buildings have been adapted for other uses, others lie in ruins.

Stratford and Lisbon, New Hampshire also grew thanks to the paper industry. Paper mills have been vitally important to the economies of Ryegate and Gilman, Vermont, and Groveton, New Hampshire, among others. As the contemporary embodiment of a way of life that goes back to the settlement period, they are a vivid expression of the culture of the northern region. The viability of manufacturing paper and finished wood products locally has been undercut by the global timber economy and cheap imports from Southeast Asia and elsewhere, raising questions about the future of the once-thriving industry in the northern valley.

Private sawmills continue a long tradition in the North Country.

The Wausau mill is a fixture of the Groveton, New Hampshire, skyline.

Textile Manufacturing

U.S. Ambassador to Spain William Jarvis introduced Merino sheep to the Connecticut River Valley—and all of New England—when he brought them to his farm on the banks of the Connecticut in Weathersfield, Vermont, in 1808.

Two decades later, the Monadnock Mills were established just across the river, the first and soon the largest textile manufacturer in the upper Connecticut River Valley. Beginning with one factory building and associated boarding houses on the Sugar River in Claremont, New Hampshire, it grew into a large complex with the arrival of the railroad.

As did the paper industry in Bellows Falls, the textile industry in Claremont transformed a rural village into an urban industrial town. As a major employer in the region, it gave young Connecticut River Valley women a local alternative to attractive jobs in the textile mills along the Merrimack River in eastern New Hampshire. Monadnock Mills owners adopted the enlightened philosophy that pleasant working conditions maximize production, and built housing for workers within a well-defined urban district.

This 1930 view of Windsor depicts the distinctive worker housing developed by industry, seen on the right, next to the river. Much survives to this day.

PRECISION MANUFACTURING

Inventors and manufacturers in our region had a hand in some of the major advances in the Industrial Revolution. A 1994 National Park Service study noted that "precision manufacturing" is a significant regional historic theme in the four-state watershed. The foremost representative of that theme in the northern valley is the American Precision Museum in Windsor, Vermont. A National Historic Landmark, the museum occupies the former 1846 Robbins and Lawrence Armory and

The American Precision Museum sits next to the power source for early precision manufacturing in Windsor, Mill Brook.

Machine Shop on Mill Brook, and houses the finest collection of precision machine tools in the nation.

The inventive genius of three men, primarily Richard S. Lawrence, produced significant improvements in the design and production of precision machine tools in the 1840s. In their first big job, for the Federal government, they mass-produced rifles with interchangeable parts, employing for the first time this simple concept that would revolutionize industry world-wide. Later, they invented machine tools such as a profiling machine, a milling machine, and a universal milling machine. After seeing Robbins and Lawrence machinery at the Crystal Palace Industrial Exhibition in London in 1851, a British parliamentary commission came to Windsor to study the details of the "American system" and ordered machines for shipment to British arsenals.

Springfield's first machine shop was built about 1810 near four other mills in what was then the village of Lockwood's Mills, where the Black River drops 110 feet in one eighth of a mile. For the next 80 years, businesses manufacturing machinery to create products in wood, iron and textiles formed Springfield's inventive machine shop tradition.

The 1880s and 1890s witnessed the launching of three companies that drew on the creative and influential leadership of James Hartness, a governor of

Invention of the Fairbanks Scale put St. Johnsbury, Vermont, on the map.

Vermont: the Jones and Lamson Machine Company, the Fellows Gear Shaper Company, and the Lovejoy Tool Company. Springfield's machine tool industry shaped the town's growth in the late 19th and early 20th centuries, resulting in the National Register district enjoyed today. Hartness started his career at Jones and Lamson in 1889 at the age of 16, becoming its president in 1900. Among his inventions were the flat turret lathe, automatic die, and double-spindle lathe.

In St. Johnsbury, Vermont, the E. & T. Fairbanks Scale Works stimulated the growth of a substantial industrial and cultural center astride terraced hillsides above the Passumpsic River, high up in hill country. Erastus and Thaddeus Fairbanks established their iron foundry in 1823. Thaddeus' invention of the platform scale in 1830 launched a company that became one of the region's foremost iron-working industries as well as the world's largest producer of platform scales for a century, and revolutionized standards for the accurate commercial measure of goods throughout the United States. Although the original scale works was destroyed by fire in 1972, the philanthropic Fairbanks family, which appreciated art and architecture, donated many public institutions to St. Johnsbury, including the Fairbanks Museum and the Athenaeum.

SCIENCE & INVENTIONS

The northern valley's general absence of light pollution from urban centers made it a favorable location for early 20th century residents interested in astronomy. Stellafane Observatory in Springfield,

Vermont had its origins in the genius and inventiveness of one man and a local group of amateur astronomers. The two-building complex, now a National Historic Landmark, was designed and built in 1924 and 1930 by Russell W. Porter, arctic explorer, artist, astronomer, architect and engineer. It consists of an observatory with a 16-inch, reflecting turret telescope, and the clubhouse of Springfield Telescope Makers, Inc. The club, founded in 1923, was the first organized group of amateur telescope makers in the country. Porter, who left Springfield for California to work on the giant Palomar telescope, is considered the founder of the amateur telescope making movement.

A related Springfield landmark is the Hartness House. The impressive c. 1904 Shingle-Style residence of James Hartness (listed on the National Register) is unusual in Vermont and includes five underground rooms and an underground passage to an observatory containing a Russell Porter telescope.

Bradford, Vermont, was the birthplace and home of Admiral Clark James Wilson, a farmer and self-taught engraver. In the early 1800s, Wilson made and sold the first geographical globes in the United States. Halifax, Vermont, is the birthplace of Elisha Graves Otis, inventor of the "safety elevator," founder of Otis Elevator Company.

The Littleton, New Hampshire, factory building still stands in which, from 1867 to 1909, the world famous Kilburn brothers, Benjamin and Edward, produced and distributed the world's largest assortment of stereoscopic views. Their collection provided popular parlor entertainment for generations.

LOCAL INDUSTRIES

Some local industries employed natural resources distinctive to particular locations. For example, clay deposits in Keene, New Hampshire, and four surrounding towns provided the raw material for nearly a million bricks for local use. The Spaulding brickyard in Woodstock, Vermont, supplied bricks for the Windsor County Courthouse, Gov. Billings's house in Woodstock, Gates Opera House in White River Junction, and many other structures. Fine sands around Keene and Stoddard, New Hampshire, were employed in glass-making in the mid-19th century.

Other industries were based on the inventions or innovations of individual entrepreneurs, related industries, or a pool of trained workers. The Estey Organ complex in Brattleboro, Vermont, was the largest organ manufacturer in the world in 1880, employing 500 men and women, turning out more than 250,000 reed organs before pianos eclipsed their popularity. In Bellows Falls, a railroad junction stimulated the growth of the Vermont Farm Machinery Company and the Bellows Falls Cooperative Creamery.

THE GENERAL STORE

While industrial manufacturing created lively commercial centers in towns up and down the Connecticut River Valley, the general store functioned as the entire commercial center for small villages. It sold groceries, hardware, dry goods, clothing, building materials, animal feed, farming equipment, candy, newspapers, and anything else that had a local market. Among the early general stores that survive in much their original setting is the Brick Store in Bath, New Hampshire, listed on the National Register of Historic Places. Built in 1824, the Brick Store is one of the earliest commercial buildings in New Hampshire, and is said to be the oldest continually operating country store in America. The front of the store features a Doric portico and second floor porch. Its exterior rear wall served as a billboard directed toward passengers on passing trains.

General stores still anchor many a village in the Connecticut River Valley, holding tight against the growing tide of multi-national corporations seeping into northern New England. Chapman's in Fairlee, Dan & Whit's in Norwich ("if we don't have it, you don't need it"), and many others like them keep dollars at home and provide informal community gathering places.

DOWNTOWN REVITALIZATION

The northern valley's commercial downtowns are remarkably intact examples of classic American "Main Streets" that were created in the late 19th and early 20th centuries. They are compact streetscapes composed of commercial buildings constructed over that period in a variety of historic architectural styles. Through the 1950s, these traditional commercial centers fulfilled the role of regional market towns, transportation centers, and social gathering places. The arrival of interstate highways in the 1960s dispersed commercial activity more widely throughout previously rural areas.

The strength of our traditional downtowns has been sapped by a variety of events and trends over the past half century. Among them was the concept that "urban renewal" required the bulldozing of older buildings and the redesign of downtowns to support automobile use. Such policies instead resulted in places that lost connection to their pasts and became degraded environments in which to do business.

The Brick Store in Bath, New Hampshire, is listed on the National Register of Historic Places, and is a favorite of bus tours.

Since 1829, this church, now the United Church of Christ, has been part of the civic streetscape at colorful Central Square in Keene, New Hampshire. Visit page 141 for a glimpse of the same scene a century earlier.
Photo by Richard J. Ewald.

A quiet adventure awaits up a back road in the northern hardwood forest, arrayed in autumn's reds and golds.
Photo by Rosamond Orford.

*Sunlight lifts morning mists from the hills above the Connecticut
River between Thetford and Lyme.*
Photo by Rosamond Orford.

The Canada Lynx, well adapted to the deep snows of the cold boreal forest, is considered endangered in New Hampshire and Vermont. This cousin of the bobcat and cougar could well recover within the boreal region in the Connecticut River Valley, assuming our communities can successfully conserve and steward the habitat it requires. Photo by Susan Morse.

The family farm at home in the hills. For centuries, the fertile soils of the Connecticut River Valley have fed its people and grown its traditions. Photo by Rosamond Orford.

The Connecticut River Valley has long been home to people with eyes for beauty and hands with talent. Late Woodland Period vessel, circa 1000 AD, from the Hunter Site at the confluence of the Connecticut and Sugar Rivers at Claremont, New Hampshire. Sargent Museum Collection. Photo by Richard Boisvert.

The gardens of Aspet, the home of sculptor Augustus Saint-Gaudens in Cornish, New Hampshire, are adorned by the blues of delphinium in the foreground, and Mount Ascutney in the distance. Photo courtesy of the National Park Service and the Saint-Gaudens National Historic Site.

Fishing the river at sunset. Many people who have spent their lives within sight of the Connecticut River are now discovering its peace and beauty for the first time, often through the simple act of floating downstream. Photo by Bob Linck.

Today's Main Street in Wells River, Vermont, retains much of the character shown here a century before.

A number of northern valley communities have adopted the "Four-Point Approach" to downtown revitalization created by the National Main Street Center of the National Trust for Historic Preservation. The New Hampshire Main Street Center and the Vermont Downtown Program assist these communities, which are among more than 1,200 communities nationwide which follow the Four-Point Approach.

The four points: Organization, Economic Restructuring, Design, and Promotion, encompass a variety of activities that chart a path to revitalization appropriate to each community. Northern valley communities with downtown programs include Claremont, Lancaster, and Littleton, New Hampshire, and Brattleboro, Bellows Falls, Springfield, Windsor, and St. Johnsbury, Vermont. For more about this approach, see FYI below.

COTTAGE INDUSTRIES

Throughout our history, the rural farmstead has been both home and workplace. Even off the farm, cottage industries and home occupations have provided income for people working at home as well as goods and services for the local economy. Today, most of the companies in our region are small businesses, employing less than 30 people, and many of these operate in or near the home of their originators. Improved communications technology, such as personal computers and the Internet, now permits self-employed "knowledge workers" to conduct more business in home offices and gives employees the opportunity to "telecommute" from home to their employers' workplaces.

❋ Threats ❋

Our traditional industrial and commercial centers are undermined by a wide variety of national and international economic and social trends and a myriad of individual and public policy choices. Unsustainable and inappropriate use and unnecessary pollutants threaten natural resources.

THE GLOBAL ECONOMY

The shift of industries to the southern U.S. and to other countries continues to undermine northern valley businesses, from precision manufacturers to saw mills. The growth of giant national retail chains similarly challenges the viability of locally-owned businesses.

CONSOLIDATION & DISINVESTMENT

The normal business cycle has always included periods when companies grew by mergers and consolidation. The creation of the International Paper Company in 1898 as a consortium of 13 companies is a good example. However, today the trend toward consolidation frequently results in the acquisition of small companies in our region by national or international corporations, and then the downsizing or closing of the local firms.

BROWNFIELDS

The term "brownfields" refers to sites polluted by industrial use. These places are the legacy of previous industrial eras when the importance of environmental health was less understood than it is

A former brownfields site finds new life as the home of Bellows Falls' new Byway interpretive center.

today. In all too many cases, historic regional industries have become obsolete or moved production to other locations, leaving large, empty buildings and sites contaminated by industrial chemicals. While many of these sites are prime candidates for adaptive reuse, prospective developers are wary of taking on liability for previous pollution. Some communities in our region are taking advantage of federal grants and programs to resolve liability issues and clean up the sites.

Invasion of the Big Box

National-chain retailers build giant cookie-cutter stores with oversized parking lots on large parcels of land claimed from agriculture and floodplains. These out-of-state corporations typically put out of business a wide variety of local stores that formerly sold such goods as groceries, books, hardware and building supplies, stationery and office supplies. This deprives our communities of the continuity of stable downtown shopping districts and the "multiplier effect" of dollars that recirculate locally.

Cell Towers

Telecommunication began in our region almost a century ago with the creation of local telephone companies. Today, the increasing popularity of cellular phones is leading to a demand for "cell tow-

ers"—without which wireless telephones cannot function—and proposals for so many that our hilly landscape appears destined to resemble a pin cushion. In some communities, like Newbury, Vermont, antennas are located within buildings such as church steeples as an alternative to placing oversized industrial structures in historic or scenic areas.

The Connecticut River Valley's most beautiful cell tower, in Newbury, Vermont. The secret is below.

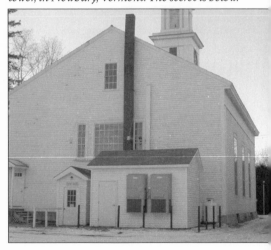

❈ Actions & Activities ❈

It is important to know how our commercial history has shaped our communities and to pursue economic development that is compatible with historic preservation and environmental protection.

LOCAL HISTORY HOMEWORK

• Identify and document archeological sites and ruins of historic industrial and commercial structures. They are an important part of community identity.

• Explore the history of your community's early efforts to provide gas lighting and electrical and telephone service.

• Assemble oral histories of residents who have worked in the manufacturing and service industries and in retail businesses in your community

• Use historic maps—including the Sanborn Insurance Company maps from the 19th and early 20th centuries—to follow the growth of local industries.

HISTORY MEANS BUSINESS

• Promote the rehabilitation of historic industrial structures for new commercial, residential, or educational uses. Industrial communities like Manchester, New Hampshire and Lowell, Massachusetts illustrate how old mill buildings can be used for multiple purposes in a way that reinforces community identity, preserves historic structures, and enhances the local economy.

• Promote the use of federal and state historic preservation investment tax credits for the rehabilitation of historic industrial and commercial centers.

• Support efforts to clean up and re-use brownfields areas.

• Establish a downtown revitalization program. Learn how through the "four-point approach" developed by the National Main Street Center of the National Trust for Historic Preservation.

• Visit the Stellafane Observatory for a star party or other event.

• Participate in the excavation or restoration of an historic site like Ben's Mill in Barnet.

NEW DEVELOPMENT IN OLD COMMUNITIES

• Make sure your regional and town plans and local zoning bylaws influence commercial development to be consistent with your community's character. Consult your town office and regional planning commission. These policies and regulations should make clear to potential developers and investors what kind of development your community wants and in what locations. (Be specific... would your town's zoning allow an industrial-sized water amusement park to be built on prime agricultural soils, in the floodplain, on the banks of the Connecticut River?)

• Does your town have site plan review which addresses how new development fits into old streetscapes, protects the town from light and noise pollution, and provides for screening of parking lots?

• Does your town have a signage ordinance? If not, work with the local business community to ensure that commercial development is compatible with the character of your town.

• Check your local zoning to see if it encourages cottage industry to operate in some or all designated areas of the town, as long as performance standards are met.

• Support your local businesses, downtown merchants, and farmers. While some items may cost more than they do in national big-box chain stores, the money you spend in locally-owned businesses will stay in your community and help maintain your quality of life.

• Encourage local retailers to carry locally produced items.

FOREST REVIVAL

• Visit Weeks State Park in Lancaster, New Hampshire, and climb the historic stone fire tower there to look out over the region's vast forests and scenic vista of the Presidential Range and the White Mountain National Forest.

• Support sustainably harvested forest products.

• Arrange for your local library or community center to host an exhibit from the Northern Forest Center.

• Tour a paper making plant or visit a woodworking shop.

❧ Q & A ❧

• Where was early trade in your community focused? Boston? Connecticut? New York?

• Which industries in your community are locally owned and run, and which are units of companies owned elsewhere?

• Which industries in your community have historic ties?

❧ FYI ❧

RECOMMENDED READING

Locating Telecommunications Towers in Historic Buildings by Nancy E. Boone, et. al, Preservation Books, National Trust for Historic Preservation, 2000. (www.nthpbooks.org)

Logging Railroads of the White Mountains by C. Francis Belcher, Appalachian Mountain Club, Boston, MA, 1980.

The Northern Forest by David Dobbs & Richard Ober, Chelsea Green, Chelsea, VT, 1996. (The character, politics, and economics of the forested northern portions of New Hampshire, Maine, Vermont, and New York, reflecting the variety of people whose lives are bound to the land.)

Over the River and Through the Years: Book Four, Mills and Mines by Katharine Blaisdell, The Journal Opinion, Bradford, VT, 1982.

Spiked Boots by Robert E. Pike, Yankee Books, Dublin, NH, 1956, 1959; and *Tall Trees, Tough Men* by Robert E. Pike, W.W. Norton & Co., NY, 1967, 1984. (Compelling

histories and narratives of logging and log drives on the upper Connecticut River and Maine, by a master storyteller.)

Time and Change in Vermont: A Human Geography by Harold A. Meeks, Globe Pequot Press, Chester, CT, 1986 (History and inventory of settlement and industry.)

200 Years of Soot, Sweat and Toil: The History and Archeology of Vermont's Iron, Charcoal, and Lime Industries by Victor Rolando, Vermont Archeological Society, 1992. (An indispensable source for the history and surviving evidence of the state's early rural industries.)

The Upper Valley: An Illustrated Tour Along the Connecticut River Before the Twentieth Century by Jerold Wikoff, Chelsea Green Publishing Co., Chelsea, VT, 1985. (Interesting collection of images not found elsewhere.)

GOOD LINKS

The National Main Street Center of the National Trust for Historic Preservation: www.mainst.org

New Hampshire Main Street Center: www.nhcdfa.org/mainstreet.html

Vermont Downtown Program: www.dhca.state.vt.us/DHP/programs/downtown.html

Vermont Division for Historic Preservation: www.dhca.state.vt.us/DHP/

Orton Family Foundation: www.orton.org   (The Orton family operates the Vermont Country Store in Weston and Rockingham, VT. Among its many programs, the Orton Foundation supports local country stores.)

Businesses for the Northern Forest: www.businessnorthernforest. org

The Northern Forest Center: www.northernforest.org (The Northern Forest Center serves as a convener of ideas and dialogue on issues ranging from cultural heritage to economics, ecology, and community development in northern Vermont, New Hampshire, Maine, and New York.)

New Hampshire Stories: www.nhstories.org (The New Hampshire Stories program promotes the people, products, and services of New Hampshire.)

Vermont-made products: www.1_800_vermont.com/products/index.asp

Vermont Independent Country Stores: http://vaics.org (A nonprofit organization dedicated to promoting and enhancing country stores, while preserving their unique heritage and contributions to their communities.)

CHAPTER SEVEN

Transportation

Traveling Places

When we say a location is "an hour away," we imply a transportation mode without measuring the distance. Getting from here to there has not always been so easy. Old bridges, roads, and rails are like footprints on the landscape left by previous generations. Historic transportation structures and settings express the pace and aesthetics of their times, illustrate technological change, and establish a human scale in the realm of machines. It is important that modern modes and technologies contribute positively to community character and that public transportation spaces be designed to be compatible with their natural and built environment.

❊ The Basic Story ❊

THE hilly, forested, and water-riven topography of the northern valley has always been a challenge to travelers and builders. From footpaths to sidewalks, from wagon roads to interstate highways, a network of routes and a variety of travel modes imprint the region with a legible history of transportation. The origins of many communities can be traced to decisions about where to locate a bridge, a road crossing, a rail depot, and even an interstate exit. Similar decisions today continue to affect community character and vitality.

Our region can claim several transportation firsts—the first bridge over the Connecticut River any-

---

Travelers on the Coös Turnpike depart from a stagecoach inn in Haverhill.

The first bridge across the river anywhere was the Enoch Hale Toll Bridge connecting Bellows Falls and Walpole, built in 1785.

where in its entire length, the nation's first chartered canal company, and one of the first steamboats. Sprinkled throughout our local histories are the stories of speculators and inventors and tinkerers whose breakthroughs changed society, like the man who built a steam-propelled, charcoal-fired, four-wheel automobile in 1875, in an old brick mill that still stands.

Before the arrival of European settlers, Native Americans traveled by canoe on rivers and streams and by foot through the forest. The Connecticut itself was a main travel corridor, linking people from Canada to Long Island Sound. The West and White Rivers provided routes to Lake Champlain by way of Otter Creek and the Winooski River, respectively. The Passumpsic and Nulhegan Rivers offered similar routes between the Connecticut River and Lake Memphremagog and the Canadian interior.

European explorers and settlers also traveled by canoe or adopted Abenaki footpaths. Early roads became corridors for settlement and commerce. The first roads in Vermont were built for military purposes while the first turnpikes in New Hampshire led directly to fertile floodplains suitable for agriculture. Some of the early roads followed Indian travel routes. Some of these and early "post roads" constructed in the late 1700s and early 1800s survive as our "river roads" all over the northern valley. These primitive roads were the focus of immigration, settlement and commerce. For the most part, early travel on land was slow and difficult, over roads that were too hard or too soft, depending on the season. Snow, ice, mud, or dust usually made travel unpleasant, if not impossible.

These difficulties help us understand the "canal fever" that gripped the public imagination around 1800. It was a vision of convenient travel for flat boats navigating a network of natural and built waterways. Canal lock systems would raise and lower boats around waterfalls and impassible narrow or shallow gorges. Speculators and governments dispatched surveyors and engineers all over New England. Many returned with wildly impractical and expensive schemes that resemble overly-optimistic marketing plans of our own day. Among the possi-

Guardrail technology and surfaces may have changed, but "river roads" still follow the waterway throughout the valley.

HISTORIC INDIAN TRAILS OF NEW HAMPSHIRE

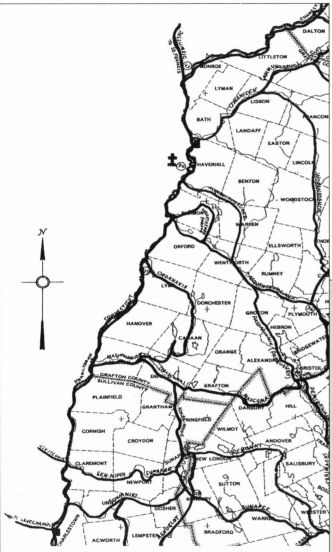

The first English colonists were greatly indebted to the Indians for the use of their trails. A trail paralleled the entire Connecticut River, and many of our modern highways follow the routes of these ancient footpaths.

At what is now Newbury, Vermont, across the river from Haverhill, was the Indian village Koisek, "people of the pine mountains." There was also a Jesuit mission here. The Asquamchumaukee trail led from Lake Winnipesaukee to the village.

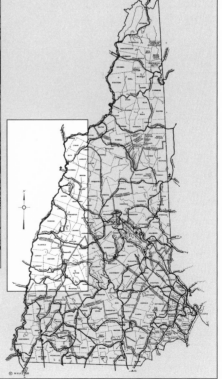

"Historic Indian Trails of New Hampshire" by Chester B. Price in *The New Hampshire Archeologist*, Vol. 14 (June 1967). © New Hampshire Archeological Society, used by permission.

An 11x17-inch map and pamphlet with detailed annotations on each trail are available from the New Hampshire Archeological Society (see Appendix B).

bilities dreamed of were routes between the Connecticut River and Lake Champlain by way of the White, Waits, or Wells Rivers.

The Connecticut was the first large river in America to be altered for a significant distance for transportation. By the time ground was broken for the famous Erie Canal in 1817, a series of canals on the Connecticut already had opened it to river boat traffic from Long Island Sound as far north as Barnet, Vermont. Hartford, Connecticut, was the tidal head of the river and the transfer point between ocean-going vessels and smaller boats that plied the upper river. Some flatboats were 72 feet long and almost twelve feet wide, and had a capacity of 30 tons, yet drew only two to three feet of water. Sometimes propelled by men with poles, they also carried square sails. At least ten flatboats from the northern valley made regular round trips to Hartford, carrying lumber and farm produce down river and returning with goods shipped from American and foreign ports.

The invention of the steamboat represented the next advance in transportation technology. One of the first launched anywhere in the country was built by Samuel Morey, of Orford, New Hampshire, and Fairlee, Vermont in 1793. After 1815, the lower Connecticut River was lively with steamboat travel. Large ships steamed between Hartford, Connecticut, and New York City. But steamboats turned out to be commercially impractical and uneconomical on the upper river, where populations were smaller and the river more shallow, rocky, and narrow.

Artist's conception of the first steamboat on the Connecticut River, Samuel Morey's "Aunt Sally."

By the 1840s, canals on the upper river had deteriorated into decrepit relics. Government-regulated tolls from small numbers of flatboats and steamboats failed to keep canal companies financially solvent, and locks fell into disrepair. The construction of railroads around 1850 made commercial traffic obsolete on the river. Some canals were modified for power generation and manufacturing purposes.

Rail depots were busy places for a century. The elegant Lancaster station (above) is no longer standing. The crowded Thetford depot (below) is now a quiet corner of the hamlet of East Thetford.

Railroads transformed the physical and cultural landscape of the region. For the first time, there was year-round transport to hamlets formerly inaccessible due to poor roads and seasonal snow and mud. Farmers and manufacturers alike shipped products directly and quickly to major markets. Virtually overnight, daily trains served the once-isolated region to and from Burlington, New York, Boston, and

Montreal. This weakened the region's previous cultural ties to other parts of central Connecticut and Massachusetts via the river, a relationship which dated back several generations to the earliest settlers.

The railroads focused industrial, commercial and residential development in the vicinity of rail lines and intersections. In northern New Hampshire, rail permitted paper companies to expand logging operations beyond previous limitations set by seasonal river flows for floating out logs. Tourist trains rode steep grades and rickety bridges to resort hotels high in the White Mountains. Passenger cars brought in travelers from around the U.S. and Europe, and permitted residents to broaden their horizons through travel outside the valley. Immigrants from Europe who constructed and operated the railroads introduced new cultures among the previously homogenous valley population. Urban downtowns evolved, employing the same styles of major American cities elsewhere.

The next major shift in transportation occurred in the first decades of the 20th century when residents of the region obtained automobiles. Roads were improved and some were paved for the first time. Road construction and widening increased in the 1950s, and accelerated dramatically in the 1960s when interstate highways opened up the northern valley to high-speed travel. The automobile became an integral part of peoples' lives and the truck replaced rail cars as the principal carrier of freight.

Interstate 91 arrived in the 1960s, delivering as much change as the railroad had a century before. Here it spans the Williams River near Bellows Falls.

The arrival of the interstate highway in the northern valley required the construction of high, long-span bridges, engineering on a scale not seen since the railroads required similar daring a century before. All of our historic bridges—whether made of wood, steel, stone, or concrete—collectively represent two centuries of changing technology, engineering and style. Some 80 bridges in the region are listed on the National Register of Historic Places, including more than 60 functioning covered bridges.

Modern bridges typically are supported by structures beneath the road surface while many historic bridges are formed of trusses and arches that soar above the road. They stand prominently in a landscape in which the predominant elements establishing a vertical scale are trees, and the tallest structures are church steeples.

Huge changes in land use, leisure, and lifestyle were wrought by the automobile.

Occupying an even higher vertical scale, airplanes played a colorful role in the region's early 20th century transportation. Small rural airfields featured barnstorming air shows and provided rapid transport to and from distant locations, contributing to the cultural homogenization of the region. Vermont's first airport was constructed in 1919 in Springfield.

❦ Resources & Revelations ❦

EARLY ROADS AND TURNPIKES

Most early road builders generally avoided low-lying wet areas in favor of hilltops where the ground was drier, although rocky, and the smaller upland streams were easy to bridge or ford. Oxen teams were equal to the task of pulling wagons over the hilly terrain.

Rough road ahead.

Military purposes motivated the construction of early roads in Vermont. The Crown Point Military Road was the first, built across Vermont in 1759–1760 by military forces supporting the settlers during the French and Indian War. It linked the northernmost outpost on the Connecticut, Fort at No. 4 in Charlestown, to Chimney Point and the garrison at Crown Point on Lake Champlain.

For nearly 150 years, most river crossings were by chain ferry.

Beginning at a Connecticut River ferry crossing, the road extended some 90 miles, much of it over hilltops. It passed through the river and tributary towns of Springfield, Weathersfield, Cavendish and Plymouth. Obliterated now by paved roads in many places, a few portions of the main route and its spurs may still be seen in substantially their early condition. There is a published guide to the trail and its extant mile markers.

The second road set out for military reasons was the Bayley-Hazen Road. Newbury, Vermont, was settled in 1763 when General Jacob Bayley, veteran of the Indian wars, led a migration of settlers from Newbury, Massachusetts, to the fertile land of a great ox-bow, or sweeping curve, in the river. Beginning in 1776, Bayley constructed a road 14 miles northwest from Newbury to Peacham, intending to create a better route for American Revolutionaries to invade Canada than through British-controlled Lake Champlain. It was never used for an invasion, ut after Moses Hazen extended the road to Westfield, the Bayley-Hazen Road became an avenue for trade and settlement. Resulting hilltop settlements along the highland roads remain like guide fossils to the early road that produced them.

In New Hampshire, the first major road was the Province Road from Concord to Haverhill, built about 1773 to promote settlement of the rich alluvial floodplains known as the Cohass or Coös Meadows. Returning veterans of the French and Indian Wars had brought back news of the area's agricultural possibilities as early as 1761, and later motivated the Assembly to construct the road.

By the early 1770s, there was regular mail service between Hanover and Portsmouth, through Concord. In 1795, work was begun on a post road in Vermont from the Massachusetts border north to Newbury, a route that approximates today's Route 5.

A decade of turnpike construction greatly accelerated the settlement of western New Hampshire

and eastern Vermont. Claremont was the terminus of the Second New Hampshire Turnpike (1799) leading from Amherst, Massachusetts. The Third New Hampshire Turnpike (1799) came up from central Massachusetts through Keene to Walpole. The Fourth New Hampshire Turnpike (1800) led from from Boscawen on the Merrimack River to Lebanon. Haverhill also became the terminus of the Coös Turnpike in 1808.

Haverhill Corner owes its handsomely displayed history to its location at the terminus of the Province Road, and later, the Coös Turnpike.

In some places, these early pikes have been widened and paved over for continued use. One example is the Grafton Turnpike, which brought travelers from Boston through Grafton, New Hampshire, and on to Lyme and Orford. Two centuries after its construction, most of its length is now a two-lane, wide-shouldered, paved highway, but some still snakes through the forest as a one lane unpaved adventure. In other places, the early roads are only traces through the woods, fit only for travelers on foot. After two centuries of development, many local roads in our rural region remain unpaved due to economics, aesthetics, a desire to keep vehicle speeds down, and advancements in the grading and compacting of dirt and gravel. Of nearly 70 miles of public road in Lyme, for example, only 28 miles are paved. Many towns designate their unpaved roads as "scenic" to deter

The path of progress followed turnpikes connecting the valley with Boston and Portsmouth.

large-scale clearing of the trees that may frame them. Muddy in the spring and dusty in summer, these country roads are an integral part of our regional character.

CANALS AND RIVER BOATS

The Bellows Falls Canal Company was the first canal company chartered in the nation, in 1791. A flood washed out its first construction efforts, however, so by the time it was completed, in 1802, it was the third canal constructed on the Connecticut, after two in Massachusetts, at South Hadley (1795) and Turner's Falls (1798). Other smaller canals were constructed 1810-1812 at Sumner Falls, at Cornish-Windsor, and at Olcott Falls at Lebanon-Wilder.

A narrow, rocky gorge between Bellows Falls and Walpole had required unloading of river boats and transport of their cargo—and sometimes the rafts themselves—around the Great Falls. A wing dam above the gorge diverted water into a long canal with eight locks—two stone and six wood—that raised and lowered boats a total of 54 feet. After the canal had ceased to serve a transportation function, it provided water and hydro power for a variety of industries, principally for paper manufacture. The upper section of the canal has since been widened and deepened several times, and now delivers water to an electricity generating station. However, unaltered walls of the lower canal section appear to survive in the basement of paper mill structures situated to use its waters in the second half of the 19th century.

STEAMBOATS

In 1793, six years after the first successful operation of a steamboat in America, by John Fitch on the Delaware River, Samuel Morey successfully ran the first steamboat on the Connecticut River, the "Aunt Sally." First to use two side wheels, Morey received a patent signed by George Washington for his engine design. Lacking the finances to make his venture profitable, Morey loaned his plans to a potential investor, who showed them to Robert Fulton. Fulton

based his "Clermont" on Morey's designs and ultimately received credit for inventing the steamboat when the Clermont ran up the Hudson River in 1811. Tradition has it that, upset by Fulton's success and fame, Morey sank his boat in the Fairlee lake later named after him.

Morey went on to patent an internal combustion engine in 1826, advancing technology later employed in automobiles and airplanes. Morey's Orford residence is among the "Ridge Houses" on a terrace facing the river, and is listed on the National Register of Historic Places.

In 1826, the "Barnet," named after the Vermont town it was intended to reach, traveled from Hartford, Connecticut, 125 miles upriver to Bellows Falls, Vermont. Even steamboats designed for the upper river such as the "Vermont" and the "John Ledyard," were restrained by narrow locks, sandbars, and shallow rapids, and were not efficient or profitable for their owners.

George Long, of Hinsdale, New Hampshire, adapted a steam engine for a four-wheel, charcoal-fired automobile in 1875. He built another automobile, propelled by gasoline, which is now housed in the Smithsonian Institution in Washington, D.C. Long's workshop was in the Holman and Merriman Machine Shop, which still stands.

The Connecticut River Valley has long been home to creative minds.

White River Junction begins to grow in response to the arrival of the railroad.

RAILROADS

Railroad construction began in New Hampshire in 1835, and by 1840 there were 15 miles of track. In 1847, the Northern Railroad was completed from Boston, through Concord, New Hampshire to Lebanon. There, Daniel Webster (Dartmouth Class of 1801), stood on brand new tracks and declared, "It is an extraordinary era in which we live." By 1850 there were 376 miles of track in the state, and thirty years later there were 1,200 miles.

When Webster made that comment, a single farmhouse stood on the Vermont side of the Connecticut opposite Lebanon, at its confluence with the White River. The next year, 1848, the river was spanned by a bridge that brought the railroad west to Vermont. Rail yards quickly rose on a broad terrace, creating White River Junction, in the township of Hartford. The construction of five railroads between 1848 and 1863 established White River Junction as one of the region's major transportation centers, and, as one without manufacturers, completely dependent on the railroad. A National Register historic district contains commercial buildings associated with the village's role as a rail center.

Also in 1848, Vermont's first rail line opened for traffic from White River Junction up the White River Valley to Bethel. Quickly following was a line from Boston through Fitchburg, Massachusetts, to Keene, New Hampshire, and Bellows Falls, Vermont (1849). St. Johnsbury, was linked by 1850, and Littleton by 1853. By then, most of the northern river valley was interconnected by tracks, linking formerly remote towns and villages to Boston and coastal New Hampshire. While Woodsville and Keene, New Hampshire, became rail centers, and each retains some flavor and architecture associated with the railroads, the most significant rail hubs in the region probably were White River Junction, St. Johnsbury, and Bellows Falls, Vermont.

Bellows Falls, a village in Rockingham, developed as both a transportation, manufacturing and commercial center after an east-west rail line was brought in from New Hampshire in 1849 and in 1851 was connected to a north-south line along the

Travelers in 1850 were astonished to learn that they could leave Wells River and arrive in Boston the very same day.

Connecticut River. In response to restrictive topography, a distinctive railroad tunnel was constructed in 1851 underneath the village's central square, which is within a downtown National Register district. The 275-foot-long tunnel, cut through solid rock, is lined with a continuous stone arch.

Bellows Falls, like many other downtowns and remote villages, retains its railroad depot, and this one, built in the 1920s, now serves as an Amtrak station. Many of the region's late 19th- and early 20th-century train stations have been adapted for other uses. The oldest surviving railroad structure along the Connecticut is probably a c. 1860 wood-framed depot in Fairlee. Lyndonville is a commercial and residential village that was set out by the Boston & Maine Railroad in 1866, when it was the headquarters and terminal for the company's Passumpsic Division, and is the only known such planned railroad community in Vermont.

Rail accidents have been relatively few but spectacular, such as the one that occurred a few miles north of White River Junction on February 5, 1887.

Fairlee's c. 1860 rail depot is the longest survivor of its species in Vermont.

In below zero temperatures, four passenger car separated from the rest of their train and plunge off a bridge into the river below, where much of th wreck remains to this day. Thirty-nine people wer killed and 49 injured. One of New England's wors train wrecks, it stimulated passage of the 1893 federal Railway Appliance Act, the first national legislation setting standards for railroad equipment.

In the northernmost New Hampshire town o Pittsburg, there are still traces of abandoned loggin; railroad rights-of-way. In other parts of the region track has been pulled up but the rights-of-way hav been retained for traveling by foot, bicycle, ski o snowmobile. These "rails-to-trails" conversion: provide alternative means of transportation while maintaining the rights-of-way until such time as rail roads might re-emerge as economically viable.

Since railroad companies preferred the gradua grades found in river valleys, and had the politica clout to obtain the rights-of-way, railroads tended to be built adjacent to waterways, creating a patter of private ownership of shorelines. Particularly along the Connecticut River in Vermont, that pattern has both prevented further development o shorelines and severely limited public access to waterways.

LIGHT RAIL TROLLEYS

Light rail systems, or trolleys, served the northern valley's urban centers for about three decades beginning about 1890 and lasting into the 1920s. The Springfield Terminal Railway linked Springfield and Charlestown across the Connecticut. The Bellows and Saxton's River Street Railroad served those villages in the town of Rockingham. The Brattleboro Street Railroad ran between Brattleboro and West Brattleboro.

Ashley's Ferry linked Weathersfield producers and Claremont processors.

FORDS & FERRIES

Before materials and technology were improved to construct bridges—or at places too wide to bridge—water crossings were made at shallow, rocky fords or upon flatboats poled or cabled from one shore to the other. The mark of these transits lasted no longer than ripples in the current. But every "Ferry Road" in the region today is a place-marker for those ephemeral crossings, as are the historic buildings clustered around what were once important cross roads.

In Weathersfield, Vermont, for example, along the 200-year-old river road, now called Route 5, there is a Ferry Road that leads down to the sandy

west bank of the Connecticut River. Directly across the water is the Ashley Ferry Ramp, a public boat launch, whose name is a reminder of the original purpose for the steep, twisting road that now descends to the water from Route 12A in Claremont, New Hampshire. On Ferry Road in Weathersfield in 1811, William Jarvis began to breed Merino sheep that stimulated New England's economy for a half-century. It is likely that the imported sheep were introduced into New Hampshire by the ferry in this place, which also probably transported wool to textile mills in Claremont.

BRIDGES

Bridges are vivid elements in our physical and cultural landscape. More than two centuries of changing bridge technology and design have created a useful museum of historic structures throughout the northern valley. They include timber-framed covered bridges, steel truss bridges, and concrete bridges. They have historic value due to their age, their association with noted designers or manufacturers, advances in technology or materials, and their links to the growth of our communities and industries. New Hampshire owns all the bridges that span the Connecticut, up to the point where they are supported on Vermont soil.

Natural events have dramatically shaped the character of the region's bridge inventory. Large-scale destructive weather events were followed by periods of

The 1856 covered wooden truss bridge linking Orford (r.) and Fairlee succumbed in 1936, when flood waters crested several feet above its deck, but not without a fight. The massive timbers were so difficult to dismantle that the bridge was ultimately dynamited.

The well-loved Cornish-Windsor Covered Bridge, fourth to link these two towns.

have been retired for pedestria use only. Within a couple c miles of each other, spanning th West River in Dummerstor Vermont, are two significa bridges made of differer materials—an 1872 Town lattic truss covered bridge, at 280 fee the longest covered bridg wholly within Vermont, and a 1892 Hilton through truss stee bridge.

In the northern Connecticu watershed there are 63 function ing covered bridges, 28 in New Hampshire and 35 i Vermont. Not so unusual in its day, but significant nov because of its length, high use and visibility, is th Cornish-Windsor Covered Bridge, spanning th Connecticut River between those towns. Built i

rebuilding, which replaced one group of structures having distinctive materials and styles with another group representative of the new period. The most significant events were major floods in 1927 and 1936 and a hurricane in 1938. The flood of 1927 washed away—in Vermont alone—1,200 bridges, including 200 covered bridges. Some, like the North Thetford-Lyme bridge, were never replaced.

Hilly topography and the great number of rivers, streams and brooks in the region rendered overland travel difficult until the establishment of sawmills that could manufacture bridge materials from locally abundant timber resources. Timber framing techniques widely known for centuries were adequate for spans up to about 50 feet. Builders adapted barn-framing techniques to develop a variety of wood trusses that supported spans of greater length. Stone arches were widely employed for short railroad bridges (and some highway bridges) while long spans for heavy loads motivated the design of iron and steel bridges by railroad companies. Steel and reinforced highway concrete bridges became predominant in the late 19th and early 20th centuries.

Timber truss bridges—also known as covered bridges—are to many people one of the symbolic icons of our region and New England. Many of our covered bridges are still in full service, while others

The double concrete arch Vilas Bridge spans the rocky gorge at Bellows Falls at the site of the first bridge anywhere on the Connecticut River. Behind it is the 1899 double stone arch Cheshire Railroad Bridge.

Lebanon's c. 1848 railroad overpass arch is on the National Register of Historic Places.

866, it is the longest wooden bridge in the United States (460 ft.) and the longest two-span covered bridge in the world. The fourth covered bridge on this site, it employs a lattice truss patented by Ithiel Town.

The 1930 concrete Vilas Bridge, spanning the gorge between Walpole, New Hampshire, and Rockingham, Vermont, is considered to be of national significance. A rare concrete arch bridge in its original condition with outstanding architectural and engineering details, it has unusually fine proportions in an outstanding setting. Supported by two open spandrel arches, the bridge stands in the same location as the very first bridge on the entire length of the Connecticut, built in 1785. The observer with just a passing knowledge of architectural history may easily recognize features that link the bridge's design to Colonial Revival Style buildings of the same era.

Notable stone arch bridges include a c. 1848 railroad overpass bridge in Lebanon, unique in western New Hampshire, an 1862 stone arch in Gilsum, New Hampshire, and an 1899 masonry railroad bridge over the Connecticut River near the Vilas Bridge. In Townshend and Putney, Vermont, there are eight c. 1900-1910 vernacular stone arch bridges by James O. Follett, a local artisan. Another, slightly altered, spans the Cold River in Walpole, New Hampshire.

The region also includes unusual, one-of-a kind bridges such as the floating bridge in Brookfield, Vermont, set out in 1812 on 390 oak barrels across wide Sunset Lake, and recently reconstructed in the same location. The Monadnock Mills complex in Claremont includes an 1870 Moseley truss iron footbridge. Bethel, Vermont, is home to a rare survivor—an 1896 wrought-iron, pin-connected lenticular pony truss bridge.

Surviving from the pre-automobile era is a c.1885 steel Pratt truss bridge over the Connecticut River at Stratford, New Hampshire-Maidstone, Vermont. Long closed to traffic, its rehabilitation and reopening will reinforce the close link between these two communities. An early (1911) steel arch bridge spans Quechee Gorge in Hartford, Vermont.

Among steel bridges of the auto era that span the Connecticut, the most notable are a 1923 steel through-arch bridge at Haverhill, New Hampshire-Newbury, Vermont, a 1929 steel Petit truss bridge at Piermont, New Hampshire-Bradford, Vermont, a 1930 steel Parker truss bridge at Monroe, New Hampshire-McIndoe Falls, Vermont, and a 1937 steel Petit truss bridge at Charlestown, New Hampshire-Springfield, Vermont. Residents of Fairlee and

The dramatic Samuel Morey Bridge receives a facelift. It is one of three remaining steel arch bridges built over the Connecticut in the 1930s. All are being preserved.

Orford successfully nominated their 1937 steel arch bridge, the "Samuel Morey Memorial Bridge," to the National Register of Historic Places, saving the dramatic bridge from replacement by a one-size-fits-all modern highway crossing. Like large-scale models made with old Erector Set® kits, steel truss bridges are honest expressions of the forces of tension and compression that permit them to "fly" from one place to another.

High style concrete may seem an oxymoron to some, but it has served artistic bridge designers well.

Scores of modest concrete bridges built since the floods of the 1920s and 1930s stand as testimony to the modern bridge-builder's art and the adaptability of concrete. Their designs include side walls that resemble wood paneling, and poured concrete ballusters that look like classic urns and vases or the staircase turnings in Colonial-era homes. Some of these bridges still retain paired electric lamp posts at each end, creating gateways for villages and downtowns.

Air Travel

Hartness State Airport, in Springfield, was the first airport built in Vermont, constructed in 1919 by James Hartness. A governor of Vermont (1921-1922), Hartness was an influential leader in both the national air transportation movement and the regional machine tool industry. In 1915, at the age of 54, he became one of the first one hundred licensed pilots in America, earning his wings in a Wright bi-

plane. In 1916, he was the founding president of th Aero Club of Vermont. In 1927, Charles Lindberg landed at Hartness Airport and was a guest at th home of his friend Hartness.

Hang-gliding, more of a sport than a transporta tion mode, is particularly popular on two hillside in West Windsor, Vermont, and Charlestown, Ne Hampshire. Hot air ballooning is another mode recreational "travel." On many an early summe evening, colorful balloons drift over the landscap from an airfield in Post Mills, Vermont.

Interstate Highways

The arrival of the interstate highway system in th 1960s dramatically altered our regional culture, as ha the arrival of railroads slightly more than a centur before. The new divided highway displaced or seg mented farms, cut off old roads, directed traffic int small towns at new exits, promoted a rush of deve opment in selected areas, and opened up the north ern valley to travelers and new immigrants fro eastern metropolitan areas. Today people can driv between the Massachusetts and Canadian borders i a small fraction of the time it took to walk or canc half that distance two hundred years ago. Such spee costs us the experience of all the places in betwee While the interstates reduce unwanted through tra fic in historic downtowns, they also deprive dow towns of potential customers and reward stri development and sprawl at exits and interchanges.

The Connecticut River Byway is an opportunity for motorists to leave behind the generic monotony of the interstates to travel on local roads that border scenic waterways, wind through historic villages and downtowns, and offer a more intimate experience of the landscape, history, and culture of the region.

ARCHEOLOGICAL FEATURES

Remnants of historic transportation modes are visible in the landscape. The ages of buildings by the side of the road are a good indication of how long a road has existed in that location. Stone bridge abutments stand in midstream and on riverbanks like monoliths of a previous civilization. Here and there in the northern valley, when traveling down a straight road it is possible to see traces of an older road, looping away and back like the dry oxbow of a former riverbed. Old railroad beds follow gradual grades on built-up berms easily legible in the landscape. A sharp eye can see these remnants in many places. For example, trolley rails are still visible in a steel truss highway bridge over the Black River in Springfield about a mile upstream from its confluence with the Connecticut.

❈ Threats ❈

Our traditional everyday transportation environments are threatened by poor maintenance, as well as by unnecessary alterations that go beyond reasonable safety provisions. Many bridge and road replacements ignore evidence that merely increasing road capacity will not relieve traffic congestion or improve safety. Narrow focus on automobiles hampers the development of other modes.

ROAD & BRIDGE DESIGN STANDARDS

Only recently have state standards for the design of roads and bridges begun to reduce the impact of construction projects on natural and historic resources. The accumulation of small details of

designs—such as long runs of shiny metal guardrails, wide road shoulders and clear zones, unnecessary road straightening, higher design speeds—produce "improvements" that are out of scale with their setting, physically intrusive, aesthetically unpleasant, and sometimes wastefully expensive.

Federal weight limits on the interstates are lower than New Hampshire and Vermont weight limits on state highways. The result is that heavy freight trucks travel on state roads, which often run directly through historic villages, residential areas, and other non-industrial settings. This, in turn, creates a strong temptation for the kind of widening and straightening of roads that destroys their scenic and historic character and contributes to speeding and other fac-

Today's Route 10, at the southern entrance to Lyme Village, has invaded front yards, taken street trees, and eliminated walkways past the mid-19th century homes lining the road. Greek revival gable-front home, above left c. 1916, appears below behind utility pole, 2002.

tors that residents say makes them feel unsafe and diminishes their quality of life.

LACK OF INFORMED PUBLIC INVOLVEMENT IN HIGHWAY PROJECTS

Without input from local communities, transportation engineers are more likely to produce new roadway designs that do not take community values into account, thus altering the look and feel of the community. Among such changes are the addition of the urban amenity of curbing in a rural setting, loss of street trees through widening or salt poisoning and root compaction, loss of front yards, the elimination of angled parking, the creation of one-way streets, the paving of country lanes, and widening of narrow country roads.

LACK OF MAINTENANCE & FUNDING

Roads and particularly historic bridges are permitted to deteriorate due to deferred maintenance. Subsequent high costs of repair frequently are used to justify historic bridge demolitions. Financially strapped small towns are required to maintain historic bridges on state highways. Others are left standing as bridges to nowhere. Although covered bridges are icons of the rural countryside, they are threatened by vandalism and fire.

The handsome 1906 Arch Bridge between Walpole and Bellows Falls, lost in 1982 but not forgotten.

Historic wooden rail overpass at Birch Meadow Farm i Fairlee, Vermont. Farmers must rely upon the railroad sometimes poorly maintained overpasses to reach their riverfront cropland.

INTERSTATE HIGHWAY INTERCHANGE:

Some communities zone all their highway interchanges for commercial development. Others hav no zoning, which means anything goes. Lack of lane use controls at highway interchanges is likely to produce sprawl and strip development, sapping the economic vitality of traditional commercial center and ruining whatever pastoral landscape had remained there.

RAILROADS

A lot of infrastructure and prime real estate is devoted to the railroad, which is vastly underutilize and offers a means to reduce traffic on highways Some historic rail overpasses on farms could benefit from maintenance by the rail company. The national bias toward subsidizing the automobile a the expense of other modes leaves passenger rail service in an ever-precarious financial situation. Pas senger rail service is a critical component of the region's continuing economic development.

OVEREMPHASIS ON THE AUTOMOBILE

A transportation system balanced among different modes—automobiles, buses, trains, bicycles, and pedestrian—is most likely to enhance our cultural landscape and maintain our quality of life.

❀ Actions & Activities ❀

It is important that our transportation systems provide mobility while retaining the quality of life represented by the balance of our built and natural environments.

PLANNING

• Become familiar with your town and regional plans' policies and goals for transportation. Your regional planning commission employs planners who specialize in transportation issues and can assist you in gathering information.

• Learn about new concepts in transportation design such as "traffic-calming" and "pedestrian-friendly environments" and advocate for them in your community.

• Attend public hearings for proposed highway projects in your town and participate in discussions about how to balance community needs.

• Investigate the use of "enhancement funds" available from state transportation agencies for historic preservation, environmental, and bicycle and pedestrian activities related to transportation. Many towns have tapped such funds to restore historic transportation buildings, enhance visitors' centers, build bicycle and footpaths, and improve water quality.

BRIDGES

• Research and publicize the importance of historic bridges to encourage their maintenance, protection, and retention.

• Encourage local groups to take responsibility for unused covered bridges, and maintain them as foot, ski, bicycle, or horse crossings.

• When changes to bridges are proposed, advocate for addition of public access for fishing, boating, and swimming. By federal

The 1866 Bedell Bridge between Newbury and Haverhill, and the toll-house, in a 1950s postcard view. The fifth bridge on the site, it was closed in 1958 and in 1973-8, determined citizens raised funds to restore it. The reconstructed bridge, pride of the community, was dashed off its piers only ten months later by a sudden windstorm, and never rebuilt. The New Hampshire side is now a state park.

law, these options must be considered but are some-times bypassed if support from the public is not ex-pressed.

• Take steps to protect historic wooden covered bridges in your town, by documenting their history and establishing fire protection.

• Encourage science projects in which children construct toothpick bridges and test their strength, to help them better appreciate the engineering in-volved in constructing an historic or modern bridge.

RAILS

• Visit the Vermont Transportation Museum in the White River Junction railroad station.

• Find out when the first railroad line was brought into your area and who were the local people in-volved in decisions about where it would be built.

• Ride an excursion train such as the Green Moun-tain Railroad in Bellows Falls.

• Attend the annual Glory Days of the Railroad event in White River Junction.

• Follow the progress of the restoration in Claremont of the Flying Yankee, one of only three articulated Streamliners ever built. After restoration it will re-turn to the tracks in the Connecticut River Valley and White Mountain Valley.

• Gather oral histories from elders who remember previous transportation modes such as horse-drawn carriages, trains, and trolleys, and the arrival of the interstates. Compile into videotape or exhibit.

• Use public transportation whenever possible, particularly Amtrak.

• Use park-and-ride parking lots and carpools.

• Support "rails to trails" —the conversion of un-used former railroad beds to trails for people on foot, bicycles, skis and snowmobiles.

Bridge to rail trail.

ROADS

• Through maps and local histories, identify the first roads built in your town. Create an atlas of your town's roads, with notes on when the road was laid out, consulting historic maps to see how long it was in repair and if it was abandoned, when.

• Seek early photographs of your town's intersec-tions, and compare them with the view today.

• Organize or participate in Green Up Day in your town. Many valley towns hold such an event on the first weekend in June, when residents get together to pick up roadside trash.

• Learn about the legal classification of roads in your state and what the implications are for the fu-ture use and development of each class of road in your town.

❧ Q & A ❧

• Was there an early ford or ferry in your area? Why was it located there? Where were people going when they crossed and what do you think they were car-rying? Is there anything left to see, above ground or under water?

• What transportation features were influential in the establishment and growth of your village or town? Was it an early road or turnpike? A crossroad? Bridge crossing? Railroad crossing or station stop?

The North Stratford depot.

Transportation and communications technology are ever-evolving fields. This early-1900s postcard view shows a transportation planner's ambitions for White River Junction.

• Where were the earliest bridges located? Does any evidence of them remain such as stone piers or traces of approach roads? What else visible today might have resulted from that location, such as mills, houses, or roads?

• Study your town's road names for clues to historic places (for example, Ferry Road, Lime Kiln Road, etc.) or notable families.

• What is the full range of bridge types in your community? Is there at least one covered bridge, one steel truss bridge, and one concrete bridge?

• How do historic bridges compare to modern bridges in your town in their materials, individual features, and overall feel?

• What is it like to travel by foot around your village or town? Are there sidewalks? Are there places you feel more comfortable than others? Are crosswalks clearly marked? Do traffic lights stay red long enough to cross safely? Are there street trees and public benches?

• Canoe, kayak, walk, or bicycle from your village or town to another village or town nearby. How long does it take compared to making the same trip by car? Of what you see, what do you think existed 20-50-100 years ago? How can you tell?

• Find historic photographs of your community's streets in commercial and residential neighborhoods and take contemporary photographs from the same vantage points, and compare. What's changed and what's remained the same?

• What is the most important road to you in your village or town? What do you like about it? What would you least like to see change about it? What could you do to make sure the road retains those qualities and still provides safe passage to users of multiple travel modes?

• Are there places in your town that suffer aesthetically from such unnecessary things as "litter on a stick" and other signs that could be eliminated or consolidated? Unnecessary light pollution from streetlights and parking lot lighting? Overhead utilities that intrude upon village character?

❅ FYI ❅

RECOMMENDED READING

Covered Bridges of Vermont by Ed Barna, The Countryman Press, Woodstock, VT, 1996. (A loving inventory of the state's transportation antiques with photography recommendation.)

Getting There: The Epic Struggle Between Road and Rail in the American Century by Stephen B. Goddard, Basic Books, Harper Collins, 1994. (How and why automobiles and highways replaced trains and railroads, and the implications for today.)

Historical Markers on the Crown Point Road, Vermont's First Road, Crown Point Road Association, 1965, 1992. (Documenting the mile markers set out along the road are the basis for this guide, which also includes maps that make it possible to locate portions of the early road.)

On the Road North of Boston: New Hampshire Taverns and Turnpikes by James L. and Donna-Belle Garvin, New Hampshire Historical Society, Concord, NH, 1988. (Very readable history of New Hampshire's earliest roads, and the buildings and towns that resulted from them.)

Spanning Time: Vermont's Covered Bridges by Joseph C. Nelson, The New England Press, Shelburne, VT, 1997. (An engineer's comprehensive history of the bridges, their designers, and their structural systems, with color photographs and suggested driving tours.)

A State Highway Project in Your Town? Your Role and Rights: A Primer for Citizens and Public Officials by Jim Wick, The Preservation Trust of Vermont, Burlington, VT, 1995, 1998. (A workbook with a point of view. Covers Vermont but is somewhat applicable to New Hampshire.)

Take Back Your Streets: How to Protect Communities from Asphalt and Traffic by Stephen H. Burrington and Veronika Thiebach, Conservation Law Foundation, Montpelier, VT, 1995. (Policies, practices and laws for making communities pedestrian friendly for people of all ages and conditions.)

Trails for the Twenty-First Century by Charles A. Flink, Kristine Olka, and Robert M. Searns, Rails to Trails Conservancy, Island Press, Washington, D.C., 2001. (Planning, design, and management manual for multi-use trails.)

MAP

"Historic Indian Trails of New Hampshire" by Chester B. Price in *The New Hampshire Archeologist*, Vol. 14, June 1967. (An 11x17-inch map and pamphlet with detailed annotations on each trail are available from the New Hampshire Archeological Society [see Appendix B].)

GOOD LINKS

The Surface Transportation Policy Project: http://transact.org and http://www.tea21.org (A rich source of information and publications. Their goal: "To ensure that transportation policy and investments help conserve energy, protect environmental and aesthetic quality, strengthen the economy, promote social equity, and make communities more livable. We emphasize the needs of people, rather than vehicles, in assuring access to jobs, services, and recreational opportunities.")

New England Rails to Trails Conservancy: www.railtrails.org (The role of this organization is to promote voluntary cooperative efforts for on/off road multi-use trails, particularly those which link across state lines.)

Vermont's Better Back Roads program: www.anr.state.vt.us/dec/waterq/lakespro.htm#backroads

The Green Mountain Railroad: www.rails_vt.com/grn_mtn_flyer.html

Flying Yankee: www.flyingyankee.com

CHAPTER EIGHT

Architecture

Narrators in Stone & Wood

Architecture has been called "frozen music." Although that sounds a bit elegant for some of our modest old buildings, it captures the sense that every structure is a design expression of a past moment suspended in time. These expressions by previous generations narrate nearly two-and-a-half centuries of our local, regional and national history. It is important to maintain and rehabilitate historic buildings for continued use, both for the information they contain about the past and to preserve a built environment that enriches our sense of place.

❉ The Basic Story ❉

OUR history is told, day in and day out, by narrators who stand by the side of the road. These narrators—our historic buildings—are the northern valley's longest-surviving inhabitants. Having sheltered families, businesses and industries for the past two centuries, they tell the story of our region's settlement and growth since the late 1700s. Each building or group of buildings was shaped by a particular con-

stellation of need, aspiration, location, resources, materials, and fashion. Along with new buildings now under construction, they tell the layered stories of the people who have lived here over time.

Our communities are full of storytellers in many shapes and sizes: homes, churches, town halls, court houses, libraries, post offices, grange halls, barns and

An unusual early 19th-century Greek Revival duplex in Lebanon, complete with original glass in the side-lighted entry, and double Connecticut River Valley porch.

Beauty in simplicity: the 1836 Congregational Church, also home of the Historical Society, in Saxton's River Village, Rockingham.

silos, carriage houses, garages, bridges, old mills, industrial buildings and downtown commercial blocks.

Buildings, however, are silent narrators. They communicate by sign. Fortunately, using the language of architectural styles we can translate their symbolic speech and have a good idea what they're saying, and when they first said it. Like hairstyles and clothing in old photographs, historic buildings date themselves. Like the "guide fossils" that geologists find in the same strata of sedimentary rock the world over, building styles also date from particular time periods all over

Beauty in detail: Queen Anne style residence in Lebanon, c. 1870.

the United States. Given knowledge of architectural styles, building features, construction materials, and a general time-line of events and trends, anyone can walk down any road or street in our region and "read" the history of the place.

For some people, identifying architectural styles is like bird watching. "There goes a Greek Revival entrance! Quick, look, it's a Queen Anne porch!" But houses, unlike birds, and more like their human builders and occupants, display individualism. Cross breeding is common. A specimen may represent more than one species. You may spot a house as unusual as a robin with a blue jay's tail. Taking stock of the corresponding details of a house, as well as its overall form

The piazza—leisure hallmark of the Industrial Revolution. At Lake Morey, Fairlee, Vermont.

leads to an understanding of its architectural style. Part science and part aesthetics, it's a matter of studying building's anatomy—its structure and ornament—while keeping the mind as open and empathetic as when reading poetry, alert for subtlety and nuance. Architectural styles help us bring some order to the creative disorder of human invention.

Throughout the northern valley, many communities include good examples of most major American architectural styles (see Appendix C). The most widespread styles are Federal, Greek Revival, Gothic Revival, Italianate, French Second Empire, Queen Anne, and Colonial Revival. Less common but also important are others such as the Romanesque, Stick, Shingle, Classical Revival, Beaux Arts, Art Deco, and International styles. Some styles survived from one generation to the next with only minor changes, while some flourished and faded within a single decade. Some styles were recycled in "revivals" more than a century after they first appeared.

Among the simplest indicators of period and style are building materials. Indigenous people built the first human structures in our region from materials they found in nature. They employed saplings for frames, tree bark and animal skins for walls, and bound these materials together with plant roots and animal sinews. The record of these dwellings is found in archeological sites, ethno-histories and oral histories. Early European immigrants—and the next generation of settlers born in America—built with more processed natural materials. They constructed frames of hewn timbers or bricks made from local clays or from stone quarried nearby, and laid them with mortars of local lime and sand. They covered exterior walls with clapboards or shingles milled from local trees, and finished roofs with slate quarried locally or wood shingles made from trees close at hand. As transportation methods improved, materials were brought in from other parts of the region, and then from outside the region and the country.

Along with these outside materials came building ideas and fashions, imported from the immigrants' previous homes in coastal New England, and from continental Europe. Most of the historic architectural styles in the northern valley were based on forms previously popular in England, Italy, and France, which themselves drew on traditions established in ancient Greece and Rome. Trained architects, when they did arrive, based their designs on established styles. Pattern books published in the late 18th and 19th centuries provided carpenters and joiners with detailed examples for such buildings as churches and courthouses. Later, in the early 20th century, manufacturers like Sears & Roebuck published plans for small suburban houses, and even prefabricated houses that were shipped in pieces and assembled on-site.

Those Sears houses were set down all over the country, blown like a certain species of architectural spore into a variety of cultural landscapes. As building fads and fashions swept the nation, similar buildings rose at the same time thousands of miles apart. So we share many architectural traditions with other parts of our country, although each region tends to put its own stamp on a style.

One architectural feature that *is* distinctive to our region is the "Connecticut River Valley porch," a recessed second-floor porch in the gable end of Greek Revival and Gothic Revival-style residences. The openings above the porches may be semi-cir-

Built of local bedrock and serving still.

Variations on a theme: Connecticut River Valley porches. (Above, N. Haverhill; below, Chesterfield)

cular, elliptical, trapezoidal, square, or rectangular, depending on the preference of the owners or builder. In our region, only a handful of these are found outside of the immediate river valley.

Taken all together, these styles and their variations represent our architectural heritage. If we lose too many buildings of a certain style or period, we lose that part of our authentic collective story forever, just as a species of plant or animal becomes extinct. (Modern reproductions of historic architectural styles are somewhat like taxidermy of extinct animals.) And just as bio-diversity may reflect a healthy natural ecosystem, what we might call "archi-diversity" reflects the richness of our cultural landscape. We can see evidence of the vitality of residential neighborhoods and downtowns—or the

lack of it—in the survival, condition and use of ou authentic historic architecture.

We've noted elsewhere that historic preservatio today seeks the preservation of communities, rathe than isolated particular buildings. Preserved com munities are favorable "habitats" for historic archi tecture. Our region is notable for having many o these "habitats," in which buildings survive in thei historic contexts. Sometimes, buildings survive bu lose their historic context, for example when onl one house stands where once there was an entire resi dential neighborhood of older homes, and the sur vivor is encircled with gas stations and strip malls A much different and richer story is told when a col lection of buildings survives in an intact historic con text, along with it natural environment. Then it i possible to see, for example, historic brick mills, the residences that housed mill owners and workers and the Main Street commercial buildings tha served the thriving community spurred on by the mills, all in one setting.

Much of our rural agricultural architecture stil stands in the recognizable working landscape fron which it sprang, and offers its own strong context. I many cases, a number of separate buildings wer connected to the residence, forming a "continuous" architecture. In the colloquial, this succession i known as "big house, little house, back house, barn." The northern valley contains many examples of suc "continuous" architecture.

Connected farmstead complex, Jaffrey, New Hampshire, prior to 1910.

High style Greek Revival in McIndoe Falls, Vermont, a community which has researched and documented its unusual history.

Many of these context-rich "habitats" are found in the historic downtowns and rural villages of the northern Connecticut River Valley, many of which have been documented and recognized as historic districts listed in the National Register of Historic Places. The nomination forms for these historic districts contain what amounts to short community histories. They include thumbnail descriptions and histories of each building, and trace the development of local industries and commercial and residential areas. They are available to us in libraries and town halls all over our region, and are largely

West Fairlee, Vermont, 1906. Note Connecticut River Valley porch at far left.

unread and unappreciated. The architectural historians who compile this information are actually translating for our "silent narrators," the buildings that embody our history and building traditions.

❧ Resources & Revelations ❧

WHAT MAKES SOMETHING HISTORIC?

What makes a building, district, object, or structure "historic"? First, it must survive mostly intact from the historic period, which is generally defined as at least fifty years ago.

A property's historic significance could derive from a number of factors. It could be part of a pattern of events that contribute to history. These patterns could include the growth of a commercial downtown or residential neighborhood, the expansion of railroad lines, the creation of parks to display Civil War statues, or the establishment of a town government, church congregation, or important business enterprise.

Detail over entrance to Bank Block, on Bradford's Main Street. Note symbol in keystone of brick arch.

A property may be associated with an important person who owned it or lived in it, such as a high ranking government official, industry leader, artist, or inventor. The building could be either an outstanding or representative example of a type of construction or architectural style. It could have high artistic value or be the work of a master builder or architect.

In short, historic buildings and sites derive their significance because of people—the people who designed them, built them, lived and worked in them, and passed them on to us as one of the most important parts of our cultural landscape.

BUILDING TYPES

All structures may be categorized within the context of the evolution of other historic buildings which all share a general use. This is one of many analytical tools that permit architectural history—as well as particular buildings—to be considered objectively and not merely subjectively as a matter of personal taste. Such tools are critical to evaluating the relative importance of the wide variety of our architectural inheritance.

Lebanon City Hall (left) and Rogers Hotel, in matching Colonial Revival style.

Historic architecture takes many forms. The National Park Service has developed categories of building types according to their general use, such as domestic, commerce/trade, social, government, education, religion, funerary, recreation and culture, agriculture/subsistence, industry, defense, health care, landscape and transportation. Each category includes a variety of subcategories. For example, a *domestic* building could be a single dwelling, multiple dwelling, secondary structure, hotel, institutional housing, or camp. A *government* building could be a city hall, correctional facility, fire station, customhouse, post office, or courthouse. Buildings in the *education* category could be schools, colleges, libraries, or research facilities.

HISTORIC PROPERTIES

While *buildings* and *districts* make up the majority of our historic resources, they are not the only kind.

Historic properties also can be *sites* (archeological sites, gardens, battlefields, ruins of historic buildings, land areas having cultural significance), *structures* (bridges, tunnels, dams, towers, roadways, kilns, locomotives and cars, telescopes), and *objects* (sculpture, monuments, fountains, statuary).

NATIONAL HISTORIC LANDMARKS

The northern valley is rich in buildings and sites that have earned recognition as National Historic Landmarks by the National Park Service, Department of the Interior, for being among the foremost historic properties in the nation. They are important for their architecture, for their use, and for the influential people who built, lived, and worked in them. To qualify for inclusion in this select group, the buildings and sites must survive in nearly their original condition.

The handsome Romanesque Coös County Courthouse, Lancaster, New Hampshire.

The Fairbanks Museum and Planetarium, a grand Richardsonian Romanesque brownstone, gift of the Fairbanks family to the community of St. Johnsbury.

Wealthy benefactors and community organizations produced two sites in the northern valley worthy of National Historic Landmark status. The 1872 St. Johnsbury Athenaeum *(see Civic Life & The Arts)*, in St. Johnsbury, Vermont, is one of the best preserved late 19th-century art galleries and libraries in the country. It was donated by the Fairbanks family. Stellafane Observatory *(see Industry & Commerce)* in Springfield, Vermont, constructed 1924-1931, had its origins in the genius and inventiveness of Russell W. Porter and a local group of amateur astronomers.

Marsh-Billings-Rockefeller National Historic Park in Woodstock, Vermont, is one of the foremost sites in America for the interpretation of the history and evolution of conservation and agriculture. George Perkins Marsh's boyhood home, part of the site, is a National Historic Landmark. Beginning in 1805 and continuing through the middle of the 20th century,

the site has been home to the Marsh family, Frederick Billings, and Laurance S. Rockefeller. *(For more, see Natural Communities.)*

The American Precision Museum in Windsor, Vermont, erected in 1846, interprets the invention of the manufacturing of interchangeable parts, which stimulated mass production and "precision manufacturing." *(See Industry & Commerce.)*

The rural village of Plymouth Notch, in Plymouth, Vermont, is a National Historic Landmark and a State Historic Site. The preserved 19th century agricultural village includes President Calvin Coolidge's birthplace in 1872, his boyhood home in which he was sworn in as President in 1923, and his summer White House.

Perhaps the finest Gothic Revival-style residence in the region is the c. 1848-1851 homestead of Justin S. Morrill, in Strafford, Vermont. This National Historic Landmark and State Historic Site is located south of the common, in a National Register district. Morrill himself designed the large cottage, whose masonry-like details actually are rendered in wood. The variety of gardens, orchards and buildings located on the property reflect Morrill's diversified interests in farming and the needs of a rural homestead in the 19th century. Morrill, a U.S. Representative and Senator, was responsible for the so-called "Morrill Acts" (1862 and

Justin Morrill's high style Gothic Revival home is set in the hills of Strafford, Vermont.

1890), which established the nation's system of land grant colleges. The Land Grant Act created colleges whose agricultural research programs stimulated and aided settlement of the West at a time when free land was offered to homesteaders and the transcontinental railroad was completed.

Residences and work places of three singular men are honored as National Historic Landmarks. In Cornish, New Hampshire, is the c. 1790 dwelling that was the birthplace and boyhood home of Salmon P. Chase, a political figure of national significance who served in all three branches of the federal government. The Saint-Gaudens National Historic Site, in Cornish, New Hampshire, with buildings that date from 18th and 19th centuries, includes the home and studio of the northern valley's most illustrious artist, the sculptor Augustus Saint-Gaudens (1885-1907). Rudyard Kipling once lived and wrote at Naulakha, the unique Shingle-style home he helped to design. It was constructed in 1893 in Dummerston, Vermont. *(For more about all three men, see Civic Life & The Arts.)*

NOTABLE ARCHITECTS

Perhaps foremost among the region's designers of historic buildings is Asher Benjamin (1771-1845). Benjamin adapted the ideas of English architects Robert Adams and William Pain to create *The Country Builder's Assistant*, the first work of original architecture by an American, published in 1797. A native of Greenfield, Massachusetts (a Connecticut River town), Benjamin was a joiner by trade, and intended his volume to be a practical guide for fellow craftsmen. In the first book, and in his 1806 *The American Builder's Companion*, Benjamin presented plans for building features such as doors, windows, mantelpieces, and all manner of decorative moldings. These volumes exerted a profound and widespread influence upon the buildings of New England and popularized what became known as the Federal Style. While he resided in Windsor, Benjamin designed the 1798 Old South Church on

Asher Benjamin's beautifully proportioned Old South Church, slightly altered by the addition of a portico, is the pride of Windsor, Vermont.

Main Street, which has since been somewhat altered. Benjamin also designed three residences in Windsor, constructed 1800-1803, all of which have been demolished.

Alexander Parris (1780-1852), who had a distinguished architectural career in Portland and Boston, designed another of Windsor's churches. Built between 1820 and 1822, St. Paul's Episcopal Church was an important precursor of the Greek Revival style, which would flourish after 1830.

The prolific Ammi Burnham Young (1798-1874), first supervising architect of the U.S. Treasury Department (1852-1862), left a legacy of many buildings in river towns. Born in a circa 1790 Georgian-Federal–style residence, which survives in Lebanon, New Hampshire, Young designed works in the Federal and Greek Revival styles, which are found in Vermont and New Hampshire as far away as Burlington and Portsmouth. The Doric portico

Ammi Burnham Young's Shattuck Observatory, left foreground, from an early 1900s view of the Dartmouth campus.

of the 1833 Vermont State House he designed in Montpelier survived a fire and was incorporated into the 1857 structure.

His earliest work is found in the Connecticut River Valley near his hometown, including the 1828 First Congregational Church in Lebanon. At Dartmouth College, in Hanover, he designed Wentworth Hall and Thornton Hall (1828-29), and the Shattuck Observatory (1854). With a two-story cylindrical center and a rotating dome, the Observatory is one of the oldest of its type surviving in the United States. At the Shaker Village in Enfield, New Hampshire, Young designed the Great Stone Dwelling (1837), the community's largest building. Across the river in Windsor, Vermont, is his U.S. Post Office (1857).

An interesting comparison involving the work of Richard Upjohn (1802-1878), architect of New York City's Trinity Episcopal Church, appears in two of his churches built in neighboring towns at about the same time. In the village of Bellows Falls, Vermont, is his Immanuel Episcopal Church (1863-1867), a stone church in the Gothic Revival style he helped to popularize. Across the river in Charlestown, is St. Luke's Episcopal Church (1863-1869), also in the Gothic Revival style, and Upjohn's only wooden church in New Hampshire. Both churches are in National Register historic districts.

Lambert Packard was known as the architect to the Fairbanks family of St. Johnsbury, where he designed the Fairbanks Museum and fifteen other buildings on the town's main street. Among his other remarkable works in the region is a 1903 round barn at the West View Farm in Waterford, Vermont.

SOME NOTABLE BUILDINGS

Orford, New Hampshire, is home to one of the most remarkable collections of historic houses in northern New England. Set on a river terrace east of the main street are seven houses built between 1773 and 1839. They are now known collectively as The Ridge, or Bulfinch Row, for their resemblance to the

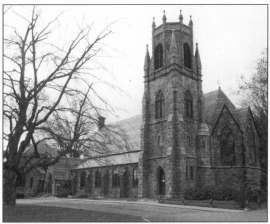

Richard Upjohn's 1860s Gothic Revival churches in Bellows Falls (above) and Charlestown.

work of Charles Bulfinch. The National Register of Historic Places nomination's statement of significance declares: "The Bulfinch-style house of John B. Wheeler, built 1814-1816, was designed by a Boston architect, probably Asher Benjamin, an associate at that time of Charles Bulfinch. Other Ridge houses also display the influence of Asher Benjamin." Professional and business men of the town, including steamboat inventor Samuel Morey, built the Federal-style residences which are listed in the National Register as part of the larger Orford Street Historic District. After visiting Orford, Washington Irving remarked, "In all my travels in this country and Europe, I have never seen any village more beautiful than this."

Sometimes architectural gems survive intact due to long-term ownership by families and individuals who resist change. Such is the case with the Burtch-Udall-Boyd Homestead in Hartford, Vermont, which is significant for the integrity of its well-preserved interiors. The heart of the property is a 1786 Georgian-Federal-style house with an early 1800s brick ell. Alterations have been extraordinarily few, with no modern improvements. Its floor plan is unaltered, and it still retains its massive central chimney and fireplaces, original paneling and woodwork, two early 19th-century

Across from the bridge which bears his name is Samuel Morey's 1804 fine Federal home on The Ridge in Orford, with its graceful entry.

The Lyme Congregational Church built by an ambitious 25 year old and dedicated in 1812.

cast stoves and wallpaper. The property is owned by the State of Vermont.

Historic buildings are often linked intimately to interesting details of local history. For example, construction of the Wilder-Holton House, in Lancaster, New Hampshire, which was Coös County's first two-story dwelling, was halted temporarily during the "Dark Day" of May 19, 1780. The house was built with boards planed and nails wrought on the site, and originally possessed a four-fireplace chimney and Indian shutters. The building is now a museum.

Historic buildings stand in special relationships with their neighbors. Adjacent to the Congregational Church in Lyme, New Hampshire, for example stands a long row of carefully preserved horse sheds where owners tied their animals while attending services or visiting the village. Taken together, these two structures built for quite different purposes tell a more complete story than either could by itself.

The Lyme horse sheds, built to shelter parishioners' mounts, represent the longest surviving structure of this type in New England, and possibly the United States.

Historic Districts

In comparison to the example given just above, historic districts are collections of many stories. Whether they are rural areas, commercial downtowns, industrial complexes, or residential neighborhoods—and some districts encompass more than one of these—historic districts tell the layered stories of changes over time. The changes are visible in the progression of architectural styles that each evolved in succession. Exactly how all these changes have produced each community's character is the cherished story of each place. *(See Settlement.)*

Among towns in the northern valley there are 75 National Register Historic Districts (15 in New Hampshire and 60 in Vermont) and scores of local historic districts designated by municipalities. In addition to the examples above, historic districts may also be college campuses, rural villages, large farms and estates, and transportation networks such as canals. See Appendix D for a list of the districts.

A recent tabulation found that in New Hampshire towns in the northern valley, the National Register of Historic Places lists some 933 historic buildings, 762 of which are within 17 historic districts. In Vermont towns in the region, the National Register lists some 2,777 buildings, 2,518 of which are within 47 historic districts.

Meeting Houses

One of our emblematic New England building types is the meeting house. The oldest meeting houses in the northern valley date from the period when buildings used for religious purposes were constructed at least in part with public funds, reflecting a unity of church and state that since has been dissolved. Two distinctive examples may be found not far from each other in Rockingham, Vermont, and Westmoreland, New Hampshire.

The Rockingham Meeting House (1787-1799) is Vermont's oldest public building found in nearly its original condition. A National Historic Landmark, it contains a fine pulpit and box pews. It was modeled after an earlier meeting house in Charlestown, New Hampshire, that was torn down in 1818. In its vicinity are a number of early 19th

The 1836 Unitarian Church in Chester, Vermont, is part of a well-preserved historic district remarkable for its stone buildings constructed by Scottish masons.

The Rockingham Meetinghouse, an elegant example of an early public gathering place.

century wood frame homes and a late 19th-century Grange Hall. Across the river and slightly south in New Hampshire, the Park Hill Meeting House was built in 1762 and then moved in 1799 to its present site on Federal Hill. A steeple with a bell cast by the Paul Revere Foundry was added in 1826, when the church was extensively remodeled in a Greek Revival style.

Historic Religious Buildings

Our historic churches, with their steeples pointing toward the heavens, are one of the universally recognized iconic images of the northern valley. Beginning with the spare meeting houses from which they evolved, these churches illustrate the same progression of architectural styles shared by commercial and residential buildings in the same neighborhoods. Most of the historic churches in our communities were built in the Federal, Greek Revival, and Gothic Revival styles.

The examples of buildings in the religion cat egory listed by the National Park Service provide wide and interesting context for our familiar steepled landmarks, and broaden our conventiona notions of what constitutes a "church." Subcatego ries include *religious facility* (church, temple, syna gogue, cathedral, mission, mound, sweathouse, kiva dance court, shrine) and *ceremonial site* (astronomi cal observation post, intaglio, petroglyph site).

Historic Industrial Buildings

The many industries that formed the economic ba sis for our towns and village centers are still repre sented in the stone, brick, and wood frame buildings that housed their many enterprises. Th architectural styles of these structures were not a important to their designers and builders as thei function. However, glimpses of styles and construc tion periods appear in such details such as overal massing, roof pitch, windowsills and lintels, and cor nice embellishments. These buildings date from the early 1800s to the mid-20th century, and housed manufacturers of textiles, paper, and machine tools among others. Many former mill buildings have found new life as museums and retail, office, and residential complexes. *(For more about these enter prises, see Industry & Commerce.)*

Farmstead Architecture

Two-and-a-half centuries of agriculture have been characterized by changing technology and changing markets, and its practitioners have ranged from hardscrabble survivors to gentlemen farmers. It's no surprising, then, that farm architecture reflects thi history in a variety of materials, styles, and types o structures. The typical farmstead includes a residence and a variety of shelters for humans, animals, anima feed, equipment, food storage—such as barns, sheds silos, corn cribs, milk houses, root cellars, and suga houses for boiling maple sap into syrup or sugar.

Among barns, their purpose and period of con struction is reflected in their location, size and hape, and the size nd location of win- lows, whether for ows or horse stalls, or example. Their imber frames, de- ived from English raditions, create pen spaces that nay be adapted to a ariety of functions. Timber frames also rovided the struc- ural frames for overed bridges.) Among the types are

One of a several historic out- buildings at Alpenglo Farm in Newbury, Vermont.

English barns, bank barns, high-drives, and round barns. Silos, too, reflect changes in grain and silage torage. From barrel-like constructions of wood taves encircled with iron hoops, to ceramic tiles, to oncrete and steel, silos have been the church teeples of the agricultural landscape.

Constantly changing agricultural technology has added and subtracted forms on the landscape. Con- crete bunkers are now employed to store silage. Hay s rolled and wrapped in white plastic, giant marsh- mallows in the field leaving hay barns empty and without purpose.

Round barns are survivors of an architectural con- cept that intrigued some farmers in the Connecticut River Valley. Rarely really round, their 8-, 12-, or 16- sided shape appealed to innovative dairy farmers in the early 1900s. At the time, these barns were con- sidered the model of efficiency in feeding cows whose stalls were arranged as spokes of a wheel around a central feeding chute. Only one survives in the entire state of New Hampshire—in Piermont, where it has been joined by a look-alike commercial retail build- ing across the road. Another stands across the river in Newbury, Vermont, but many others have succumbed to fire or decay, or have been taken down by their owners because of the tax burden they represented.

All of these farmstead structures stand in a par- ticular relationship to each other amid surrounding pastures, crop lands and wood lots. Some twenty farms in the upper Connecticut Valley survive in nearly enough their historic form to qualify for list- ing on the National Register of Historic Places. Many more appear eligible for listing. This region- wide inventory of historic agricultural buildings— which includes both the natural and cultivated landscape of which they are a part—forms one of our most important architectural treasures.

Continuous Farm Architecture

Nineteenth century farming was a home occupation business that required space for daily tasks involving animals in close proximity to living quarters in a cold climate. The phrase "big house—little house—back house—barn" describes the interconnected buildings, or "continuous architecture," sometimes displayed with all the structures joined in a straight line.

Connecting sheds and outbuildings to the house—or arranging the buildings in a U-shape to create a sort of courtyard—provided sheltered and more efficient work areas that made the most of the elusive winter sun. These ideas were handed down and disseminated by word-of-mouth, by example, and by articles in agricultural journals of the day.

The connected barns, sheds, and domestic structures in this early farmstead complex in Charlestown, New Hampshire, shelter a dooryard work area from the prevailing wind.

❧ Threats ❧

Our historic architecture faces a variety of threats, the worst as simple as gravity, weather, and time. Others are: the dearth of resources necessary to keep it in good repair; lack of awareness, appreciation, and commitment to preserve it appropriately; private beliefs and public policies that favor new construction over repairing older buildings; and lack of imagination in finding new uses for functionally obsolete buildings. Changing agricultural technology diminishes the previous usefulness of farm buildings like hay barns and silos. Time and taxes take their toll on old wooden structures that lack current uses.

THE TOLL OF TIME
Belfries threaten to hit the cellar, the barn roof meets its last snowstorm, carpenter ants set up shop, and centuries of wet summers finally win.

A LIMITED RESOURCE
"They" just don't make old houses any more. While many attempts at reproduction of historic architecture are pleasing and comfortable within their setting, there is no substitute for the real thing.

LACK OF INFORMATION
Sometimes, a venerable historic building is to be redeveloped for a new public function, and the new owner thinks it's necessary to tear the guts out of the building to bring it up to the standards of modern building codes. In many cases, there is flexibility in applying building codes to historic structures.

"REMUDDLING" INSTEAD OF REMODELING
Lack of information or appreciation of historic architecture can turn a beautiful if functionally dated building into a hybrid monster that may function better but with less grace and diminished value. This is what happens when sliding French doors are sub-

These two late 1700s cape houses started life as nearly identical twins. While both have been thoroughly updated, the original character of the house below was lost along the way.

stituted for a pair of American Colonial 8 over 12 light antique sash windows, when gorgeous Greek Revival side-lighted entries are obscured by plain pressure-treated access ramps, and when the design and texture of wooden ornament and trim are cut away during application of a new vinyl "skin." It's possible for people who own historic buildings to remodel them in a manner that is sensitive to the venerable old style, while making them comfortable, energy efficient, functional, and even handicapped accessible, without destroying their historic values.

RELUCTANCE TO APPLY LOCAL ZONING
Some communities have withheld from establishing historic districts or considering aesthetics in their zoning, whether related to architecture or otherwise. Many communities have found that active efforts to

ncourage protection of historic buildings have resulted in an increase in their value. In New Hampshire, the Supreme Court stated in a 1992 case,
"....We now conclude the municipalities may validly
exercise zoning power *solely* to advance aesthetic
values, because the preservation or enhancement of
the visual environment may promote the general
welfare ...." (RSA 674:16 and Opinion of the Justices,
103 NH 268).

❧ Actions & Activities ❧

It is important to preserve historic architecture in
your community for the information it contains
about the past, for the economic benefits inherent
in its continued usefulness, for the richness it adds
to our lives, and for its aesthetic value over the de-
pressing uniformity of much modern design. Fortunately, the value of original building materials and
ornament is becoming more widely appreciated, and
some businesses now specialize in salvage and re-
sale of these materials.

LOCAL PLANNING & PUBLIC POLICY

• Check your town plan to see if it has an historic
resources section; if not, enlist the help of your regional planning commission to guide you in writing
one.

• Advocate for flexibility in fire and life safety
codes for historic buildings to allow their redevelopment while also providing public safety and
access.

• Establish a heritage commission in your
community.

• Establish a local historic district in your community. If one already exists, gather a group of fellow
residents and seek help to develop design guidelines—based on local design traditions—and a review process, as part of zoning regulations. These
will guide appropriate decisions for proposed alterations to historic buildings and new construction in
the district to maintain quality and community character. Among these guidelines should be height re-
strictions to prevent new construction from
overwhelming the scale of earlier structures.

• Help strengthen the role of your local historical
society, historic district commission, or heritage
commission, in protecting and celebrating historic
resources. If these organizations don't exist, establish them.

LEARN MORE ABOUT YOUR HISTORIC PROPERTY

• Consult your state's preservation organization
(see Appendix B) to learn more about the architectural style of your property, and how to repair or rehabilitate it in a way that respects its historic features.

• Visit your county registry of deeds to trace the
ownership and history of your house.

• Consult your local historical society for old photographs of your neighborhood.

• Visit Vermont Salvage in downtown White
River Junction, a business that functions informally
as a museum of historic architectural building
materials.

*The owners of this unusual Guildhall fence researched
its original design before restoring it.*

The 1936 Latchis Hotel in Brattleboro, well-known for its bold Art Deco design.

Seek Grants for Projects That Protect Local History

• Explore the possibilities offered by the Certified Local Government program through your state historic preservation office. Communities which have established historic districts, even if the district consists of a single building, are eligible for grants which can bring an architectural historian to town, design and write a walking tour brochure, provide date plaques, and more.

• Promote the use of the federal Rehabilitation Investment Tax Credits for the rehabilitation of historic income-producing commercial properties. (Contact your state historic preservation office for information.)

• If Congress has not yet passed a bill, advocate for passage of the federal homeowners' historic preservation tax credits so that homeowners who carry out appropriate restorations to their own residences can

have access to a similar set of tax credits as the owners of income-producing properties.

• Consider restoring a local landmark with help from the Connecticut River Joint Commissions Partnership Program.

Support Protection of Local Landmarks

• Support the continued use and restoration of community-owned public buildings such as town halls, community centers, libraries, fire stations.

• Nominate a building or a district to the state Register of Historic Places.

• If there is a National Register Historic District or a building listed on the National Register of His

Carpenters at the Putney Tavern are installing windows and wooden siding compatible with the building's original appearance.

The portico of the elegant Guildhall Public Library receives careful repair. The building once served as a Lutheran church.

• Engage an architectural historian to work with interested citizens to do a windshield survey of the town's architecture, and present a program to the community.

• Hand out awards to property owners who maintain and restore their historic buildings in an appropriate manner.

• Promote the use of preservation easements to preserve the appearance and upkeep of historic buildings. Contact the Preservation Trust of Vermont or the New Hampshire Preservation Alliance.

oric Places in your community, share its description with current property owners to be sure that they are aware of the significance of each structure's history and architectural features.

• Encourage owners of architecturally significant properties to consider preservation easements. Contact your state's Historic Preservation Office for more information on these easements.

• Advocate for the remodeling of historic buildings to provide accessibility in a manner that preserves architectural integrity.

• Rehabilitate a historic downtown commercial block in your community for retail on the first floor and apartments on upper floors.

• Create a walking or driving tour booklet about your town or neighborhood from the information contained in local histories and documentation forms for historic buildings listed on the National Register and state surveys. Arrange for people knowledgeable about architecture and local history to lead walking tours.

• Create a program for schoolchildren to participate in a "treasure hunt" of architectural features on buildings in a residential neighborhood.

The 1839 Lyme Center Academy was carefully restored by the community, which employed an array of imaginative fund-raising tools.

The projecting bay on this house in Hartford, Vermont, is rich in texture and detail.

nesses which will fabricate the coverlets using photographs.

• Design and collectively stitch a town quilt depicting favorite town architectural landmarks, as a celebration of local history and fund-raiser.

• Publish a book or even a calendar with "then and now" photographs of the same street scene, the same buildings, the same landscapes, to illustrate positive and negative changes over time.

• Publish note cards or postcards, or even Christmas ornaments depicting well-known historic buildings in town (useful as a fund-raisers).

Ornament portrays mill at Tannery Falls, shown pg. 61.

• Encourage the historical society to maintain a collection of historic photos from your town, and make copies easily available.

• Obtain a copy of the Secretary of the Interior's Standards for Rehabilitation (from your State Historic Preservation Office) and hold a workshop with qualified historic preservation consultants to discuss what they mean and what they encourage.

• Advocate for the repair and preservation of historic building materials (such as brick, slate, and wooden clapboards) rather than their replacement with modern materials (such as vinyl and aluminum) that lack durability, detail, and texture. Provide information to property owners.

• Hold a workshop for homeowners on how to date an old house, employing maps, deeds, probate records, architectural styles, and building "archeology."

CREATE VISUAL CELEBRATIONS

• Create woven coverlets or quilts depicting local historic landmarks and sell them as a fund-raiser and awareness-raiser for the historical society. Contact your state historical society for the names of busi-

PROTECT THE FUTURE OF HISTORIC FARM BUILDINGS

• Conduct a survey of historic farm buildings in your town (contact your state historic preservation office for survey forms and guidelines).

Time, taxes, and other troubles are bringing down historic barns throughout the valley.

Encourage owners of historic barns to apply for barn restoration grants, and inquire about historic agricultural preservation easements which may help reduce tax burdens on historic barns and other farm structures.

❈ Q & A ❈

What are the architectural landmarks in your community? Are they publicly or privately owned? What condition are they in?

• What are the predominant architectural styles of your town? How many can you identify?

• What's the oldest building in your town? The oldest site? Structure? Object?

• How many different building types can you identify in your town?

• Are there any community or school programs that celebrate your community's architectural heritage and try to preserve it?

• Do you think your community does a good job of preserving its historic architecture and special places? What could you or your organization do to improve those efforts?

• Are there non-historic buildings or structures (less than 50 years old) in your town that are an important part of your community's identity? As they approach 50 years, will someone nominate them to the National Register of Historic Places and move to protect them?

• What would your community be like if *all* its historic buildings disappeared? Which buildings would be especially painful to lose? Is anything being done to preserve them now and protect them for the future?

• Who are the "keepers" of your community's history and historical awareness? Are they organizations or individuals? What would happen if those organizations folded or the individuals no longer fulfilled the role? Who would step forward to take up the work?

❈ FYI ❈

GUIDES TO ARCHITECTURAL STYLES

A Building History of Northern New England by James L. Garvin, University Press of New England, Hanover, NH 2001. (An excellent overview of the architecture of Vermont, New Hampshire and Maine, including the evolution of building technology and styles, with a comprehensive bibliography of resources.)

A Field Guide to American Houses by Virginia and Lee McAlester, Alfred A. Knopf, New York, 1991. (Copiously illustrated, depicting variations on historic residential styles.)

New Hampshire Architecture: An Illustrated Guide by Bryant F. Tolles, Jr., University Press of New England, Hanover, NH, 1979. (An inventory of New Hampshire's significant buildings, with thumbnail descriptions and histories.)

Haverhill's handsome Alumni Hall, once the Grafton County Courthouse, is the focus of a major citizen-led restoration effort.

Old House Dictionary: An Illustrated Guide to American Domestic Architecture, 1600 to 1940 by Steven J. Phillips, Preservation Press, Washington, D.C., 1992. (Good glossary of architectural and building terms.)

What Style is it? A Guide to American Architecture, by John C. Poppeliers, S. Allen Chambers, Jr., and Nancy B. Schwartz, the Preservation Press, 1983. (An excellent, illustrated pocket-sized guide to most American styles.)

See Appendix C.

The graceful fountain at the Mountain View Grand hotel in Whitefield, New Hampshire.

HISTORIC BARNS & AGRICULTURAL BUILDINGS

Big House, Little House, Back House, Barn by Thomas C Hubka, University Press of New England, Hanover, NH 1986. (An excellent historical narrative of the development of the distinctive "continuous architecture" of New England farms.)

Field Guide to New England Barns and Farm Buildings by Thomas Durant Visser, University Press of New England, Hanover, NH, 1997. (Definitive, amply illustrated guide to more kinds of farm buildings than one could ever guess exist.)

Preserving Old Barns: Preventing the Loss of a Valuable Resource by John Porter and Francis Gilman, University of New Hampshire Cooperative Extension, 2001. (Generously illustrated, covers history and architectural features of New Hampshire barns, structural repair and restoration, information on disassembling and reassembling a barn, maintenance plans, resources and references.)

"Taking Care of Your Old Barn: Ten Tips for Preserving and Reusing Vermont's Historic Agricultural Buildings" by Curtis B. Johnson and Thomas D. Visser, Vermont Division for Historic Preservation, Montpelier, VT, 1995 (Booklet of practical information; also available on-line at www.uvm.edu/ffvhnet/hpres/publ/barnb/bbtit.html)

GOOD LINKS

Caring for Your Historic Building—National Park Service Technical Preservation Services for Historic Buildings: www2.cr.nps.gov/tps/care/ [help for home owners, preservation professionals, organizations, and government agencies by publishing printed pamphlets and books— easy-to-read guidance on preserving, rehabilitating and restoring historic buildings. Also interactive "web classes"]

Online Preservation Briefs, addressing a wide range of historic preservation topics, technology, and treatments. Go to www2.cr.nps.gov/tps/briefs/presbhom.htm.

The Preservation Education Institute: www.historicwindsor.com

CHAPTER NINE

Civic Life & The Arts

Public Agreements & Personal Achievements

The first generations of European descendants to settle the northern valley established homes, businesses, churches, schools, courts, and local governments, and joined in achieving statehood and establishing a nation. The civic stability and social cohesiveness we inherit is woven into the fabric of the agreements they created and which we ratify by our participation. Our democratic traditions support individual expressions found in religious practice, artistic creation, and scientific invention. The two poles of The One and The Many in the northern valley are represented by rugged individualism, our popular self-image, and Town Meeting, our most famous political institution.

❈ The Basic Story ❈

CONNECTICUT River Valley residents today say that regional issues sometimes don't get enough attention in state capitols located far outside the Connecticut's watershed. Our predecessors in the northern valley generally shared this point of view for more than two centuries, whether the decisions were made by Colonial-era British governors

in Albany, Portsmouth, or Boston, or by the powers that be in Montpelier and Concord. Valley towns frequently have perceived they have more in common with communities just across the river than with the rest of their own state.

This perception reinforced the evolution of a regional culture in the Connecticut River Valley. The

Keene Square bustled with activity around 1900.

men and women who came here in the second half of the 18th century brought with them the society-building habits of coastal New England. Building on these traditions, but in the absence of today's culturally homogenizing influences, they put their own stamp on a new landscape somewhat isolated by distance and topography from their previous homes. With extraordinary leadership and tenacity, they established local governments, public meeting places, schools, and churches. English and French settlers later were joined by immigrants from the rest of Europe and around the world. The river valley's landscape attracted entrepreneurs, inventors, artists, and writers who responded to their new experiences in a distinctive way and gave voice and image to a regional identity.

The Connecticut River now defines the entire length of the political boundary between New Hampshire and Vermont. But during the formative years of the United States, settlers in the watershed on both sides of the river believed they shared a social unity that deserved recognition as a separate political entity. Their vision was not endorsed by others who had the power to draw political boundaries.

The right to grant town charters in our region was claimed variously by Colonial governors in New York, New Hampshire, and Massachusetts. In 1735, the Colonial governor of Massachusetts chartered four towns along the river in present-day southern Vermont and New Hampshire. These towns were numbered One through Four. Present Charlestown, New Hampshire, was known as Number Four, a name passed on to its frontier fort and the fort's 20th-century museum reconstruction, the Fort at No. 4. In 1740, King George II settled a boundary dispute between New Hampshire and Massachusetts by setting the northern boundary of Massachusetts slightly further to the south, at its present location.

The King also named new governors for his colonies of Massachusetts and New Hampshire. How-

ever, the description of the Massachusetts–New Hampshire boundary—as proceeding west "til it meets with his Majesty's other Governments"—exacerbated rather than resolved questions about New Hampshire's western boundary with New York.

Beginning in 1749, New Hampshire's provincial governor Benning Wentworth granted charters to towns west of the Connecticut as well as east. Present-day Vermont became known as the "New Hampshire grants." A modern map showing town boundaries reflects Wentworth's intent to straddle the river. It appears that when it came time to establish northern and southern boundaries for 14 new towns on both sides of the Connecticut, a straight edge was laid directly across the river, creating seven matched pairs of towns, from Weathersfield, Vermont, and Claremont, New Hampshire, in the south to Fairlee, Vermont, and Orford, New Hampshire, in the north. This displeased Governor George Clinton of New York, who complained to the Crown. New York refused to honor the New Hampshire grants, particularly after King George attempted to settle the matter in 1764 by declaring the western bank of the Connecticut River as the eastern boundary of New York.

This sat well with neither Ethan Allen and the Green Mountain Boys in western present-day Vermont nor among settlers of the Connecticut River Valley, who had closer ties to communities downriver, and didn't want to be governed either from Albany or coastal New Hampshire. With leadership coming from Hanover, where Dartmouth was founded in 1769, an association of Connecticut River towns spoke up for an independent status.

After Vermont declared itself an inde-

Westminster, VT, cemetery.

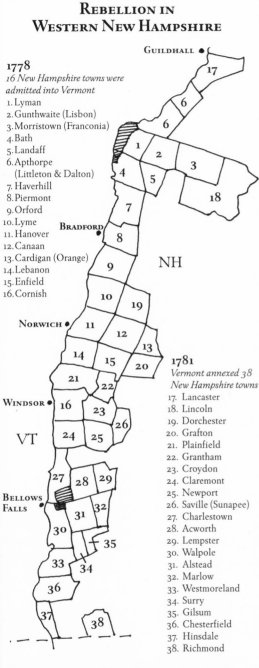

REBELLION IN WESTERN NEW HAMPSHIRE

GUILDHALL ●

1778
16 New Hampshire towns were admitted into Vermont

1. Lyman
2. Gunthwaite (Lisbon)
3. Morristown (Franconia)
4. Bath
5. Landaff
6. Apthorpe (Littleton & Dalton)
7. Haverhill
8. Piermont
9. Orford
10. Lyme
11. Hanover
12. Canaan
13. Cardigan (Orange)
14. Lebanon
15. Enfield
16. Cornish

BRADFORD ●

NORWICH ●

WINDSOR ●

VT

BELLOWS FALLS ●

NH

1781
Vermont annexed 38 New Hampshire towns

17. Lancaster
18. Lincoln
19. Dorchester
20. Grafton
21. Plainfield
22. Grantham
23. Croydon
24. Claremont
25. Newport
26. Saville (Sunapee)
27. Charlestown
28. Acworth
29. Lempster
30. Walpole
31. Alstead
32. Marlow
33. Westmoreland
34. Surry
35. Gilsum
36. Chesterfield
37. Hinsdale
38. Richmond

(In 1781, Monroe and Langdon were the only New Hampshire towns near the Connecticut River south of Lancaster that did not join with Vermont).

pendent Republic in 1777, sixteen river towns on the New Hampshire side of the river opted to join Vermont, claiming that independence from Britain freed them from obligations to New Hampshire which had been granted by the King. Vermont towns bordering the river petitioned to withdraw from Vermont unless the eastern towns were accepted. A convention of river valley towns in Cornish in December, 1778, considered forming a new and separate state, called New Connecticut, encompassing the valley towns on both sides of the river and having as its capital Dresden, that part of Hanover where the college is located. In 1779, New Hampshire responded by claiming all of Vermont's territory.

In 1781, delegates from towns on both sides of the river met at a widely attended convention in Charlestown, and agreed that they wanted to remain united, condemning the idea of making the Connecticut River a state boundary. Governor Chittenden of Vermont wrote to George Washington, seeking Vermont's admission to the Union with territories extending into both present-day New York and New Hampshire. Meeting in Philadelphia later that year, Congress voted to accept Vermont into the union, but left out the lands claimed by New Hampshire on the east and New York on the west. The Vermont Assembly did not acquiesce, but offered to appoint commissioners to review the situation in conjunction with Congress.

In January of 1782, New Hampshire sent 1,000 soldiers to enforce its jurisdiction. Trying to avoid turf battles while waging a war against England, General Washington advised that Vermont accept Congress's proposal that Lake Champlain and the Connecticut River be its west and east borders. The Vermont Assembly agreed, and the river towns on the eastern shore were drawn back, unhappily, into the New Hampshire fold.

It wasn't until 1934 that the U.S. Supreme Court reaffirmed the official boundary between New Hampshire and Vermont as the ordinary low-water mark on the western bank, which was identified with markers and is now, in some places, inundated by dams later constructed. Since their settlement, the towns on both sides of the river have had more in common with each other than they did with their distant state capitols, a situation that continues today.

New Hampshire ("Live Free or Die"), one of the thirteen original colonies, achieved statehood on June 21, 1788, the ninth state in the Union. Vermont ("Freedom and Unity") was granted statehood on March 4, 1791, as the fourteenth state.

The terms of the 1783 settlement that ended the Revolutionary War set off another boundary dispute, this time in the north involving the U.S.-Canadian border, and centered on varying interpretations of which streams were actually the headwaters of the Connecticut River. In the region of present-day Pittsburg, New Hampshire, residents finally took things into their own hands in 1832 by declaring themselves the United Inhabitants of Indian Stream Republic. They drafted a constitution and created a militia—of 41 men. But they couldn't agree among themselves about whether to form an alliance with Canada and Great Britain or the United States, and civil war seemed likely. When the New Hampshire Assembly proposed that the Republic become part of New Hampshire, it agreed. In 1840 the former Republic was incorporated as the town of Pittsburg.

Our political stability was—and still is—reinforced by a variety of political, social, and religious organizations and traditions. Annual Town Meeting is foremost among these traditions, at the top of a pyramid of similar institutions within which we carry out the common purposes of government. These include: town select boards and village trustees; regional and local planning, zoning, and conservation boards and commissions; school boards, teachers' and parents' associations; churches, libraries, historical societies, granges, and service clubs; museums, art guilds, performing arts, and poetry groups. We celebrate our communities in gatherings large and small, such as concerts and readings, church and game suppers, festivals founded on local traditions (moose, pumpkins, zucchini), historical re-enactments, and a host of activities gathered into Old Home Days.

Over time, our cultural institutions—our museums, libraries, theaters, galleries, historical societies and historic sites—have become the repositories of our regional heritage and stages upon which the region's individual and collective accomplishments and memories are kept alive. They are also sometimes the forums within which new ideas and paradigms are introduced and evolve.

Through all of these institutions and organizations, we enact our roles as stewards of our precious natural and architectural inheritance. On any given night in the northern valley, we are gathered in kitchens and meeting halls to make important decisions about the care and stewardship of this inheritance. Sometimes we're called on to express new visions, make extraordinary efforts, and strengthen our organizations, in order to preserve and protect our communities.

C. 1908 postcard rendering of the Woods Public Library, Bradford, Vermont.

❧ Resources & Revelations ❧

POLITICAL TOUCHSTONES

vents and places in our communities are remind-
rs of the people and events that have shaped our
emocratic traditions and political landscape.

On March 11, 1775, fearing the loss of their farms
hrough foreclosure, local farmers tried to prevent a
New York court from sitting in the Westminster
Courthouse. The New Yorker sheriff and his depu-
es fired into an unruly crowd, killing two men. The
ictims became martyrs of the "Westminster Massa-
re" and the incident united Connecticut River Val-
y settlers—east-siders—with Ethan Allen and the
est-siders against New York colonial authorities.
One month later a convention at Westminster peti-
oned King George III to allow them to be "either
nnexed to some other government or erected and
ncorporated into a new one." (Just a week later, Brit-
h soldiers marched on Lexington and Concord.)

In January, 1777, another convention held in
Vestminster went beyond the earlier petition and
oted "That the district of land commonly called and
nown by the name of the New Hampshire Grants
e a new and separate State; and for the future con-
uct themselves as such." The name chosen was "New
onnecticut." The name was soon changed at a con-
ention held in Windsor where, on July 8, 1777, the
presentatives voted to adopt the first Constitution
f the "Free and Independent State of Vermont."
Iodeled on Benjamin Franklin's constitution for
ennsylvania, Vermont's Constitution went further.
was the first Constitution in America to prohibit
avery, to establish universal voting rights for all
ales, and to authorize a public school system.

The adoption of the Constitution marked the
eation of an independent Republic of Vermont.
he meeting was held in Windsor at Elijah West's
vern, now known as the Old Constitution House
d "the birthplace of Vermont." It is operated as a
ate-owned historic site and is listed on the Na-
onal Register of Historic Places.

*This 1790 Federal style home in Cornish, New
Hampshire, was the birthplace of Salmon P. Chase.*

POLITICAL PERSONALITIES

To call the early settlers of the Connecticut River
"pioneers" is not to say they were unsophisticated
or untrained. Among the first and second generations of settlers—and down the generations to the
present—have come men and women of remarkable
breadth, sophistication, and vision.

In Cornish, New Hampshire, is a 1790 residence
that was the birthplace and boyhood home of Salmon
P. Chase. Born in 1808 into a family of lawyers, Chase
studied at Dartmouth College and in Washington,
D.C., and as a lawyer himself defended the rights of
runaway slaves. After practicing in Ohio, he served
as a U.S. Senator and Governor of that state and
helped found the Republican Party. Abraham Lincoln appointed him Secretary of the Treasury (1861-
1864) and Chief Justice (1864-1873), in which
capacity he presided over the impeachment trial of
President Andrew Johnson. Chase is pictured on the
$10,000 bill. His birthplace, listed on the National
Register, is a National Historic Landmark, now used
as a bed & breakfast inn.

Among other early political notables whose stories survive in their residences is General Lewis R.
Morris, whose 1795 homestead in Springfield is
listed on the National Register. Morris was a sol-

dier of the Revolution, member of Congress (1797-1803), commissioner for Vermont statehood (1791), Secretary of Constitutional Convention (1793), and a six-term member of the Vermont Legislature.

A leader in modern conservation thinking was U.S. Senator John Wingate Weeks, born in Lancaster in 1860. He was the author of the Weeks Act (1911), which established the White Mountain National Forest, the Weeks-McLean Act of 1913 for migratory birds, and the Federal Reserve Act. Weeks began his political career as mayor of Newton, Massachusetts, and then went on to represent the state in the U.S. House of Representatives and later the U.S. Senate. He died in Lancaster in 1926, after serving as Secretary of War. His summer home on Mount Prospect in Lancaster is listed on the National Register of Historic Places, and became Weeks State Park after his family donated it to the State of New Hampshire in 1942.

The most significant political figure to come from the northern valley was Calvin Coolidge, the 30th President of the United States. His 1872 birthplace, boyhood home, and summer White House are preserved in the Plymouth Notch Historic District. His journey to the presidency was a gradual progression that Coolidge likened to the flow of water down-

hill. He attended Black River Academy in Ludlo and St. Johnsbury Academy, graduated fro Amherst College, was admitted to the bar, becam solicitor and then Mayor of Northampton, Mass. chusetts. He went on to become state senator, Pres dent of the state Senate, Massachusetts Lt. Govern and Governor, U.S. Vice President under Warre G. Harding, and then President. (For more abo Coolidge, see *Settlement*.)

Stone foundations, in Pisgah State Park, Che terfield, New Hampshire, survive from the birt place of Harlan F. Stone, Chief Justice of the U. Supreme Court, appointed by President Franklin Roosevelt.

Other places are notable for their links to t wider world beyond the valley. Canadian bord crossing stations were constructed in the 1930s Beechers Falls and Canaan, Vermont, and Pittsbur New Hampshire. Built for U.S. Customs and Imm gration and Naturalization Services personnel, th established the Federal presence in remote, rur towns. In Stark, New Hampshire, an historic mark in the White Mountain National Forest records t location of Camp Stark, a German prisoner of w camp, built in 1944. Closed in 1946, it housed a proximately 250 German and Austrian soldiers wh worked in the surrounding fo est where they cut pulp woo vital to wartime industry.

TOWN MEETING

Held once each year in ear Spring, Town Meeting is the a nual opportunity for citizens gather and take action on ma ters of importance to the con munity. Questions to be vot upon are listed as "articles" a publicly advertised, "warned" agenda known as "warrant." Some towns no schedule the Meeting in t

Constitution House in Windsor, scene of a pivotal chapter in civic life.

>wn Meeting and all its traditions knit a community together.

consolidation in the second half of the 20th century created regional high schools. As a result, some large high schools built in urban centers during the first half of the 20th century still serve educational functions, while others have been converted to other uses or lost, along with the school's traditional seat within the physical center of the community.

Several early public academies, such as those in Thetford and St. Johnsbury,

vening to accommodate residents who cannot take me off from work, while others adhere to the day-me schedule, and take a break from the meeting or the traditional potluck covered dish meal. Meetngs are presided over by a moderator, a longtime esident who typically combines a working knowldge of Roberts Rules of Order with a keen sense of umor and a knack of knowing when to use it. Despite sometimes-low attendance and rumors of s demise, Town Meeting endures.

EDUCATION

The rural northern valley is dotted with scores of ne-room brick or clapboarded district or neigh-orhood schoolhouses. Their widespread presence n the 19th century attests to the dispersed charac-r of settlements and the high value placed on edu-ation. The c. 1790 Eureka Schoolhouse in pringfield, Vermont, is operated as a state historic te. Relocated in 1968, the one room schoolhouse s sheathed with pine planks to simulate stone locks.

In the first half of the 20th century, most of these mall schools were closed as towns created consoli-ated classrooms in larger single buildings. Further

Vermont, are thriving still and approaching their third century, drawing high school students from neighboring towns and even across the river. St. Johnsbury Academy's campus includes the High Victorian Gothic-style "Brantview," formerly the Fairbanks Family home, at the south end of Main Street.

The notion of a separate state in the Connecticut River Valley didn't completely die in 1784. Since 1963, Hanover and Norwich have been united in the Dresden School District, the first interstate school district in the United States, adopting the name of the intended capital of the proposed state of "New

The Eureka Schoolhouse.

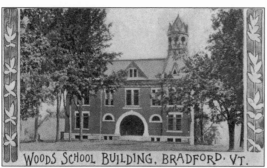

The public school, later Bradford Academy, in a c. 1916 postcard view. The building now houses town offices.

Connecticut." The Dresden School District was created by one of the last bills signed by President John F. Kennedy before his assassination. The towns of Orford, New Hampshire, and Fairlee, West Fairlee, and Vershire, Vermont went even further in 1998, establishing the Rivendell Interstate School District, the only K-12 interstate district in the country.

Dartmouth College was founded in 1769 in Hanover, in the first decade after signing of the treaty that ended the French and Indian Wars. Its first class was held in a log building. Its founder, the Rev. Eleazar Wheelock, who had been tutoring children in Lebanon since the 1740s, was motivated to educate Native Americans. In the 1760s, Wheelock sent one of his early Indian converts to England to raise money for the project. Dartmouth trustees held their first meeting in the 1762 Wyman Tavern in Keene. For thirty years, Dartmouth was the only collegiate institution in the entire Connecticut River Valley. Dartmouth Medical School, founded in 1797, helped stimulate the creation of the Dartmouth-Hitchcock Medical Center, now the largest medical center in the region.

Across the river in Norwich, Vermont, Capt. Alden Partridge founded the nation's first private military college in 1819. It moved to Northfield in 1866 and is now known as Norwich University, taking the town's name along and also leaving one behind: the Grange in Norwich is still known as University Grange. Enriching the higher education

opportunities in the northern valley are Keene State College and Antioch/New England Graduat School in Keene, Lebanon College, Marlboro Col lege and Lyndon State College in Lyndonville Vermont.

RELIGION

Churches and their steeples are a distinctive ingre dient in the visual character of our communitie Their congregations have contributed significantl to the social cohesiveness of the region. Many of th familiar white spires rose to the sky in the earl 1800s as church meetings grew too large for farm house kitchens. This was a time of religious energ and factionalism in the hills of the northern Con necticut River Valley. The Congregationalist an

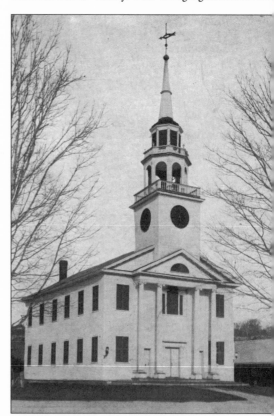

The 1817 Norwich Congregational Church. Its bell came from the Paul Revere Foundry.

Free Will Baptist traditions captured the sympathies of most families, soon joined by the Universalists. The hardships and uncertainty of life in the northern valley probably contributed to its fertility as a source of new religious thinking.

Another major religious movement also has its roots in the Connecticut River Valley. The Seventh Day Adventist Church was founded in Washington, New Hampshire, in 1842. One of the most unsettling religious doctrines of the time was William Miller's insistence that the world would end in March of 1843. Miller preached extensively in both states, drawing crowds and inviting the faithful to assemble on hilltops for their ascension.

Mormon prophet Joseph Smith grew up in Royalton, Vermont, and Brigham Young, Mormon leader and founder of Utah, was born in Whitingham. Their childhood homes are no longer standing.

A Shaker Community at Lower Shaker Village on the shore of Mascoma Lake in Enfield, New Hampshire, was active from 1793 to 1923. Named after a Shaker community in Enfield, Connecticut, at one time it extended over 3,000 acres and numbered 350 members. Known for its textiles, linen, cotton and wool products, it is now a museum.

Claremont is the site of both Old St. Mary's Roman Catholic Church (1823), the first Roman Catholic Church in New Hampshire, and the Union Church (1773, 1820, 1850), the oldest standing Episcopal church in the state, and the oldest structure in the state built specifically for religious use. Not far away in Plainfield, Kimball Union Academy was founded in 1813 by Congregationalists for the preparation of ministers.

ARTISTS & AUTHORS

The upper Connecticut River Valley has been a magnet for painters, sculptors, and writers of all kinds who came to be inspired by its scenic beauty or find as much solitude as they could away from the demands of urban society.

The 19th century primitive-realistic work of the itinerant mural painter Rufus Porter survives in several valley houses. Porter, who left murals in Maine and Massachusetts, was also an inventor and journalist, becoming the founding editor of "Scientific American" in 1845. In Orford, New Hampshire, Porter created murals in the Hinkley House, one of the Ridge Houses, just after it was built in 1824. *(For more, see Architecture.)* One fresco includes a view of the Connecticut River with a steamboat that closely resembles a steamboat constructed by Orford neighbor Samuel Morey about 1820. Between 1825 and 1830, Porter painted murals in the Daniel Carr House in North Haverhill and the Wagner House in Lyme, New Hampshire. A mural that includes the frigate "Potomac" survives in the Elwin Chase House across the river in Topsham, Vermont, painted about 1835.

A completely different image of the region is reflected in the work of painter Maxfield Parrish, who kept a studio in Plainfield, from 1898 to 1966. His painting "New Hampshire," also known as

Maxfield Parrish, artist, artisan, and machinist.

"Thy Templed Hills," has been used to extol the state's rural splendor. Parrish illustrated childrens' books, calendars, magazines, and even chocolate boxes. His landscape paintings—dramatic, accurate, and romantic, sometimes peopled with nymphs—are said by critics to constitute a 20th-century version of the great 19th century tradition of landscape painting as represented by artists like Thomas Cole. (Cole's 1823 painting of the great ox-bow of the Connecticut River as seen from Mount Holyoke, Massachusetts, is a famous and iconographic image.) Plainfield's 1846 Greek Revival-style Town Hall includes stage scenery produced by the Cornish Colony under the direction of Maxfield Parrish.

Parrish was as intrigued by precision machinery as he was inspired by the colors and landforms of the Connecticut River Valley, and his talents as a machinist have been celebrated at the American Precision Museum in Windsor. The State of New Hampshire recently designated the portion of Route 12A from Plainfield to the Cornish–Windsor Covered Bridge, past Parrish's former home, "The Oaks," as the "Maxfield Parrish Highway," indicated by a sign in Parrish's signature vivid blue.

Parrish was the son of artist Stephen Parrish, who had been drawn to Cornish by the sculptor Augustus Saint-Gaudens, the northern valley's most illustrious artist, whose home and studio, a National Historic Landmark, is operated by the National Park Service as the Saint-Gaudens National Historic Site.

Saint-Gaudens moved to Cornish in 1885 and spent many of his productive years here. He was the creator of sculpture depicting Abraham Lincoln, in Chicago, the Puritan in Springfield, the Shaw Memorial in Boston, the memorial to Mrs. Henry Adams in Washington's Rock Creek Cemetery, and the monument to General Sherman in front of New York's Plaza Hotel. Reproductions of many of these works are also displayed here for the public to enjoy.

Saint-Gaudens drew into his sphere many other artists and musicians who collectively became known as the Cornish Colony, at "little New York," from about 1885-1935. Among them were sculptor Herbert Adams, poet Percy MacKaye, and architect Charles A. Platt. Homer Saint-Gaudens, Augustus's son, wrote that what called the artists of his father's generation to the Cornish area were the "peace and dreamlike ripeness of the hills…their dark clumps of trees…their river winding south" before Mt. Ascutney in Vermont.

Members of the Cornish arts community founded the Mothers and Daughters Club in 1901 in Plainfield, part of a national movement favoring increased independence and activity for women. Colony members entertained each other with elaborate theatrical performances, staged on their terraces or in their gardens on warm summer evenings.

During the same period, Rudyard Kipling came to Vermont to marry his best friend's sister and build a home where he lived and wrote from 189

Rudyard Kipling in his library at Naulakha, Dummerston, Vermont.

o 1896. Called Naulakha, his home in Dummerston is now a National Historic Landmark.
Kipling himself designed the house, one of
Vermont's finest Shingle Style residences, to provide privacy from prying visitors while writing
uch classics as *The Jungle Books*, *Just So Stories*,
nd *Captains Courageous*. The house is now op-
rated as a bed & breakfast inn by the Landmark
Trust of America.

Nearby Brattleboro around the same time was
ome to a number of illustrious individuals. They
ncluded Larkin Mead (whose statues of Ethan
Allen and Abraham Lincoln grace the Vermont State
House and Springfield, Illinois, respectively), Wil-
iam R. Mead, architect, and William Morris Hunt,
sculptor and architect. Author Louisa May Alcott
vacationed and wrote in Walpole, New Hampshire.
Ludlow, Vermont, is the home town and burial place
of Abby Maria Hemenway, publisher of early his-
ories of every Vermont county except one, her own
county of Windsor.

The arts continue to
play a strong role in the
cultural life of the
northern valley. Per-
orming and visual arts
groups, summer stock
companies, classical
music ensembles and
chorales, and a lively
concert circuit all bring
people together around
he arts. So-called
"amateur" productions
populate the calendar

*Matt Brown works on the
wood block print for the
cover illustration of this
book in his Lyme studio.*

year-round, such as church pageants, school plays
and concerts, summer readings in historic meeting-
houses, and fund-raising benefits.

In a number of towns, community-based arts
groups have established cooperative galleries and
affordable apartments for artists. Individuals con-
inue to make strong contributions to the regional

*The Hopkins Center at Dartmouth College hosts live
performances by internationally known artists.*

identity, from crafts producers and artisans who
display at local and regional fairs to nationally
known artists such as children's illustrator Trina
Schart Hyman and authors such as W.D. Wetherell,
Reeve Lindbergh, Noel Perrin, Galway Kinnell,
and David Budbill.

CULTURAL CENTERS

Our larger towns such as Hanover, Brattleboro and
Keene are regional cultural centers. Dartmouth College is well known for its Baker Library, Hood Museum of Art, and the Hopkins Center, a leading
venue for the performing arts.

The St. Johnsbury Athenaeum is a distinctive
public library and art gallery, in St. Johnsbury, Vermont. This National Historic Landmark is a legacy
of the Fairbanks Family of St. Johnsbury, inventors
and manufacturers of the world's first platform scale,
who gave the Athenaeum to the town in 1871. The
art collection contains a number of Hudson River
School paintings. Dominating the gallery is the magnificent canvas, about ten feet by fifteen feet, of the
Domes of the Yosemite, by Albert Bierstadt. The
artist visited St. Johnsbury often until his death in
1902, touching up the canvas from time to time.

❅ Threats ❅

Our democratic traditions are threatened by our own indifference. Without our informed involvement and financial support, our local governments, schools, and community organizations will fail to live up to their capacity to maintain our sense of community, quality of life, and economic vitality. For a variety of complex reasons and despite a long and strong tradition of volunteerism, many towns find it difficult to fill all the positions on boards and committees. Attendance at Town Meetings is sometimes disappointingly slim. Lack of support and appreciation for the arts can limit our individual and collective ability to use our tactile senses and imaginations to discover and envision life's possibilities.

Brunswick, Vermont, celebrated the U.S. Bicentennial with a gathering at the Town House and re-enactment of Stark's Rangers.

❅ Actions & Activities ❅

It is important that representative forms of government remain responsive to the public, and for the public to participate actively in their municipal and educational systems. It is important to support non-profit organizations that serve immediate and long-term functions, and for non-profit organizations to remain true to their purposes and open to innovative ideas. It is important to support the arts and all their manifestations to invigorate ourselves and our communities.

EXPLORE
• Visit the Old Constitution House in Windsor, Vermont.
• Take a tour of the valley to sample the variety of town and city halls, from humble to grand.
• Enjoy a summer concert on the lawn at Saint-Gaudens National Historic Site.
• Explore the exhibits at the Hood Museum in Hanover, New Hampshire.

LEARN ABOUT LOCAL CIVIC LIFE
• If your town history has been written, read it; if there is no published history for your town, organize a committee to coordinate its compilation and publication. An initial effort can be publication of a simple collection of local historic photographs.

• Gather a group to work with your town's elders to record and publish an oral history of their recollections.

• Evaluate your municipal and educational boards' fulfillment of state open meeting laws and requirements for due process.

The Woodsville Fire Department, pride of the community.

PARTICIPATE IN VOTER EDUCATION

• Bring your children with you when you go to vote.

• Encourage students to become involved and speak up on local issues.

• Encourage the school to send out a regular newsletter to the wider community so that citizens (and taxpayers) who are not school parents are aware of school activities.

• Keep alive the memory of local political traditions and civic leaders.

Encourage local newspapers to cover town affairs.

Promote citizen participation in municipal meetings and elections.

Write letters to the editors of local newspapers on issues about which you are knowledgeable or have special information or experience.

Consider working with others to create an interactive historical web site such as that of Hollis, New Hampshire.

Help establish a web site and a listserv for your town, so that web-connected community members can keep in touch with local events.

VOLUNTEER

Volunteer to serve on a town committee or board.

Start a town-wide newsletter if your community does not already have one.

Share your experience and knowledge as a school volunteer.

Establish a "citizen of the year" award to recognize volunteerism.

SUPPORT THE ARTS

• Reinvigorate or create festivals that celebrate local history, events, traditions, ethnic groups, or anything else that is key to your community's identity or unique character.

• Maintain or restore statues, sculptures, and other artwork in parks and public places.

• Hold block party dances, and close off streets for the festivities.

Colebrook's Moose Festival draws a crowd.

Pie auctions bring out the talents of local bakers for a good cause.

- Write and perform plays based on local history and individuals.

- Dedicate a public gallery space to exhibits by local artists, perhaps at the library or town hall.

- Organize an "open studio" tour of local artists' studios.

- Hold an annual pre-holiday book-signing and sale by local authors.

- Organize a lecture or discussion series around local authors and experts.

- Start a town band, join an existing one, or attend their concerts.

- Attend a literary reading, participate in a book or discussion group.

- Start a neighborhood literary club, perhaps with dinner included.

- Create outdoor murals in visible locations to spruce up blighted areas, depict local history, and delight the eye.

- Incorporate music into public events.

- Invite local artisans to exhibit their works durin community suppers and other events.

- With property owners' permission, install histor exhibits or hang art in the windows of vacant stor fronts, and install art panels over boarded-u windows.

❋ Q & A ❋

- What year was your town chartered, and b whom? (Consult your town clerk or local writte history.)

- Who were the grantees, proprietors, or incorpo rators who signed the charter?

- Did any of them actually settle in town or wer they speculators?

- Do any of their descendants survive amon today's residents?

- Compare the first survey of your town to its natu ral resources and topography. Does the map sho how the town was intended to be established an grow? Were early plans fulfilled? If some plots wer deemed valuable at the time, has that value change over time?

- What ethnic groups have influenced you community's culture? Were they drawn to work i local industries? Does any of their cultural identit survive in festivals, foods, place names?

- Who are the authors and artists in you community's past who have contributed to your lo cal and regional identity? Which ones are good can didates for exhibits or readings?

- Do schools in your community have classes o local history and civics?

- Are young people participating in Town Meet ing, civic organizations and activities?

- Obtain attendance records for your annual Tow Meeting—and town census figures—over a lon

...he road crew—unsung heroes of the early hours, whether driving a snow ...ller or a plow truck. Seen here at work in Lebanon in 1889.

...riod of time. Has attendance generally increased ...r decreased as a percentage of population? What ...ctors have contributed to changes in this in your ...wn?

Add up the total number of volunteer positions ...n your municipal government. Include elected po-...tions such as select board, village trustees, town ...lerk, and any other positions on the ballot, right ...own to fence viewer and weigher-of-coal. Include ...ll boards and committees, such as planning com-...ission, zoning board, conservation commission, ...chool board, and cemetery overseers. (Consult ...our town report and/or town clerk.) Are all posi-...ons filled?

• What are your community's strongest civic and cultural institutions? (See Community Profile chapter and exercise.)

CIVIC TOPICS

The Great Good Place by Ray Oldenburg, Paragon House, New York, 1989. (Great concept book about the need for communities to have a "third place," neither a home or workplace, where informal public life can thrive.)

Indian Stream Republic: Settling a New England Frontier, 1785-1842 by Daniel Doan, University Press of New England, Hanover, NH, 1997. (Detailed narrative covering the Republic's laws, taxation, land use, terrain, and material conditions of life.)

Old Home Day by Donald Hall, Browndeer Press. 1996. (The origins of New Hampshire's Old Home Day. Illustrated by Caldecott Medal Winner, Arnold McCully.)

Organizing Volunteers for Preservation Projects: A How-to Guide for Using Volunteers to Save Historic Buildings by Judith Winters Bell and Stephen Brownell Harris, Preservation Trust of Vermont, Burlington, VT, 1993. (A great sourcebook for conducting activism on the local level for any kind of civic project.)

Stark Decency: German Prisoners of War in a New England Village by Allen V. Koop, University Press of New England, Hanover, NH, 1988. (An unusual story of the impact of World War II on a small New Hampshire community.)

We Had Each Other, A Spoken History of Lyme, New Hampshire edited by Mary Daubenspeck and Judith G. Russell, Friends of the Lyme Library, Lyme, NH, 2000. (Sensitively gathered, arranged, and illustrated oral history collection of reminiscences of community elders.)

THE ARTS

This American River: Five Centuries of Writing on the Connecticut; an Anthology edited and selected by W. D. Wetherell, University Press of New England, Hanover, NH, 2002.

This Land of Pure Delight: Charles C. Beaman and Blowmedown Farm by John H. Dryfhout, Augustus Saint-Gaudens Memorial, Cornish, New Hampshire, 2000.

GOOD LINKS

Vermont Arts Council: www.state.vt.us/ vermont-arts
The goals of the Council are to create an environment where artists and arts organizations flourish, and to strengthen community life through the arts.

New Hampshire State Council on the Arts: www.state.nh.us/ nharts *The mission of the State Council on the Arts is to support and promote excellence, education, and community investment in the arts for the benefit of people in NH.*

Both states have Humanities Councils that are a source of lectures, programs, and activities on cultural matters, history, and literacy:

Vermont Council on the Humanities: www.vermonthumanities.org

New Hampshire Humanities Council : www.nhhc.org

Catamount Arts, St. Johnsbury, VT 05819 802-748-260

Arts Alliance of Northern New Hampshire 603-444-15C

Vital Communities: *www.vitalcommunities.org/*

Great River Arts Institute: www.greatriverarts.org

Post Mills Hall and School, Thetford, Vermont, c. 1911.

CHAPTER TEN

Tourism & Recreation

Getting Away Means Going Back

Tourism in the northern valley illustrates more than two centuries of human desire for interaction with the natural world and the cultural past. Wayfarers and sightseers arrived alongside the earliest settlers. Today, the region's proximity to major population centers provides city dwellers easy access to our places that evoke "the way things used to be." Recreational and heritage tourism contribute significantly to the year-round economy of the region. Tourism carefully focused on the natural, scenic, historic, recreational, and cultural assets of the northern valley offers our communities the opportunity to strengthen their identity and to preserve and promote their historic and natural special places.

❋ The Basic Story ❋

THE close of active hostilities at the end of the French and Indian Wars opened New England's wild interior to settlement by European descendants in the 1760s. Immigrants from the region's coastal towns discovered a blank slate upon which to project their ideas about nature and aesthetics. Jeremy Belknap, a Congregational pastor and early New Hampshire historian, wrote that the White Mountains' "wild and rugged scenes" were "sublime and beautiful." His words were an American echo of William Wordsworth's writings about the Alps. They represented the transplantation of the English Romantic movement across the Atlantic, and foretold the idealization of nature later expressed by Thoreau and Emerson.

Cottage life at Hall's Pond near Wells River, Vermont, c. 1915.

John Ledyard, the valley's first "extreme" tourist. In 1773, he built a dugout canoe at Dartmouth College and paddled it down the river.

Almost as soon as the communities of the northern valley took root in the second half of the 18th century, travelers came seeking adventure in a wilderness only recently settled. The mountains and free-flowing rivers lured journalists, artists, painters, poets, and preachers—those with the daring and means to travel, and sometimes the motivation to publish accounts of their experiences.

The earliest "tourist stops" were turnpike taverns and stagecoach inns. Among the first tourist destinations were mineral springs hotels that promised to cure a variety of ills both real and imagined through the drinking of sometimes foul-smelling waters. The prospect of better health prompted thousands to travel by horse-drawn coaches for long distances over poor roads, and stay in accommodations having a wide range of conveniences and amenities.

Smith's Hotel, which once welcomed weary stagecoach travelers on the Coös Turnpike. Note Connecticut River Valley porch on the fourth story. It stood opposite the northwest corner of the Haverhill Common.

The Industrial Revolution and the expansic of urban areas led to overcrowding and unhealtl ful conditions in such cities as Boston, New Yor and Hartford. There grew up a class of urba dwellers whose regular employment provided bot the means to afford vacations and the need to tal them. The mountains and waters of New Hamp shire and Vermont awaited nearby as clean, wil natural places offering cooler temperatures, clear air, and regenerative relief. The construction railroads in the mid-19th century brought prev ously remote tourist destinations in the upper riv valley within a day's travel of the East Coast's ma jor urban centers.

The ample dining room of Union Station in White River Junction c. 1910, ready for the incoming train.

The railroad transformed the culture of the 19t century, propelling economic growth, entertainmer and fashion. Rail passenger cars, while cramped an sooty, permitted Americans to travel like royalty an view the passing scenery from the comfort of a pac ded seat. City dwellers boarded the train in thei downtown stations and stepped off at small depot high in the hills, to be carried by coach to grand hc tels with mountain vistas. The hotels and railroad grew symbiotically in response to the market. Wel to-do vacationers were eager consumers of amen ties and diversions such as hiking, golf, and late tennis and skiing, all of which stimulated the growt of nearby towns to supply and serve them.

arriages await urban visitors arriving by train at the fanciful Bethlehem, New Hampshire, depot in the White Mountains.

Life, specifically to promote its pastoral image. Today, both Vermont and New Hampshire promote tourism as a form of economic development. Computers and the Internet now offer tourist-oriented businesses new ways to find customers, and help potential visitors gather information and make travel decisions.

While grand resorts flourished in the mountains, both states struggled with the loss of vitality in their farming base. Their population and economy had begun to move west in the mid-19th century, and within decades the states were troubled by the prospect of hundreds of abandoned farms. State officials in both states urged farmers to earn extra money by taking in tourists who would relish their farm-fresh food and the clean air of the countryside. The governor of New Hampshire proclaimed "Old Home Week" in 1899 to create celebrations with the goal of drawing some former residents who had moved away, in hopes of stimulating the economy and resettling depressed rural areas. Vermont quickly followed suit, and the tradition remains strong in both states today.

The campaign to promote tourism in Vermont was stepped up in 1911 with the creation of the Bureau of Publicity, the first state agency of its kind in the nation. In 1947, the state became the first to publish a magazine, *Vermont*

Just as the railroad spurred the growth of tourism in the 19th century, so the automobile drove its expansion in the 20th century. As early as 1907, when roads were impassable by car most of each year, auto tour guides promoted New England. One called it "the favorite touring section of America, for nowhere else can there be found such a variety of scenery contained within a comparatively small area, so much good or so many places of historic interest."

The Woodsville Stage loaded with less fortunate travelers.

Pleasure craft plied the river and larger lakes, such as Lake Morey in Fairlee, Vermont.

After 1915, the automobile and paved roads created tourism opportunities for the growing middle class and dispersed its travelers more widely than before. Their travels no longer limited by rails and train schedules, tourists opted for short-term stays in roadside inns over long-term stays in remote grand hotels. Auto touring was promoted by the Depression-era "American Guide Series," written by workers of the Federal Writers' Project of the Works Progress Administration. The Civilian Conservation Corps, established by President Roosevelt to provide work during the Great Depression, supported the fledgling state park systems by building shelters, picnic areas, trails, bridges, and more. As

Guests at Currier's Camps in Pittsburg, New Hampshire, now Lopstick Lodge, show off their impressive catch.

the car replaced the railroad as the travel mode of choice from the 1930s through the 1950s, roadside motels and clusters of tiny tourist cabins sprang up offering an alternative to the more pricy grand hotels. Gas stations, farm stands, and an assortment of roadside attractions arose to serve the new market.

Tourists who remained in the region longer than the typical two-week vacationer were known as seasonal residents, "rusticators," or "summer people." Wealthy and middle-class summer people bought up old farms and lived on them during the fair weather months, returning to their urban residences when mud and winter conditions challenged their patience with the truly pastoral.

Thetford, Vermont, campers ascend a ridge.

During the 20th century, a cultural shift in seasonal recreation produced "winter people" who came to the region for snow sports. In January 1934 the nation's first ski tow was built in Woodstock, Vermont. On a sloping pasture of Clinton Gilbert's farm, skiers weary of climbing the hill after every downhill run could hold onto a rope hooked to a Ford Model T engine, to be pulled back up the hill. The ski tow launched a new era in winter sports. The Inn at Sugar Hill near Franconia Notch, no longer in existence, was the first ski school in the country and employed European instructors, who gave the sport a fashionable appeal. In 1940, a skiers' guide listed 49 "ski towns" in New Hampshire and 31 in Vermont. The ski industry revived some of the old grand hotels, a few of which developed into year-

The Alden Inn in Lyme in 1909, built a century before as a stagecoach inn to serve travelers on the Grafton Turnpike, still welcomes guests.

ound destination resorts with slope-side condominium communities. The northern valley today includes a number of downhill ski areas popular with residents and tourists alike, as well as miles of groomed cross-country ski trails.

In the early 20th century, long-distance hiking became popular, and winter activities such as skiing expanded seasonal tourism into a year-round industry. The development of state parks, national forests, the Appalachian Trail and scores of local and regional trails coincided with growing interest in camping, hiking, boating, and canoeing, along with steady interest in fishing and swimming. Throughout the past century, with the increase in leisure time and discretionary income, outdoor recreation has matured into a national pastime and a multibillion dollar industry.

Tourism in the upper Connecticut River Valley today draws on a combination of historic, scenic, and recreational resources that is unique in the American northeast. Communities in New Hampshire and Vermont came together in 1999 to create the Connecticut River Byway to promote heritage-based tourism and agri-tourism as a means toward economic development. The Byway is a network of scenic roads that follow and cross the river in a 275-mile-long corridor that stretches between the Massachusetts and Canadian borders, at the core of what we consider the northern valley. Ten "waypoint" communities along the river are developing interpretive centers to provide local and regional information to travelers. These places are also potential centers for community identity-building activities.

❧ Resources & Revelations ❧

INNS & TAVERNS

The community is rare in our region that did *not* have at least one tavern or inn that functioned as both travelers' stopover and local gathering place in the period from 1780 to 1850. Their guest registers and account books provide the earliest information about the tourist industry in the northern valley.

Inns and taverns typically were located beside long-distance turnpikes, spaced along the routes between population centers, or at village crossroads.

The Greek Revival-style Windsor House, an important stagecoach stop which later served rail passengers, was spared demolition in 1971 by a group of determined citizens.

Huntley's Inn in Claremont, c. 1916.

Travel by stage along the bumpy turnpikes required the same kind of traveler services that motels now provide along interstate highways. For the three days' travel from Concord to Montreal, for example, a traveler might spend the first night at the Alden Inn in Lyme, situated on the Grafton Turnpike, before changing stages to continue west.

While many stagecoach inns succumbed to fire, since they were heated with multiple shallow fireplaces, a surprising number remain in the northern valley, where they still serve as restaurants or bed-and-breakfast inns, if they have not become private homes or apartment houses. Most were built in the Federal and Greek Revival styles *(see Architecture)* and occupy prominent locations. In the late 18th century, such earlier inns tended to resemble large homes, and sometimes were indeed residences that also served a public function. By the heyday of stage traffic in the 1820s-1840s, they had reached grand proportions of three stories and more, often in brick, and frequently with imposing columns or other ornament, such as the Windsor House, located on an important stop on the Connecticut and Passumpsic Turnpike, and the Putney Tavern in Putney, Vermont.

Another fine example is the former Grafton Hotel on Court Street in Haverhill, a magnificent Fed-

eral style three story brick building with a ballroom on its top floor and a curving staircase, strategically set at both the terminus of the Coös Turnpike and across the road from the county courthouse. Intact in their exterior form are Clark's Tavern in Lisbon and another in Canaan, New Hampshire.

MINERAL SPRINGS

In the second half of the 19th century, the owner of a spring or well whose water tasted odd likely found it difficult to resist the potential benefits from selling it as a remedy for whatever ills were "popular" at the time. Small-scale "mineral springs" were scattered throughout the region and met with a wide range of longevity and financial success.

On a larger scale, a handful of mineral springs resorts attracted considerable investment. They offered the promise of health through drinking or bathing in the waters as well as a variety of cultural activities involving literature and the performing arts. A stay at such resorts also served as a badge of social status and provided opportunities to make business connections.

Several notable such enterprises blossomed in Woodstock and Brattleboro, Vermont. One of the most significant was at Brunswick Springs, at a bluff on the Connecticut River already valued by Native

The Balsams, in its spectacular North Country setting.

Americans as a healing place. Beginning in the 19th century, a succession of three hotels arose there and burned down, the last one gone to ashes in 1933.

In 1992, the land was purchased by Wobanaki, Inc., a nonprofit Abenaki corporation, and has since been conserved. Several sulfurous springs still pour out of a sloping site, and flow down into the Connecticut River.

Guests celebrate the centennial of the Mt. Washington Hotel in the styles of many periods. 2002.

GRAND HOTELS

An excellent example of the grand hotel of the Great North Woods is The Balsams, in Dixville Notch, New Hampshire. Its origins may be traced to the Dix House, built in 1866, in which guests were treated to meals prepared by the host, the cost of which was included in the room price, a system which became known as the "American Plan." In 1897, ownership passed to Henry S. Hale, who renamed it and built The Balsams into a grand resort, adding wings in 1910, 1912, and 1916. The latter was a six-story confection that was the first concrete and steel structure in New Hampshire and displayed architectural motifs drawn from the Spanish Colonial and Italianate styles. The Balsams has become such a local landmark that Dixville Notch voters congregate there in a special room just after midnight to cast their votes in the nation's first primary.

The Mount Washington Hotel at Bretton Woods, which stands on the edge of the watershed at the base of the highest mountain in the Northeastern U.S., is another of the few remaining grand

hotels. Built at the turn of the last century, it was reconstructed following World War II, when it hosted the International Monetary Conference. In 1869, a unique Cog Railway, designed by innovator Sylvester Marsh, was completed to the summit of the 6,288-foot mountain. While similar systems of cogs had been employed for steam locomotives hauling coal out of mines, Marsh's was the first in the world intended to climb a mountain.

On a smaller scale, the 1850 Greek Revival-style Thayer's Inn in Littleton, New Hampshire, was built in anticipation of the arrival of railroads and tourism in the nearby White Mountains. In Bethehem, a resort town launched in the late 1800s, the impressive casino built in 1888 for the Maplewood Hotel included a dance floor, bowling alleys, theater, and clubhouse for a surrounding golf course.

Hundreds gathered in May 2002 to celebrate the resurrection of the oldest grand hotel in New Hampshire, the Mountain View Grand in Whitefield. Established in 1865, it remained in the same family for over a century, but fell on uncertain times, closing its doors in the 1980s. The creative and ambi-

The Thayer Hotel, a Greek Revival-style centerpiece of Littleton, New Hampshire, was erected in 1850 to host tourists drawn to the White Mountains.

tious $20 million restoration included repair (not replacement) of 937 wooden windows and preservation of 78 miles of 135-year-old cedar siding, and captured an award from the New Hampshire Preservation Alliance.

As it happened, on a rainy night in 1865, a stagecoach en route from Boston to Montreal hit a large pothole and overturned on a back road in rural Whitefield. Its two passengers scrambled out and found their way up the dirt road to a farmhouse, where they were welcomed despite the late hour. Charmed by the breathtaking view of the Presidential Range and the smell of a home-cooked breakfast, they prevailed upon their host to let them stay a few days and returned the following year, inspiring the farm family to begin a small boarding house

they called the Mountain View House. Twenty years later, it could accommodate 110 guests, and was well on its way to earning the name of "Grand."

A succession of inns in the famous White Mountain pass known as Crawford Notch spanned the earliest period of tourism in the White Mountains to the late 19th century era of the grand hotels. The Crawford family, for whom the pass was named, built their first inn in 1828. Frequent fires and reconstructions ensued. The third Crawford House opened in 1859, burned in 1977.

Surviving from the late 19th century are two buildings in Carroll, New Hampshire, which were associated with the last Crawford House and are listed on the National Register of Historic Places. The picturesque Crawford House Artist's Studio was built in 1880 as a workplace for Frank H. Shapleigh, artist-in-residence at the Crawford House. The artist provided an interesting attraction for tourists who visited the unusual studio. Nearby is the small but stylish Crawford Depot, a Queen Anne-style railroad station built in 1891 next to the Crawford House.

TOURIST CABINS & ROADSIDE ATTRACTIONS

Tiny tourist cabins began popping up like mushrooms along state highways in the 1920s and 1930s.

Ice cream has long been a lure on a summer day. Riverdale Cabins, Orford, New Hampshire.

Exquisite historic gardens and landscapes distinguish the Hay Estate at The Fells in Sunapee, New Hampshire.

offering accommodations in the form of a cartoon version of "home." Not much larger than canvas tents, they provided travelers with privacy in a minimum of space. Many still function as overnight rentals.

The best-preserved example of a 1920s tourist cabin survives at the State Historic Site and National Historic Landmark at Plymouth Notch. It was one of several "Top of the Notch" tourist cabins for visitors, possibly including members of the Secret Service who guarded President Calvin Coolidge while he visited his home town.

Abandoned gas stations, farm stands and other roadside attractions stand like fossils from the mid-20th century, put out of business and out of style when the interstates diverted travelers from state and local highways.

Fortunately, the Connecticut River Valley has relatively few could-be-anywhere tourist "attractions," and many more authentic historic sites and compelling natural settings that give tourists a genuine experience of New England's heritage.

SUMMER PEOPLE

For more than a century, most small communities have increased in population with the seasonal return of summer residents. Many part-time residents have been strong supporters of year-round community cultural organizations such as historical societies and arts groups. While most live modestly, a few wealthy individuals and families have transformed vernacular rural settings into stately retreats from urban life.

An excellent representative of the latter is "The Fells," in Newbury, New Hampshire, the summer estate of John M. Hay. During the period from 1890-1905, Hay was Ambassador to Great Britain and Secretary of State to Presidents McKinley and Teddy Roosevelt. At his summer retreat overlooking Lake Sunapee he entertained international political and cultural figures. The 165-acre site is listed on the National Register of Historic Places and constitutes the John Hay National Wildlife Refuge, owned by the U.S. Fish and Wildlife Service and operated by a non-profit friends group. It includes extensive historic gardens, a large Colonial Revival-style house and subsidiary buildings, landscaped grounds and woodlands.

Among scores of villages that have attracted summer residents and visitors since the 1930s is the small village of Weston, Vermont. Outsiders are drawn to the picturesque

Girls at Camp Lochearn work on boating skills on Lake Fairlee.

Sports at Currier's Camps in Pittsburg show off their quarry.

hamlet by its village green and its collection of churches, homes, and mills that date from the late 1700s to the early 1900s. Contributing to its popularity have been the summer stock theater at Weston Playhouse and the promotions of Vrest Orton, who founded the Vermont Country Store in an historic Weston structure, and who now operates several retail outlets, including one in Rockingham.

In a number of communities—most notably Fairlee, Vermont—summer camps for children provided opportunities for out-of-state campers, their families, and camp counselors to get a taste of life in our region, beginning in the early 1900s. Many former campers returned to stay.

The tradition of rustic camps runs deep, especially in the northern forest, where industrial timberland owners leased spaces just big enough for a cabin to private individuals. In Vermont's Northeast Kingdom, private camps ringing Maidstone Lake were all originally leased from Saint Regis Paper Company. In New Hampshire's North Country, some ninety camps were leased by Diamond International Company at Nash Stream, on land since purchased by the State. St. Regis gave leases to

well over a hundred camps in the 1920s on Pittsburg and Clarksville land later sold to Champion International, then to International Paper Company, before a major conservation purchase in 2002. As large industrial landowners divest themselves of acreage in the face of pressures originating in market globalization, and find eager conservation buyers for the most publicly valued lands, the future of the little cabin in the woods precariously sitting on this land has suddenly come into the public spotlight.

Winter Sports & Ski Resorts

The cultural and economic winter landscape of the upper Connecticut River Valley was transformed in 1911 when students at Dartmouth College held the school's first Winter Carnival. Led by Fred Harris, who founded both the Dartmouth Outing Club and the annual event, the Winter Carnival introduced and popularized winter sports such as snowshoeing, ski jumping, and downhill and cross-country skiing.

Brattleboro, Vermont, holds an annual international ski jumping competition at its Harris Hill, and the Hanover, New Hampshire, high school team is still a regular winner of state ski jump meets in the only state in America that holds high school level jumping competitions.

The White River Tavern offered pleasant accommodations for travelers in Hartford, Vermont, c. 1911.

Hiking trails are accessible enough to allow a lunch-hour summit view.

OUTDOOR RECREATION TODAY

The recent boom in outdoor physical recreation appears to be inversely related to the general reduction in physically demanding outdoor occupations. In a region where many people formerly traveled by necessity on foot, and where farming, logging, and physical labor once predominated, many of us now spend our leisure time pursuing recreational exertions that contrast dramatically with our sedentary employment.

Some activities, like hiking, camping, canoeing, hunting and fishing, join a continuum of human activity that dates back to the period of settlement, if now by choice rather than necessity. Others, like bicycling, and travel by mechanized modes such as snowmobiles, power boats and jet skis, introduce a modern element. Contemporary tourism recognizes that vacationers enjoy a variety of outdoor experiences. The management of public lands should carefully balance uses while preserving natural resources. Not all uses are necessarily appropriate in all places.

Posting of some private land—typically in more developed areas of the region—has slightly reduced the total area to which hunters formerly had free access. However, the less developed areas—particularly in the north—still offer vast tracts of near-wilderness experiences, for both hunting and fishing. While the private hunting "camp" remains a tradition in many families, commercial lodges such as those in the Connecticut Lakes region attract many who appreciate a lot of elbow room in the outdoors.

The activity that puts us most physically in touch with our predecessors is the simple act of walking. The Appalachian Trail was

After the invention of the ski tow in 1934 brought attention to Woodstock, Vermont, small-scale, family-operated ski areas soon were established throughout the region, often in a farmer's hillside pasture. Through the 1950s, ski trains from New York and Boston brought flocks of winter adventurers to the mountains. Historic villages at the foot of the slopes participated directly in the economic boom. Following World War II, the return of the Tenth Mountain Division gave the ski industry a boost.

A concentration of capital in the industry rewarded those that increased mechanization through snowmaking, grooming, and high-speed, high-volume lifts. The trend continues as ski areas diversify into year-round destinations, where some have constructed condominium villages and shopping complexes on the mountains that dwarf in size the historic villages below.

Miles of snowmobile trails are open for winter travel.

The Appalachian Trail, the longest linear park in the United States.

completed in 1937 between Georgia and Maine. From the south and west, it enters the Connecticut River watershed in Killington, Vermont and passes through Bridgewater, Pomfret, Hartford, and Norwich, where it crosses the Connecticut into Hanover, New Hampshire. From there it proceeds through Lyme, Orford, and Piermont before it leaves the watershed in Warren, and then re-enters in Benton, Woodstock, Lincoln, Franconia, Bethlehem, Crawford Notch, Carroll, and Bean's Grant. The route and elevations of this 2,000-mile footpath illustrate the wide range of topography and recreational possibilities of the northern valley.

SUMMITS AND PROSPECTS

From these peaks and lesser elevations, hikers earn vistas that reveal the size and scenic beauty of the watershed. At the eastern edge of the watershed, in Jaffrey, New Hampshire, stands Mt. Monadnock (3,165 ft.), said to be the world's second-most climbed mountain, behind Japan's Mount Fuji.

The solitary mountain stands within a state park and other protected lands covering nearly 700 square miles. More than 100,000 climbers each year hike over 30 miles of trails that lead to the summit, which offers views of all New England states.

Another Mt. Monadnock (3,140 ft.) towers over the river in the Northeast Kingdom of Vermont in

Lemington. The tallest mountain close to the river is Mount Ascutney (3,150 ft.) in Windsor, Vermont, where there is a seasonal road to the top, a campground, and hiking trails. New Hampshire peaks and prominences include Mt. Moosilauke (4,802 ft.) in Benton, Smarts Mountain (3,360 ft.) in Lyme, Magalloway Mountain (3,360 ft.) in Pittsburg, Mount Prospect (2,059 ft.), in Weeks State Park Lancaster, and Mt. Wantastiquet (1,300 ft.) in Hinsdale.

Within a very short walk, modern tourists may also experience the natural wonder of Quechee Gorge, in Hartford, Vermont, where the Ottauquechee River cut down 150 feet through solid rock.

A hiker starts for the summit of Mt. Monadnock in Lemington, Vermont.

STATE PARKS

Just as accessible are a variety of state parks, such as 2,556-acre Mount Sunapee State Park, which receives about 250,000 visitors annually. A trail system connects this with Pillsbury State Park (4,579 acres), in Washington, New Hampshire. New Hampshire's biggest park is Pisgah Wilderness State Park, which covers 12,140 acres in Winchester, Chesterfield, and

Hinsdale. It includes hiking trails, the foundations of Harlan Stone's birthplace, and the ruins of the Dickinson Mill.

New Hampshire's Weeks State Park in Lancaster and Franconia Notch State Park, and Vermont's Maidstone State Park are popular North Country parks. Along the river in the south are two Vermont state parks, Wilgus, in Windsor, and Fort Dummer, in Brattleboro. In the warmer months, campers flock to many of these state parks as well as to scores of private campgrounds.

BICYCLE TRAILS

Both mountain-bikers and road-bikers find a wide variety of back roads and trails to their liking. Bicycle touring groups coordinate with rural inns for inn-to-inn riding. Conversion of discontinued rail lines to multi-use trails is gaining interest and support. After the railroad removed rails from a section of line from Concord to the Enfield, New Hampshire area in 1992, local people hoping to use the corridor for a four-season all-weather trail removed 15 miles

of ties. Because rail lines were built to connect communities, they pass through the hearts of down towns, offering people a place to get together in traditional commercial centers, and stimulating new activity along such converted rail trails.

THE CONNECTICUT RIVER

Certainly the most significant resource for tourism and recreation today is the Connecticut River itself. Carving gorges and ox-bows through scenic forested and rolling terrain, the river continues to shape and reshape its own bed. Its northernmost Connecticut Lakes region offers a near-wilderness experience. Long sections of shoreline in its northern reaches are completely undeveloped. Farther south, its tributary White River stands out as one of the last large free-flowing rivers in New England.

Almost all of the river's waters are once again suitable for fishing and swimming. Waterfalls, gorges and cascades sparkle on its tributaries. Boat launches and landings, and swimming, picnicking and camping areas provide public access, often at the many local or state parks in river-side towns, or at areas provided by the power company at its hydroelectric generating facilities along the river. Canoeists on many miles of the Connecticut may see substantially the same river that Native Americans

Dog paddling on the Connecticut River at Lancaster, New Hampshire.

saw from their dugout canoes. The Upper Valley Land Trust established a series of primitive canoe campsites that are now maintained by a variety of public and private organizations.

Truly experienced kayakers who seek white water can find it in a variety of places on the Connecticut, such as Lyman Falls at Bloomfield-Stratford and Sumner Falls at Hartland-Plainfield. (Portage is essential for canoes at Sumner Falls and for most boaters at Lyman.) Moore Dam at Waterford-Littleton creates 13-mile-long Moore Reservoir, one of the largest bodies of water in New England with an undeveloped shoreline, and permanently protected through the terms of the operating license for the hydro dams on this part of the river.

On the West River in Jamaica, Vermont, seasonal release of water from Ball Mountain Dam creates an exciting trip for white water kayakers. Also in the West River system, hikers can reach Hamilton Falls, Vermont's highest waterfall at 125 feet, by trail from Jamaica State Park. In Ludlow, Vermont, Buttermilk Falls is a dramatic series of cascades in a geologically interesting gorge. And Brockways Mills Gorge on the Williams River, in Rockingham, is one of the three largest undisturbed gorges in Vermont. In Colebrook,

The river is a good place to take a kid fishing.

New Hampshire, waterfall seekers don't even need to get out of their cars to appreciate Beaver Brook Falls, a spectacular cascade next to Route 145.

A 1996 survey of 217 New Hampshire businesses directly or indirectly dependent upon water resources along the northernmost 150 miles of the river found that water-based recreation here is a multi-million-dollar business. Owners supported public investment—particularly for increasing fishing, swimming, canoeing and kayaking access, improving water quality, and for habitat management—and government involvement to protect the watershed. The results demonstrate the economic value of clean water to area businesses, and its role in providing sustainable jobs and income in these rural communities along the Upper Connecticut River.

The bass must be biting in the Bellows Falls pool, judging from the parking lot at Hoyts Landing in Springfield.

CONNECTICUT RIVER BYWAY

A new opportunity to promote heritage- and eco-tourism in the northern valley, both to the valley's own residents and also to visitors, has been created through the Connecticut River Byway. Launched through a study coordinated by the New Hampshire Office of State Planning and the Vermont Agency of Transportation, aided by the Connecticut River Joint Commissions, the Byway took shape as regional planning commissions in New Hampshire and Vermont convened citizen advisory groups to make an inventory of tourism resources, discuss possible routes for the Byway, and identify what kind of tourism is desirable for the region. A primary focus of the effort is protection of the natural and cultural treasures which make the Connecticut River Valley so attractive to visitors, and which provide a valued quality of life to its residents.

The concept for the Byway is modeled on a string of pearls, in which the string is the byway itself and the pearls are "waypoint communities" that act as service hubs and establish informational visitors' centers. Organizers hope that the Byway will enhance the economic vitality of the region's traditional commercial centers while also supporting rural agricultural and forest products businesses. Byway interpretive centers will be found at Brattleboro, Bellows Falls, Claremont, Windsor, White River Junction, Fairlee, Wells River-Woodsville, St. Johnsbury, Lancaster, and Colebrook.

Visitors capture their memories on film.

❊ Threats ❊

Threats to our natural and cultural heritage from tourism take the form of too much, too much in the wrong places, not enough, and not enough of the right kind. The scenic and recreational assets we value are threatened by development and overuse. Sometimes, an activity that represents pleasant recreation for one is perceived as a noisy intrusion by another. For many years we have been privileged to walk across and enjoy the views offered by private property, which may not always remain intact or open to the public.

Public access to public waters is not everywhere guaranteed.

The water slide "attraction" on the right, seen here on a river elsewhere in northern New England, seems

incongruously out of place. The Connecticut is a genuine adventure experience from its source to the sea.

SPRAWL DEVELOPMENT

Unmanaged development of destination resort communities and oversized "attractions" can harm environmental resources, cut off traditional public access to publicly-owned waterways, reduce the vitality of traditional urban centers, create traffic problems for neighboring communities, and alter the historic and natural character of the area.

LACK OF COORDINATION

Tourism not directed to appropriate roads and settings can overwhelm rural communities and fragile resources. Lack of information can frustrate travelers looking for destinations and amenities.

LACK OF INFRASTRUCTURE

Inadequate rest facilities and visitor amenities can produce unmanaged trash and wastes, traffic, and trespassing.

LACK OF RESPECT

Lack of respect for the rules of the road, waterway and trail produces conflicts among multiple users and damage to natural resources, such as shoreline erosion caused by boat wakes and soil erosion

caused by motorized use of non-motorized trails Use of mountain bikes in inappropriate places or seasons can also cause erosion.

LACK OF APPRECIATION FOR DIFFERENCES

While many of us travel to experience "the other, some travelers are unwilling to adapt to local customs or a different pace of life when, for example their way is impeded by a slow-moving tractor. On the other hand, some residents cultivate an antipathy to visitors or ridicule urbanites for their lack of familiarity with rural life.

The Hanover High School girls' crew team skims the Connecticut River.

LACK OF AWARENESS

Uninformed or inattentive boaters may unintentionally introduce invasive and destructive exotics such as Eurasian milfoil and Zebra mussel to waterways.

✺ Actions & Activities ✺

Outdoor recreation is central to how we live in the northern valley. Whether it is hiking, hunting, fishing, skiing, or other pastimes, the outdoors is where we go for refreshment and healthy exercise.

Tourism offers communities a valuable opportunity to develop a sense of identity, enrich cultural institutions, and enhance the local economy. The work of building tourism potential—reinforcing your community's image, protecting natural and historic places, strengthening cultural events and festivals, supporting food and traditional lodging businesses—all build community in and of themselves. Much of our tourism is based on "visiting family and friends," so in a sense we must market our communities first to ourselves. It is important to preserve the natural and historic resources you value, focus on authenticity and quality, collaborate with others, and find the right balance of tourism for your community.

EXPLORE AND ENJOY

• Be a tourist in your own town, explore it from a visitor's point of view, and compile a list of nearby sights and sites.

• Be a tourist in your own valley—visit the Connecticut River Byway virtually at www.ctrivertravel.net, or take to the road and tour.

• Organize a seasonal festival: a fall pumpkin festival, including a parade of costumed children around the town green; a maple festival; a community paddle or river festival such as RiverFest.

At the Pumpkin Festival on the town green.

IDENTIFY YOUR COMMUNITY'S TOURISM ASSETS

• Use the Community Profile exercise—and the other chapters in this book—to elicit your community's stories and identify its special places.

• Identify your community's tourism assets by expanding on the Profile. List all the historic resources to be found in your community, such as museums, historic districts or neighborhoods, architectural landmarks, historic railroad depots, courthouses, bridges, sculptures, town greens or parks.

• List your community's visitor amenities such as: walking tour pamphlets, tourism brochures; information centers; restaurants; inns, motels, and bed-and-breakfasts; campgrounds; public rest rooms.

- List cultural resources such as theaters, galleries, museums, ethnic restaurants, artists, crafts producers, farms and farm stands, and special events and festivals.

Clark's Tavern in Lisbon, New Hampshire, once a stagecoach inn.

- List your community's natural and recreational resources such as: rivers, lakes and ponds; water access points and boat launches; parks, forests and wilderness areas; routes or trails for hiking, biking, skiing and snowmobiling; scenic vistas; special birding spots, and unusual natural places.

- Among all the items in this inventory, evaluate strengths and weaknesses, and plan for a coordinated effort to make improvements based on what has been shown to work in other communities.

WORK WITH OTHERS

- Hold a tourism "summit" with local organizations with a stake in tourism such as: the chamber of commerce and merchants' groups; downtown revitalization group; arts, civic, fraternal and religious organizations; social service agencies; local and regional planning commissions and conservation commissions.

- Identify tourism promotion partners such as: the nearest Connecticut River Byway waypoint interpretive center; regional chambers of commerce; regional marketing organizations in Vermont; the staff and nearest welcome center operated by your state tourism department.

PROTECT SENSITIVE AREAS FROM OVERUSE

- Identify places that are too fragile or sensitive to publicize, such as favorite swimming holes, that would be irrevocably altered by too much attention.

EDUCATE VISITORS TO YOUR COMMUNITY

- Get together with the chamber of commerce or other providers of tourist services, and develop a notebook of local services and attractions. Provide copies to any business in town that is likely to be asked questions by tourists.

- Create an interpretive brochure for a hiking trail or an historic district in your community.

IMPROVE RECREATION OPPORTUNITIES

- Establish a new water access or new trails. Explore possible trail connections with local organizations such as the Upper Valley Trails Alliance, the Upper Valley Land Trust, Kingdom Trails, Ammonoosuc Land Trust, and Windmill Hill Association.

- Adopt a campsite and keep it clean.

- Help coordinate trail users in your community so some trails can be available to motorized recreation and others are preserved for quiet forms, to avoid conflicts.

SUPPORT AGRI-TOURISM

- Develop and support agri-tourism efforts like farm tours and bed-and-breakfasts, pick-your-owns, hay rides, maple sugar house visits, and corn mazes.

The former Grafton Inn, situated on the early turnpike across from the original Grafton County Courthouse, now Alumni Hall, in Haverhill Corner, New Hampshire.

Frozen lakes, ponds, and river setbacks—like Retreat Meadows, off the West River in Brattleboro—sometimes become winter villages of unique and portable shacks made for ice fishing.

❧ Q & A ❧

• What has been your community's previous experience with tourism?

• Were there stagecoach inns or mineral spas, and do any survive?

• What forms of transportation did travelers use to reach your town?

CONNECTICUT RIVER BYWAY

• Every community experiences some kind of tourism. People travel to or through your community for a variety of reasons. Do you know what they are, through a marketing study or anecdotal evidence? Are your visitors interested in recreation? historic and cultural sites? Do they want to visit farms or check out the scenery? Do they come from other countries?

• How do visitors travel to your community today? How do they hear about your community and its assets and activities?

• What are the attitudes toward visitors in your community? Are they positive or negative? What could be done to improve attitudes?

❧ FYI ❧

Car-Hiking the Appalachian Trail by Jim & Dancy Duffus, iUniverse Inc., 2002. (Guide to finding auto-accessible Appalachian Trail experiences; designed for young families, seniors, and others wishing to sample the Trail.)

The Complete Boating Guide to the Connecticut River by the Connecticut River Watershed Council, Inc., and Embassy Imprint, Inc., 1990. (A comprehensive guide to the full length of the river.)

Getting Started: How to Succeed in Heritage Tourism, National Trust for Historic Preservation, Washington, DC, 1993. (The best, most concise resource for evaluating your community's potential for tourism and for developing plans to carry out the appropriate improvements.)

The Grand Resort Hotels of the White Mountains: A Vanishing Architectural Legacy by Bryant F. Tolles, David R. Godine, Boston, MA, 1998.

Inventing New England: Regional Tourism in the Nineteenth Century by Dona Brown, Smithsonian Institution Press, Washington, D.C., 1997. (Perceptions, projections and places all evolved to produce a new experience in Vermont and the White Mountains.)

Old Home Day In New Hampshire, 1899-1998 by Tom Curran, Inherit New Hampshire, Concord, NH. (A delightful, illustrated guide to both the history and the "how-to" of one of New Hampshire's fine traditions.)

A Tourist's New England: Travel Fiction, 1820-1920 by Dona Brown, University Press of New England, Hanover, NH, 1999. (Fictional stories set in our real places, from Nathaniel Hawthorne to Sinclair Lewis.)

Trails for the Twenty-First Century by Charles Flink, Kristine Olka, Robert Searns, Rails to Trails Conservancy, Island Press, 2001. (Planning, design, and management manual for multi-use trails.)

"Boating on the Connecticut River in Vermont and New Hampshire" by the Connecticut River Joint Commissions, Charlestown, NH, 2001. (This pamphlet includes maps that show boat access locations, descriptions of the river in each run, and boating safety tips. The maps are also online at www.crjc.org.)

GOOD LINKS

Connecticut River Byway: www.ctrivertravel.net
The Connecticut River Byway web site should be an essential tool for developing tourism in your community, or in planning your own vacation. It is an excellent source of information about travel assets in the northern valley, from historic sites to boat access points along the Connecticut. It provides an overall view of the cultural history and resources of the valley and identifies links for tourism partners on both sides of the river such as state tourism agencies, chambers of commerce, and Vermont's regional marketing organizations.

Official Vermont Tourism site
www.vermontvacation.com

Official New Hampshire Tourism site:
www.visitnh.gov

Connecticut RiverFest:
www.ctriverfest.org

Lancaster Rotary Club members paddle toward Lunenburg, Vermont.

CHAPTER ELEVEN

Community Profile

A Constellation of Places, Images and Stories

Each community's heritage is unique, a special combination of geography, people, and time. As appreciation of our local heritage grows, so also grows the need to understand it better, share it more widely, and be more proactive about safeguarding our legacy for the future.

HERE'S a useful exercise for figuring out what contributes most to your community's character and identity as comprised by its natural surroundings, physical layout, history, and its generations of inhabitants. While you can make a list all by yourself, it's better to do with a small group, and it's more stimulating and much more fun. (Be sure to have food and beverages on hand.) Sometimes these are called "popcorn" sessions because once people get into the rhythm, ideas come as fast as popping corn. Make sure everyone has a chance. And just gather suggestions at first, without judging or evaluating. Some communities find it useful to have an impartial facilitator from outside the community.

The checklist below is a starting point. Add more items to create a constellation or "mind map" of

On the Common in Lyme, a peaceful place.

places, images, and stories that
are unique to your community.
The results, and the relationships that develop during the
process, can be useful for resource conservation planning,
developing or revising a town
master plan, heritage tourism
promotions, community art
and theater projects, local history research, school curricula
and special programs. The
greatest reason and reward is to
foster community pride and
provide a forum to articulate a
community identity.

Getting around town in Lyme, c. 1900.

❊ Community Profile Checklist ❊

COMMUNITY SELF-IMAGE IN MYTHS & STORIES

Early conflict with Indians, captive narratives
Heroic founding settlers
Hardship and deprivation
The (fill in the blank) Capital of the World
Melting pot of industrious immigrants
Font of higher learning
Colonial Village
Victorian Village
What's in the town's seal or
    logo?
What are the untold,
    neglected stories?

North Main Street, Newport, New Hampshire, c. 1909.

NATURAL SETTINGS

Rivers, streams
Confluence of waterways
Waterfalls or cascades
Lakes and ponds
River terrace
Ledge outcrops and balds
Mountain and hilltop summits
Wetlands
Notable springs
Old growth forest
Prime agricultural soils
Unusual plant communities
Important habitats (for plants, wildlife, humans)

OTHER PHYSICAL FEATURES IN SETTLEMENT & GROWTH

Roads descended from Native American foot-
    paths
Archeological sites
River crossings by ferry, bridge, or portage,
    past or present
Mill site
Crossroads: turnpikes, local roads, ferries and
    fords
Railroad crossings, junctions, or station stops

View into the headwaters of the Mascoma River from Lambert Ridge.

The Ely, Vermont, depot, built by the Boston & Maine Railroad in 1901, is now a private residence.

Physical Presence

Downtown commercial district: corner of Main & Main

Public places, open spaces: town green or common, parks, conservation lands, neglected green margins, street trees, public gardens

Viewsheds

Public places, built: streetscape, town hall, library, school, armory, Grange hall, courthouse, parade ground, church, meeting house, performing arts, civic club, cemeteries

Residential neighborhoods

Industrial areas, abandoned or unused historic industrial sites

Agricultural areas, farms, farm or forest lands

Roads, bridges, crossroads, railroads

Recreation trails, water access, and other recreation features

Fire towers

Commercial strips, malls

White River Junction, the railroad hub of the northern valley, c. 1905.

People in History

Native Americans (archeological sites, narratives)

Immigrants of all periods

Founders, civic leaders, patrons, benefactors

War heroes

Business owners and managers, commercial and industrial

Pastors, educators, authors, artists, inventors

Homemakers

The life of children

Children enjoy an afternoon playing in the road in Jaffrey, NH, c. 1908.

ARCHITECTURAL STYLES
(See Appendix C for a sampler of periods and styles.)
Houses
Downtown commercial buildings
Industrial buildings
Civic (town hall, library, etc.)
Farm buildings

Trinity Church, a classic example of simple New England style, 1808.

INDUSTRY AND COMMERCE
Agriculture:
    dairy farming, sheep, horse, horticultural, fruit,
    Christmas trees, diversified, other crops;
    central market town for rural agriculture
Grist mills, sawmills, tanneries
Logging
Stores, liveries, inns
Lime kilns, mineral mine, stone quarry, iron
    foundry
Manufacturing:
    wool, wood products, precision, machine tool,
    paper, clothing, farm implements, other
Railroad
Dams, hydroelectric power
Tourism

Blow-Me-Down Mill, Cornish, New Hampshire, now part of the Saint-Gaudens National Historic Site.

Some towns have created quilts depicting their favorite local landmarks, such as this one from Putney.

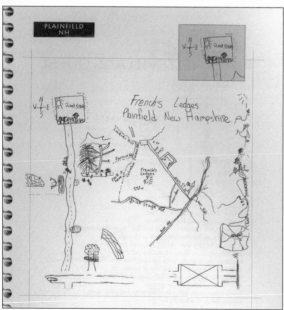

Page from a "quest" designed by the Plainfield, New Hampshire, Second Grade to help others discover French's Ledges, in ValleyQuest, 89 Treasure Hunts in the Upper Valley. *Vital Communities of the Upper Valley is experienced at assisting a community in conducting a self-profile.*

COMMUNITY TRADITIONS

Town Meeting
Holiday parades
Church suppers
Annual celebrations, festivals,
    performances, and gatherings
Old Home Day or Old Home
    Week

PARTNERS IN NATURAL & CULTURAL HERITAGE IDENTITY

Local historical societies
Local garden clubs
Regional and state arts and
    humanities councils
Local and regional watershed
    organizations
Land trusts & conservation
    organizations
Chambers of commerce, downtow
    revitalization groups, business
    and civic groups
Museums, libraries, performing ar
    groups
Schools and institutions of higher
    learning
Statewide archeological societies
State historic preservation offices
Individual and district National
    Register nominations, survey
    information
State natural resource agencies

❈ Towns of the Connecticut River Watershed ❈

Looking down Littleton's Main Street toward its historic Opera House a century ago.

The Connecticut River Watershed encompasses a full third (33 percent, 93 towns) of New Hampshire's land area, and even more (41 percent, 114 towns) of Vermont. The streams and rivers flowing through this area eventually run into the Connecticut River, and on to Massachusetts, Connecticut, and Long Island Sound. Listed below are the towns which lie within this drainage area.

NEW HAMPSHIRE
.cworth
.lstead
.ath
.enton (part)
.erlin (part)
.ethlehem (part)
.anaan
.arroll
.harlestown
.hesterfield
.laremont

Clarksville (part)
Colebrook
Columbia
Cornish
Croydon
Dalton
Dixville (part)
Dorchester (part)
Dublin (part)
Dummer (part)
Easton
Enfield

Erving's Location
Fitzwilliam
Franconia (part)
Gilsum
Goshen
Grantham
Hanover
Harrisville (part)
Haverhill
Hinsdale
Jaffrey (part)
Jefferson

Keene
Kilkenny
Lancaster
Landaff
Langdon
Lebanon
Lempster
Lisbon
Littleton
Lyman
Lyme
Marlborough

Marlow
Milan (part)
Millsfield (part)
Monroe
Nelson (part)
New Ipswich (part)
New London (part)
Newbury (part)
Newport
Northumberland
Odell
Orford (part)
Piermont (part)
Pittsburg (part)
Plainfield
Randolph (part)
Richmond
Rindge (part)
Roxbury
Springfield (part)
Stark
Stewartstown (part)
Stoddard (part)
Stratford
Sugar Hill
Sullivan
Sunapee
Surry
Swanzey
Troy
Unity
Walpole
Washington (part)
Westmoreland
Whitefield
Winchester

Also small portions of
Grafton
Lincoln
Orange
Warren
Woodstock

*Unincorporated Places
on the west slopes of
Mt. Washington:*
Chandler's Purchase,
Crawford's Purchase,
Low & Burbanks
Grant, Sargent's
Purchase, and Thomp-
son & Meserves
Purchase

VERMONT
Andover
Athens
Averill (part)
Avery's Gore (part)
Baltimore
Barnard
Barnet
Bethel
Bloomfield
Bradford
Braintree
Brattleboro
Bridgewater
Brighton (part)
Brookfield (part)
Brookline
Brunswick
Burke
Canaan
Cavendish
Chelsea
Chester
Chittenden (part)
Concord
Corinth
Danville
Dover
Dummerston
East Haven
Fairlee

Ferdinand
Glastenbury (part)
Grafton
Granby
Granville (part)
Groton (part)
Guildhall
Guilford
Halifax
Hancock (part)
Hartford
Hartland
Jamaica
Killington (part)
Kirby
Landgrove
Lemington
Lewis
Londonderry
Ludlow
Lunenberg
Lyndon
Maidstone
Marlboro
Mount Holly (part)
Newark
Newbury
Newfane
Norwich
Orange (part)
Peacham (part)
Peru (part)
Pittsfield
Plymouth
Pomfret
Putney
Randolph
Reading
Readsboro (part)
Rochester
Rockingham
Roxbury (part)
Royalton

Ryegate
Saint Johnsbury
Searsburg
Sharon
Sheffield (part)
Somerset
Springfield
Stockbridge
Strafford
Stratton
Sutton (part)
Thetford
Topsham
Townshend
Tunbridge
Vernon
Vershire
Victory
Walden (part)
Wardsboro
Washington (part)
Waterford
Weathersfield
West Fairlee
West Windsor
Westminster
Westmore (part)
Weston
Wheelock (part)
Whitingham
Wilmington
Windham
Windsor
Winhall (part)
Woodford (part)
Woodstock

Also small portions of
Mount Tabor
Shrewsbury
Stamford
Stannard
Williamstown

❈ Agencies & Organizations ❈

U.S. Fish & Wildlife Service stocking Atlantic salmon.

Environmental Quality & Conservation

FEDERAL AGENCIES

U.S. Environmental Protection Agency Region 1
JFK Building, Boston, MA 02203
617-918-1111   www.epa.gov

Silvio O. Conte National Fish and Wildlife Refuge
38 Avenue A, Turners Falls, MA 01376
413-863-0209   www.fws.gov/r5soc

US Fish & Wildlife Service
www.fws.gov

New Hampshire Office   603-223-2541
70 Commercial St., Suite 300, Concord, NH 03301

Vermont Office   802-872-0629
11 Lincoln St., Essex Junction, VT 05452

Connecticut River Coordinator
103 East Plum Tree Rd., Sunderland, MA 01375
413-548-9138   www.fws.gov/r5crc

U.S. Geological Survey
New Hampshire/Vermont District
361 Commerce Way, Pembroke, NH 03275
603-226-7837 http://nh.water.usgs.gov

U.S. Forest Service

Green Mountain National Forest
231 North Main St., Rutland, VT 05701
802-747-6700   www.fs.fed.us./r9/gmfl

White Mountain National Forest
719 Main St., Laconia, NH 03246
603-528-8721 www.fs.fed.us./r9/white

US Army Corps of Engineers, New England District
696 Virginia Road, Concord, MA 01742-2751
978-318-8238 www.nae.usace.army.mil

New England Interstate Water Pollution
Control Commission
Boott Mills S., 10 Foot of John St., Lowell, MA 01852
978-323-7929 www.neiwpcc.org

National Park Service
www.nps.gov/rtca/contactus/regions/northeast.html

New Hampshire office   603-226-3436
18 Low Ave., Concord, NH 03301

Vermont office   802-457-3368
PO Box 178, Woodstock, VT 05091

USDA Cooperative Extension
University of New Hampshire offices
www.ceinfo.unh.edu

Coos County   603-788-4961
629A Main St., Lancaster, NH 03584

Grafton County   603-747-6944
3785 Dartmouth Coll. Rd., N. Haverhill, NH 03774

Sullivan County   603-863-9200
24 Main St., Newport, NH 03773

Cheshire County   603-352-4550
800 Park Ave., Keene, NH 03431

University of Vermont offices
www.uvm.edu/extension

Essex/Caledonia Counties   802-676-3900
PO Box 20, Guildhall, VT 05905

Orange/Windsor Counties   802- 296-7630
121 Holiday Dr., White River Junction, VT 05001

Windham County   802- 257-7967
157 Old Guilford Rd, Brattleboro, VT 05301

STATE AGENCIES
Bi-state
Connecticut River Joint Commissions
PO Box 1182, Charlestown, NH 03603
603-826-4800 www.crjc.org

New Hampshire
Department of Environmental Services
6 Hazen Drive, PO Box 95, Concord, NH 03302-0095
603-271-3503 www.des.state.nh.us/water_intro.htm

Fish & Game Department
2 Hazen Dr., Concord, NH 03301
603-271-3211 www.wildlife.state.nh.us/

Department of Resources & Economic Development
172 Pembroke Rd., P.O. Box 1856
Concord, NH 03302-1856
603-271-2411 www.dred.state.nh.us

Division of Forests and Lands
603-271-2214 www.nhdfl.org

Natural Heritage Inventory Program
603-271-3623 www.nhdfl.org/heritage

Land & Community Heritage Investment Program
10 Dixon Ave., Concord, NH 03301
603-224-4113   www.lchip.org

Vermont
Agency of Natural Resources
103 S. Main St., Waterbury, VT 05671-0501

Dept. of Environmental Conservation 802-241-3770
www.anr.state.vt.us/dec/dec.htm

Department of Fish and Wildlife
802-241-3700 www.anr.state.vt.us/fw/fwhome/

Nongame and Natural Heritage Program
802-241-3700

Dept. of Forests, Parks & Recreation
802-241-3670 www.state.vt.us/anr/fpr/index.htm

Housing & Conservation Board
149 State St., Montpelier, VT 05620
802-828-3250 www.vhcb.org/

PRIVATE ORGANIZATIONS
Regional
Connecticut River Watershed Council
15 Bank Row, Greenfield, MA 01301
413-772-2020 www.ctriver.org

The Conservation Fund
Box 1080 Smith Ln., Shrewsbury, VT 05738
802-492-3368 www.conservationfund.org

New England Wild Flower Society
180 Hemenway Road, Framingham, MA 01701
508-877-7630 www.newfs.org

River Network, New England Office
RR 1, Box 209, Hartland, VT 05048
802-436-2544 www.riverwatch.org

Student Conservation Association
PO Box 550, Charlestown, NH 03603
603-543-1700 www.theSCA.org

The Trust for Public Land
3 Shipman Place, Montpelier, VT 05602
802-223-1373 www.tpl.org

Upper Valley Land Trust
19 Buck Rd., Hanover, NH 03755
603-643-6626 www.uvlt.org

New Hampshire
Ammonoosuc Conservation Trust
80 Old Post Rd., Sugar Hill, NH 03585
603-823-8119

Audubon Society of New Hampshire
3 Silk Farm Rd., Concord, NH 03301
603-224-9909 www.nhaudubon.org

Conservation Law Foundation
27 N. Main St., Concord, NH 03301
603-225-3060

Hanover Conservation Council
PO Box 516, Hanover, NH 03755
603-643-3433

Hubbard Brook Research Foundation
6 Sargent Place, Hanover, NH 03755
603- 653-0390
www.aber.sr.unh.edu/hbrook/hbfound/hbfound.htm

Monadnock Conservancy
P.O. Box 337, Keene NH 03431
603-357-0600 www.monadnockconservancy.org

The Nature Conservancy, NH Chapter
2 Beacon St., Suite 6, Concord, NH 03301
603-224-5853
http://nature.org/wherewework/northamerica/states/
newhampshire/

NH Association of Conservation Commissions
54 Portsmouth St., Concord, NH 03301
603-224-7867 www.nhacc.org/nhacc.htm

NH Rivers Council
54 Portsmouth St., Concord, NH 03301
603-228-6472 www.nhrivers.org

Society for Protection of New Hampshire Forests
54 Portsmouth St., Concord, NH 03301
603-224-9945 www.spnhf.org

Vermont
Association of VT Conservation Commissions
114 Sparrow Rd., Adamant, VT 05640
802-223-5527

Audubon Society
255 Sherman Hollow Rd., Huntington, VT 05462
802-434-3068 www.audubon.org/states/vt

Conservation Law Foundation
15 E. State St - Suite 4, Montpelier, VT 05602
802-223-5992

Keeping Track
PO Box 444, Huntington, VT 05462
802-434-7000 www.keepingtrackinc.org

National Wildlife Federation
58 State St., Montpelier, VT 05602
802-229-0650 www.nwf.org

The Nature Conservancy of Vermont
27 State St., Montpelier, VT 05602
802-229-4425   http://nature.org/wherewework/
northamerica/states/vermont

Passumpsic Valley Land Trust
PO Box 624, St. Johnsbury, VT 05819
802-748-8089

Rockingham Area Land Trust
23 Pleasant St., Springfield, VT 05156
802-885-3220

Vermont Land Trust
8 Bailey Ave., Montpelier, VT 05602
802-223-5234 www.vlt.org

Vermont Leadership Center
PO Box 220, East Charleston, VT 05833
802-723-6551 www.vtlc.org

Vermont Natural Resources Council
9 Bailey Ave., Montpelier, VT 05602
802-223-2328 www.vnrc.org

Vermont River Conservancy
RR 5, Box 920, Montpelier, VT 05602
802-229-9282
www.vermontriverconservancy.org

ENVIRONMENTAL EDUCATION CENTERS
Bonnyvale Environmental Education Center
Old Guilford Road, Brattleboro, VT 05301
802-257-5785 www.beec.org

Fairbanks Museum & Planetarium
1302 Main St., St. Johnsbury, VT 05819
802-748-2372 www.fairbanksmuseum.org

Montshire Museum
One Montshire Rd., Norwich, VT 05055
802-649-2200 www.montshire.net

Nature Museum at Grafton
PO Box 38, Grafton, VT 05146
802-843-2111 www.nature-museum.org

Vermont Institute of Natural Science
Church Hill Rd., Woodstock, VT 05091
802-457-2779 www.vinsweb.org

TRIBUTARY WATERSHED ORGANIZATIONS
*Others are forming—contact your regional planning
commission to learn more about the waterway near you.*

Mascoma Watershed Conservation Coalition
PO Box 704, Enfield, NH 03748
603-632-5160

Ashuelot River Local Advisory Committee
19 Spring St., Swanzey, NH 03446
603-352-0987 www.des.state.nh.us/rivers/ash1.htm

Cold River Local Advisory Committee
PO Box 26, Acworth NH 03601
603-543-1700
www.des.state.nh.us/rivers/cold1.htm

Friends of the West River
PO Box 2, S. Newfane, VT 05351
802-348-7877

Mill Brook Association
32 Elm St., Windsor, VT 05089
802-674-2326

Sugar River Watershed Association
PO Box 404, Sunapee, NH 03782

Tributary Trails of the Connecticut River Watershed
PO Box 353, Whitefield, NH 03598
603-837-3800
http://users.ncia.net/ffjoe/tribtrail

White River Partnership
99 Ranger Rd., Rochester, VT 05767
802-767-4261   www.whiteriverpartnership.org

A woman and her horse tedding hay at the Upper Valley Land Trust's "First Cutting" of newly conserved land in Lyme.

Agriculture

FEDERAL AGENCY
USDA Natural Resources Conservation Service
   New Hampshire offices   www.nh.nrcs.usda.gov
   Coos /Grafton Counties   603- 747-2001
   250 Swiftwater Rd., Woodsville, NH 03785

   Sullivan/Cheshire Counties   603-756-2988
   11 Industrial Park Dr., Walpole, NH 03608

   Vermont offices   www.vt.nrcs.usda.gov
   Essex/Caledonia Counties   802-748-3885
   1153 Main St. -Suite 2, St. Johnsbury, VT 05819

   White River   802-295-1662
   617 Comstock Rd. - Suite 1, Berlin, VT 05602

   Ottauquechee   802-295-7942
   12 Gilman Office Ctr., White River Junction, VT 05001

   Windham County   802-254-5323
   28 Vernon St. - Suite 2, Brattleboro, VT 05301

STATE AGENCIES
NH Department of Agriculture, Food & Markets
25 Capitol St., 2d Floor
P.O. Box 2042, Concord, NH 03302-2042
603-271-3551   www.state.nh.us/agric/aghome.html

VT Department of Agriculture, Food & Markets
116 State St., Montpelier, VT 05620-2901
802-828-2500   www.state.vt.us/agric/index.htm

Natural Resource Conservation Districts
   New Hampshire offices
   Coos County   603-788-4651
   4 Mayberry Ln., Lancaster, NH 03584

   Grafton County   603 747-2001
   250 Swiftwater Rd., Woodsville, NH 03785

   Sullivan County   603-863-4297
   24 Main St., Newport, NH 03773

   Cheshire County   603-756-2988
   11 Industrial Park Dr., Walpole, NH 03608

   Vermont offices
   Essex/Caledonia Counties   802-748-3885
   1153 Main St. - Suite 2, St. Johnsbury, VT 05819

   White River and Ottauquechee   802-295-1662
   28 Farmvu Dr., White River Junction, VT 05001

   Windham County   802-254-5323
   28 Vernon St. - Suite 2, Brattleboro, VT 05301

The Arts

STATE AGENCIES

New Hampshire State Council on the Arts
40 N. Main St., Concord, NH 03301
603-271-2789   www.state.nh.us/nharts

New Hampshire Humanities Council
19 Pillsbury St., PO Box 2228, Concord, NH 03302
603-224-4071   www.nhhc.org

Vermont Arts Council
136 State Street Drawer 33, Montpelier VT 05633
802-828-3291   www.state.vt.us/vermont-arts

Vermont Council on the Humanities
200 Park St., Morrisville, VT 05661
802-888-3183   www.vermonthumanities.org

PRIVATE ORGANIZATIONS

Arts Alliance of Northern New Hampshire
PO Box 892, Littleton, NH 03561
603-323-7302   www.aannh.org

Brattleboro Museum & Arts Center
10 Vernon St., Brattleboro VT 05301
802-257-0124

Catamount Arts
PO Box 324, St. Johnsbury, VT 05819
802-748-2600   www.catamountarts.com

Great River Arts Institute
PO Box 639, Walpole, NH 03608
603-756-3638   www.greatriverarts.org

Rockingham Arts & Museum Project
7 Canal St., Bellows Falls VT 05101
802-463-3252   www.ramp-vt.org

The arts have always been alive and well in Wells River.

Planning, Transportation, & Community Development

STATE AGENCIES

Connecticut River Joint Commissions
PO Box 1182, Charlestown, NH 03603
603-826-4800   www.crjc.org

New Hampshire Office of State Planning
2½ Beacon St., Concord, NH 03301-4497
603-271-2155 www.state.nh.us/osp/ospweb.htm

New Hampshire Department of Transportation
John O. Morton Bldg., Hazen Drive
Concord, NH 03302-0483
603-271-3734   http://webster.state.nh.us./dot

Vermont Agency of Transportation
1 National Life Dr., Drawer 33, Montpelier, VT 05633
802-828-3960 www.aot.state.vt.us

Vermont Downtown Program
Agency of Commerce and Community Development
135 State Street, Drawer 33 , Montpelier, VT 05633-1201
802-828-3042
www.uvm.edu/ffvhnet/hpres/org/vdhp/com1.html

Vermont Scenery Preservation Council
℅ Two Rivers/Ottauquechee Regional Planning Comm.
King Farm, 5 Thomas Hill, Woodstock, VT 05091

REGIONAL PLANNING COMMISSIONS

North Country Council
107 Glessner Rd., Bethlehem, NH 03574
603-444-6303 www.nccouncil.org

Upper Valley/Lake Sunapee Regional Planning Comm.
77 Bank St., Lebanon, NH 03766-1704
603-448-1680 www.uvlsrpc.org

Southwest Region Planning Commission
20 Central Square, 2d Floor, Keene, NH 03431
603-357-0557 www.swrpc.org

Northeastern Vermont Development Association
P.O. Box 640, St. Johnsbury, VT 05819
802-748-5181 www.nvda.net

Two Rivers-Ottauquechee Regional Commission
King Farm, 5 Thomas Hill, Woodstock, VT 05091
802-457-3188 www.trorc.org

Southern Windsor County Regional Planning Comm.
Box 320 Ascutney Prof. Bldg., Rt. 5, Ascutney, VT 05030
802-674-9201   www.swcrpc-vt.org

Windham Regional Commission
139 Main St., #505, Brattleboro, VT 05301
802-257-4547   www.rpc.windham.vt.us

PRIVATE ORGANIZATIONS
NH Minimum Impact Development Partnership
18 Low Ave., Concord, NH 03301
603-226-1009   www.nhmid.org

Main Street Center
14 Dixon Avenue, Suite 102, Concord, NH 03301
603-223-9942   www.nhcdfa.org/mainstreet.html

Northern Forest Alliance
58 State St., Montpelier, VT 05602
802-223-5256   www.northernforestalliance.org

The Northern Forest Center
PO Box 210, Concord NH 03302
603-229-0679   www.northernforest.org

Vermont Forum on Sprawl
110 Main St., Brattleboro, VT 05401
802-864-6310   www.vtsprawl.org

Vital Communities of the Upper Valley
104 Railroad Row, White River Junction, VT 05001
802-291-9100   www.vitalcommunities.org

Tourism & Recreation

STATE AGENCIES
NH Dept of Resources & Economic Development
172 Pembroke Rd., P.O. Box 1856, Concord, NH 03302

  Division of Parks & Recreation
  603-271-3556   www.dred.state.nh.us

  Division of Travel & Tourism
  603-271-2665   www.visitnh.gov

Vermont Department of Tourism & Marketing
134 State St., Montpelier, VT 05602-3403
802-828-3237   www.travel-vermont.com

Vermont Dept. of Forests, Parks & Recreation
103 S. Main St., 10 South, Waterbury, VT 05671-0601
802-241-3670   www.state.vt.us/anr/fpr/index.htm

PRIVATE ORGANIZATIONS
Appalachian Mountain Club
5 Joy St., Boston, MA 02108
617-523-0655   www.outdoors.org
New Hampshire Chapter: www.amc-nh.org

Appalachian Trail Conference
PO Box 312, Lyme NH 03768
603-795-4935   www.appalachiantrail.org

Cohos Trail Association
252 Westmoreland Rd., Spofford, NH 03462
603-363-8902   www.cohostrail.org

Connecticut River Scenic Byway Council
P.O. Box 1182, Charlestown, NH 03603
603-826-4800   www.ctrivertravel.net

Green Mountain Club
4711 Waterbury-Stowe Rd., Waterbury Ctr, VT 05677
802-244-7037   www.greenmountainclub.org

Kingdom Trails Association
PO Box 204, East Burke, VT 05832
802-626-9924

New England Rails to Trails Conservancy
2 Washington Square, Suite 200
Union Station, Worcester, MA 01604
508-755-3300   www.railtrails.org/newengland

Northern Forest Canoe Trail
PO Box 565, Waitsfield VT 05673
802-496-7126

Nulhegan Gateway Association
743 Victory Rd., PO Box 239, East Burke, VT 05832
802-626-8321

Upper Valley Trails Alliance
104 Railroad Row, White River Junction, VT 05001
802-291-9100   www.uvtrails.org

Vermont Outdoor Guide Association
PO Box 10, No. Ferrisburg, VT 05473
802-425-8747   www.voga.org

A venerable 1808 riverside farm house in the shadow of Smarts Mountain in Lyme, shown c. 1900 (at right) was facing an uncertain future by the year 2000 (center right). The care of an appreciative owner returned it to health without sacrificing the handsome building's historic value (below right 2002).

Historical and Archeological Resources & Preservation

FEDERAL AGENCY
National Park Service
15 State Street, Boston, MA 02109
617-223-5131   www.cr.nps.gov

STATE AGENCIES
New Hampshire Division of Historical Resources
19 Pillsbury St., P.O. Box 2043, Concord, NH 03302
603-271-3558   http://webster.state.nh.us/nhdhr

Vermont Division for Historic Preservation
135 State St., 4th Floor, Drawer 33, Montpelier, VT 05633
802-828-3211   www.historicvermont.org

PRIVATE ORGANIZATIONS
New Hampshire Preservation Alliance
P.O. Box 268, Concord, NH 03302-0268
603-224-2281   www.mv.com/ipusers/nhpreservation

The Sargent Museum of Archeology and Anthropology
PO Box 4212, Concord, NH 03302-4212
603-229-4966   www.sargentmuseum.org

NH Archeological Society
c/o Don Foster, Phillips Exeter Academy
20 Main St. msc #81337, Exeter, NH 03833-2460
(The Indian Trails map on pg. 103 is available in an 11x17-inch version with pamphlet for $5.00 from NHAS.)

Preservation Trust of Vermont
104 Church St., Burlington, VT 05401
802-658-6647   www.ptvermont.org

Vermont Archeological Society
PO Box 663, Burlington, VT 05402-0663
www.uvm.edu

National Society for the Preservation of Covered Bridges
P.O. Box 910, Westminster, VT 05158

The Preservation Education Institute
54 Main St., PO Box 1777, Windsor, VT 05089-0021
802-674-6752   www.historicwindsor.com

❧ A Sampler of Domestic Architectural Styles ❧

by Adair D. Mulligan

The northern Connecticut River Valley is rich in the architectural "vocabulary" of various eras from Revolutionary times to the present. Homeowners often updated their houses as their families or fortunes grew. One might find, for example, a fanciful Queen Anne porch added in the 1890s to a clean-lined Federal home built a century earlier. Time frames given for each style are approximate.

Although new styles bloomed almost everywhere at about the same time, their popularity and persistence varied from one community to another.

Individual builders left their marks by embracing the newest styles, sticking to familiar forms, or creating their own variations. Buildings designed during transitional periods between styles sometimes display features of both. All examples are local.

THE COLONIAL ERA (BEFORE 1789)

GEORGIAN STYLE

Very rare in our region, usually a simple, one- or two-story box shape, two rooms deep, with symmetrical doors and windows. Paneled front door, usually centered. Look for transom lights, or small rectangular window panes directly above the main entry. Little or no roof overhang on gable ends. Relatively plain, narrow corner boards. Chimney is most often massive and centered. There may be a decorative tooth-like molding under the eave. Windows are separate with small panes of glass (8 over 12 or more), although these were sometimes replaced a century later with larger panes. Look for earlier windows in out-of-the-way parts of the house.

THREE-ROOM HOUSES & CLASSIC CAPES

Some of the earliest homes were small, square houses built by settlers to fulfill the requirement to build a dwelling and clear a certain acreage in order to confirm a land grant. They normally have a nearby or attached barn for animals. The chimney is off-center, usually piercing the roof about one-third of the way from one end of the house. These tiny houses were often enlarged on one end to appear more like a common Cape Cod (one-story colonial) house, or attached as an ell to a larger, later house. See page 134 for an example of an early cape.

The hip roof, twin end chimneys, and more delicate massing suggest transition to Federal style, next page.

THE AMERICAN CLASSICAL ERA (1789–1860)

FEDERAL STYLE (1790-1830)

Look for graceful semi-circular or elliptical windows above doorways. More elegant examples have tracery in the small windows surrounding the entry, and urns, swags, and other delicate decoration. Sometimes a small entry porch. Windows are symmetrical with usually over 6 panes. Some feature a "Palladian" three-part window in the front upper story. Sometimes a hipped roof on two-story houses. See also pages 107, 122, 130, and 145.

Note swags over windows and door, and decorative corner boards.

Federal house with tracery in entry surround.

Variations on entry fans in glass and wood.

Triangular gable reflects Greek Revival influence on Federal-style building.

THE AMERICAN CLASSICAL ERA (1789–1860)

GREEK REVIVAL (1820–1860)

America's pride in its infant democratic republic led to a passion for everything Greek, recalling the ancestral home of our form of government. Because the northern Connecticut River Valley experienced a burst in population and development in the 1820s and 30s, the Greek Revival style is probably the most common historic architectural style in our region.

Look for the ghosts of Greek temples in this style of building, whether in actual columns or in corner boards and entry surrounds that resemble flat columns. Triangular decorations over doorways and windows, and outlined gables recall the Parthenon of Athens. Another clue to the style is sidelights, or a series of tiny rectangular windows on either side of the main doorway, and often also over the top, with thicker muntins than in the Federal style. Look for wide bands of trim under the roof and around doors. Porches are common on this style of house, often a Connecticut River Valley porch. The gable is often on the front of the house. Windows usually 6 over 6 panes.

For other Greek Revival examples, see pages 5, 115, 121, 124, 125, 133, 158, 161, and 164.

THE VICTORIAN ERA (1860–1910)

tyles shifted dramatically in this era to more omantic, picturesque designs drawn from ngland, France, and Italy. Look for plenty f curves and ornaments.

GOTHIC REVIVAL (1840–1880)

teeply pitched roof, usually with steep cross ables and elaborately decorated vergeoard. Windows often appear in the gables, nd sometimes have a pointed arch shape or ther decoration. One story porches are ommon. Another example appears on page 27.

FRENCH SECOND EMPIRE (1855–1885)

Mansard (dual-pitched, ipped) roof, with doner windows on steep ower slopes. Eaves usully have decorative aired brackets below. ometimes there are towrs. Roof often has a ecorative shingle patrn. Entry doors may be aired. For another exmple, see page 166.

The curved porch and columns (above) are a later Colonial Revival addition to this Second Empire home.

This elegant entry porch is under restoration.

THE VICTORIAN ERA (1860–1910)

ITALIANATE (1840–1885)

Usually two or three stories. Low-pitched, often hipped roof has widely overhanging eaves with decorative brackets beneath the roof, often in pairs. Tall, narrow windows, often arched or curved above, often with decorative hoods. Many have a square cupola or tower. Most have porches, at least at the entry. Paired, narrow doors are common. For another example, see page 63.

Look for paired brackets under the eaves, and tall, slender windows.

Note paired doors, double brackets supporting porch and under eave, bay window and distinctive cupola.

Decorative window trim on this connected complex is repeated on the carriage barn and ell.

THE VICTORIAN ERA (1860–1910)

STICK (1860–1890)

Look for "stickwork"—horizontal and vertical bands raised from the wall surface, and decorations in the gables. Gabled roof, usually steeply pitched, often with steep cross gables, and wide overhanging eaves with brace supports. Multi-textured walls are covered with clapboards or shingles. Porches and rectangular towers are common. For another example, see page 162.

A gallery of gable elements: decorative brackets of infinite designs, Stick and Queen Anne styles.

A Sears house. The plans were mail ordered, but the lumber was cut on the farm and milled across the road.

THE VICTORIAN ERA (1860–1910)

QUEEN ANNE (1880–1910)

Decoration is often extravagant, from patterned shingles and wall textures to delicately turned supports and spindlework ornaments on porches and gables, to cut-away bay windows. Lacy woodwork, knob-like beads, and other fancies sometimes called "gingerbread" distinguish this elaborate style. Steeply pitched roof of irregular shape, sometimes with a round or rectangular tower and even roof cresting. Partial or full porch, usually one story high. Asymmetrical layout, usually with few plain flat walls. Window sashes usually have only a single pane of glass. Bay windows, and large window panes surrounded by smaller ones, provide further decoration. Some round towers even feature curved glass.

An earlier photograph of this well preserved house appears on page 122. For other examples of Queen Anne houses see pages 138 and 159.

Other styles of the Victorian era more often seen in institutional buildings include Richardsonian Romanesque, such as Dartmouth College's Rollins Chapel, the Coös County Courthouse in Lancaster (page 126), and the Fairbanks Museum (pictured on page 127).

No surface left without decoration.

Half-timbering is a Queen Anne variation known as Tudor Revival.

THE VICTORIAN ERA (1860–1910)

This Queen Anne features fish-scale shingles in the second story, a flare above the first story, and diamond-paned windows.

Note window design and surface texture detail in gable.

SHINGLE (1880–1900)

Walls of continuous wood shingles, without corner boards. Look for curving edges and ample porches. Free-form, asymmetrical facade with irregular, steeply or double-pitched roof line. Little decorative detailing. Windows usually multi-paned above and single pane below, sometimes in strips of three or more windows together. In the roof, look for a variety of dormer window shapes, including narrow sloping "eyebrow" windows.

THE VICTORIAN ERA (1860–1910)

VERNACULAR VICTORIAN (1870–1910)

This familiar house form features front porches with turned spindlework details or flat jig-saw cut trim. The front porch indicated the new era of leisure. Before the Victorian Era, porches were rare, and had only a decorative function. By the 1860s, the Industrial Revolution had brought with it the mind-set and

the moments to linger with the family on the porch. The style was made possible by the railroads, which provided local lumber yards with pre-cut detailing from distant mills. Many are front-gabled, often with entries to the side of the front. Details are much less elaborate than the Queen Anne, Stick, or other Victorian styles they mimic. For another example, see page 77.

THE CRAFTSMAN ERA (1890–1955)

COLONIAL REVIVAL (1880–1955)

Following the nation's centennial, interest grew in reviving the Classical elements from the 18th century, and this became the dominant style for homes during the first half of the 1900s. It sometimes takes a sharp eye to separate the Colonial Revival of the 1900s from the original, and it often comes down to the former's machine-made finish or the latter's hand finish. Paired or bay windows, entries with "broken" pediments or split decorations over the door, and heavy eave overhangs usually indicate a later house. For more examples, see pages 126, 134, and 165.

The distinctive roof shape of a "Dutch" Colonial Revival (right).

The Craftsman Era (1890–1955)

PRAIRIE (1900–1920)

Two-story homes with low-pitched, usually hipped, roof and widely overhanging eaves. Often called the American Foursquare, for their four square sides, many of these houses have massive front porches, carports, or one-story wings. Hipped dormers are common. Windows sometimes have diamond- or honeycomb-shaped pane designs over large single panes, or long narrow panes over single panes.

CRAFTSMAN (1905–1930)

Low-pitched, gabled roof, occasionally hipped, with wide eave overhangs and often exposed false beams or braces under the gables. Porches have square columns, often resting on large sloping supports, and are usually shingled or clapboarded but sometimes built of stone cobbles. The one-story Craftsman house, often called a bungalow, was once the most popular smaller house in the country.

Note hip-roofed dormer window, arched shingle-clad porch supports, and diamond-paned entry surround.

❋ National Register Historic Districts ❋

NEW HAMPSHIRE

Canaan:	Canaan Street Historic District
Charlestown:	Charlestown Main Street Historic District
Claremont:	Claremont Downtown Historic District
	Lower Village Historic District
	Monadnock Mills Historic District
Dorchester:	Dorchester Common Historic District
Enfield:	Enfield Shaker Community Historic District
Haverhill:	Haverhill Corner Historic District
Jaffrey:	Jaffrey Center Historic District
Lebanon:	Colburn Park Historic District
Lyme:	Lyme Center Historic District
	Lyme Common Historic District
Newport:	Newport Downtown Historic District
Orford:	Orford Street Historic District
Washington:	Washington Common Historic District

VERMONT

Barnet:	Barnet Center Historic District
Bethel:	Bethel Village Historic District
Bradford:	Bradford Village Historic District
Brattleboro:	Brattleboro Downtown Historic District
	Canal St./Clark St. Historic District
Brookfield:	Brookfield Village Historic District
Chelsea:	Chelsea Village Historic District
Chester:	Stone Village Historic District
	Chester Village Historic District
Dummerston:	Scott Farm Historic District
Guildhall:	Guildhall Village Historic District
Hartford:	Jericho Rural Historic District
	Taftsville Historic District
	Quechee Mill Historic District
	White River Junction Historic District
	Wilder Village Historic District
Londonderry:	South Londonderry Village Historic District
Newbury:	Newbury Village Historic District
	Bayley Historic District
	Oxbow Historic District
	South Newbury Village Historic District
	Wells River Historic District
	West Newbury Village Historic District

Newfane:	Newfane Village Historic District
Norwich:	Norwich Village Historic District
Plymouth:	Calvin Coolidge Homestead Historic Distri
	Plymouth Historic District
Putney:	Putney Village Historic District
Randolph:	Randolph Center Historic District
	Depot Square Historic District
Rockingham:	Bellows Falls Downtown Historic Distric
	Bellows Falls Island Multiple Resource Are
	Bellows Falls Neighborhood Historic Distri
	Parker Hill Rural Historic District
	Saxton's River Village Historic District
Royalton:	South Royalton Village Historic District
St. Johnsbury:	St. Johnsbury Historic District
	Main Street Historic District
	Railroad Avenue Historic District
	Maple St./Clarks Ave. Historic District
	Summer Street Historic District
Springfield:	Parker Hill Rural Historic District
	Springfield Downtown Historic District
Stockbridge:	Stockbridge Common Historic District
Strafford:	Strafford Village Historic District
Thetford:	Thetford Hill Historic District
Townshend:	Follet Stone Arch Bridge Historic Distric
	West Townshend Village Historic Distric
Tunbridge:	Tunbridge Village Historic District
Weathersfield:	Weathersfield Center Historic District
West Dover:	West Dover Village Historic District
Weston:	Weston Village Historic District
Westminster:	Westminster Village Historic District
Wilmington:	Wilmington Village Historic District
Windham:	South Windham Historic District
	Windham Village Historic District
Windsor:	Windsor Village Historic District
Woodstock:	Woodstock Historic District
	Slayton-Morgan Historic District
	South Woodstock Village Historic Distric

❄ Photo Credits ❄

Photos are identified by page number, a brief description, and the photographer or source.

INTRODUCTION
Canoe, Richard J. Ewald
Map, Cheryl J. Sallen, in the *Connecticut River Corridor Management Plan.*
Aerial of the northern valley, Adair D. Mulligan
Horse and buggy, from the collection of Frank J. Barrett, Jr.
Sharon, VT, from the collection of Frank J. Barrett, Jr.
Woodsville church, from the collection of Frank J. Barrett, Jr.
Bridge interior, Richard J. Ewald

CHAPTER 1 - ANCIENT WATERWAY
Connecticut River view, Adair D. Mulligan
Beaver Brook Falls, antique postcard from the collection of Frank J. Barrett, Jr.
, Map of Lake Hitchcock, Tammy M. Rittenour, 1999, *Drainage History of Glacial Lake Hitchcock, Northeastern USA*, MS thesis, Univ. of Mass. Cited in *Dinosaurs, Dunes, and Drifting Continents: The Geohistory of the Connecticut Valley* by Richard D. Little, 2003.
, Aerial of meanders, Adair D. Mulligan; Mt. Ascutney, Richard J. Ewald
, Glacial erratic, from the collection of Frank J. Barrett, Jr.
, View from the Palisades, from the collection of Frank J. Barrett, Jr.; Flooding, collection of Katharine Blaisdell
, Riverbank erosion, from the collection of the Connecticut River Joint Commissions; Flooding in Wells River, from the collection of Katharine Blaisdell
, Dam, from the collection of Frank J. Barrett, Jr.
, Wellhead protection sign, Adair D. Mulligan; stenciling of storm drain, courtesy of the New Hampshire Department of Environmental Services; Residential shoreline, Adair D. Mulligan
, Grant Brook, Adair D. Mulligan
, Sediment sampling, Adair D. Mulligan

CHAPTER 2 - NATURAL COMMUNITIES
, Reflection, photo by Jill Brooks, courtesy of the *Coös County Democrat*
, Ladyslippers, Kathy Francke; Second Connecticut Lake, David Deen
, Geese in flight, Adair D. Mulligan; Eagle chick, photo by Peter Nye, courtesy of the Audubon Society of NH
, Connecticut River in Pittsburg, from the collection of the Connecticut River Joint Commissions
, Stream survey, NH Fish and Game Department

24, Salmon parr, NH Fish and Game Department; illustration of Dwarf Wedgemussel, Ethan Nedeau
25, Cobblestone Tiger Beetle habitat and marbled salamander, courtesy of the Silvio O. Conte National Fish & Wildlife Refuge; Cobblestone Tiger Beetle, photo by Jonathan G. Leonard, courtesy of the University of Vermont
26, Wood duck, USDA Natural Resources Conservation Service; River setback, Adair D. Mulligan
27, Wild turkeys, USDA Natural Resources Conservation Service; Peregrine falcon, photo by Chris Martin, courtesy of the Audubon Society of New Hampshire; Climber/researcher, photo by Michael Pelchat, courtesy of the Audubon Society of New Hampshire
28, Osprey platform, photo by Chris Martin, courtesy of the Audubon Society of New Hampshire; Moose crossing sign and deer track, Adair D. Mulligan
29, Bear hug, Susan Morse
30, Beaver dams and birch pioneer, Adair D. Mulligan
31, Long log, from the collection of the Lyme Historians
32, Claremont's Broad Street, from the collection of Frank J. Barrett, Jr.; Ice storm, US Forest Service
33, Spruce grouse, courtesy of The Nature Conservancy, New Hampshire chapter; Aerial of Moore Reservoir, courtesy of US Gen New England
34, Aerial of oxbow, Adair D. Mulligan
35, Silky dogwood, Adair D. Mulligan; Floodplain forest, photo by Matt Collins, The Bioengineering Group
36, Robbins cinquefoil, US Fish & Wildlife Service; Moss community, Adair D. Mulligan
37, Warbler, US Fish & Wildlife Service; Trail to Fourth Lake, Richard J. Ewald
38, Bunnell Tract, courtesy of The Nature Conservancy, New Hampshire chapter
39, Riverbank restoration, Sharon F. Francis; Fisherman, Richard J. Ewald
40, Hemlock wooly adelgid, US Forest Service; Phragmites, Adair D. Mulligan
41, Junked tire, Adair D. Mulligan; Herrick's Cove heroes, Ruthanne Batchelder
42, Riverbank, Richard J. Ewald; Bear tree, Susan Morse
43, Students stocking salmon, US Fish & Wildlife Service; Montshire Museum, Adair D. Mulligan
44, Hemlock, child with binoculars, Adair D. Mulligan
45, Bear Pond Natural Area, Peter Stettenheim, courtesy of the Upper Valley Land Trust

CHAPTER 3 - AMERINDIANS
46, Petroglyphs, Richard J. Ewald
47, Charcoal feature, photo by Wesley Stinson, Sargent Museum Collection; Fluted point, Richard Boisvert

48, Gouge, Howard Sargent, Sargent Museum Collection
49, Abenaki couple, courtesy of the City of Montreal. Records management and archives; Archeological dig, photo by Wesley Stinson, Sargent Museum Collection
50, Screening, Adair D. Mulligan; Archeological dig, photo by Howard Sargent, Sargent Museum Collection
51, Abenaki shelter, Richard J. Ewald
53, Archeological dig, Adair D. Mulligan

CHAPTER 4 - SETTLEMENT

55, Corinth Center, from the collection of Frank J. Barrett, Jr.
56, Family on sleigh, collection of the Lyme Historians
57, Guildhall sign, Adair D. Mulligan; Civil War soldiers, from the collection of the Lyme Historians
58, Fort at No. 4, Adair D. Mulligan
59, Norwich green, Richard J. Ewald; Map of Barnet, 1840 copy of the 1785 map, which is now lost. Published by the Barnet Bicentennial Committee in 1975.
60, Colburn Park, from the collection of Frank J. Barrett, Jr.; Sanborn family, courtesy of Adair D. Mulligan
61, Tannery, from the collection of Frank J. Barrett, Jr.; Guildhall Common, Richard J. Ewald
62, Coolidge plowing, courtesy of Calvin Coolidge Presidential Library and Museum, Forbes Library, Northampton, MA; Aerial of Hinsdale/Brattleboro, Richard J. Ewald
63, Downtown Brattleboro, Richard J. Ewald; Map, 1869 Beers Atlas of Windsor Village, courtesy of Jill Michaels
64, Street scenes in Jaffrey, from *Jaffrey Then and Now, Changes in Community Character*, by Robert B. Stephenson and Catherine L. Seiberling, Jaffrey Historic District Commission, 1994. Early scene, W.F. Allen, contemporary scene, Robert B. Stephenson. Parking lot, Richard J. Ewald
65, Last harvest at West Lebanon, courtesy of Dartmouth College Archives
66, Condo sign, Adair D. Mulligan
67, Valley Quest, photo by Donald Cooke, courtesy of Vital Communities of the Upper Valley
68, Subdivision variations, Randall Arendt, in *Conservation Design for Subdivisions*, Island Press, 1996
69, Man and child, courtesy of the Lyme Historians
70, Bird's Eye View of Lancaster, Library of Congress

CHAPTER 5 - AGRICULTURE

71, Round barn, Richard J. Ewald
72, Sky Farm, from the collection of Sharon F. Francis; Cattle grazing, Richard J. Ewald
73, Springfield, Hay wagon, antique postcard views from the collection of Frank J. Barrett, Jr.
74, Sheep at Major Farm in Westminster, VT, and River Valley Farm, Orford, NH, Adair D. Mulligan
75, Cohass Meadows and stone wall, Adair D. Mulligan
76, Tullando Royal Maxima, courtesy of Rendell and Karen Tullar, Tullando Farm, Orford, NH; Cheese cave, courtesy of Vermont Shepherd-Major Farm, Westminster, VT

77, University Grange and collecting sap, Adair D. Mulliga
78, Sign at River Valley Farm, Orford, NH, and house i field, Adair D. Mulligan
79, Gourds and farmstand at Harlow's, Westminster, V Adair D. Mulligan; Preserves labels, courtesy of Nanc Franklin, Riverview Farm, Plainfield, NH
80, Sign at Auburn Star Farm, Lunenburg, VT, Adair I Mulligan; Horse-drawn wagon at the First Cutting, Jea McIntyre, courtesy of the Upper Valley Land Trust
81, Grant Brook Trail sign, Adair D. Mulligan, with thank to the Upper Valley Land Trust
82, Celebration, courtesy of Rendell and Karen Tulla Tullando Farm, Orford, NH
83, Sign at Bailey Farm, Lyme NH, Adair D. Mulligan Milking parlor at Tullando Farm, courtesy of Rendell an Karen Tullar

CHAPTER 6 - INDUSTRY & COMMERCE

85, Claremont mills, from the collection of Frank J. Barrett, J
86, Waits River and mill, Richard J. Ewald
87, Log drive and house boat, in *The Connecticut River an the Valley of the Connecticut*, by Edwin M. Bacon G.P.Putnam's Sons, New York, The Knickerbocker Press. 191
88, American Precision Museum exhibits, courtesy of th American Precision Museum; Smith & Son scenes, antiqu postcard views from the collection of Frank J. Barrett, Jr.
89, Appalachian Sulphides scene, from the collection o Frank J. Barrett, Jr.; tailing pile, Dr. Robert Christie
90, Ben Thresher's Mill, courtesy of Ben's Mill Trust, Lt
91, Wyoming Valley Dam, from the collection of the Con necticut River Joint Commissions
92, Comerford Dam, collection of the Connecticut Rive Joint Commissions; sign at Vernon Dam, Richard J. Ewal
93, Groveton, Richard J. Ewald; Poulsen Lumber, Littletor NH, Adair D. Mulligan
94, Windsor panorama, courtesy of the Vermont Divisio of Historic Preservation; Mill Brook and American Preci sion Museum, Adair D. Mulligan
95, Fairbanks scale, courtesy of the Fairbanks Museum an Nathaniel Tripp
96, Bath Brick Store, Richard J. Ewald
97, Wells River, from the collection of Frank J. Barrett, Jr.
98, Groundbreaking at Bellows Falls, Joseph Ferrari, EP/ Brownfields program, courtesy of Susan McMahor Windham Regional Commission; Newbury church, tw views, Adair D. Mulligan

CHAPTER 7 - TRANSPORTATION

101, Stagecoach, from the collection of Frank J. Barrett, J
102, Enoch Hale Toll Bridge, postcard from the collectio of Frank J. Barrett, Jr. of a reproduction of oil on canvas b Frederick J. Blake, about 1792; river road in *The Connect cut River and the Valley of the Connecticut*, by Edwin M Bacon, op.cit.

03, Historic Indian Trails of New Hampshire, highlight om map by Chester B. Price in *The New Hampshire Ar-heologist*, Vol. 14, (June, 1967). An 11 x 17-inch map and amphlet with detailed annotations on each trail are avail-ble from the NH Archeological Society (see Appendix B)

04, Steamboat, illustration by Susan Berry Langsten; ancaster Station and Thetford Depot, antique postcard iews from the collection of Frank J. Barrett, Jr.

05, Automobile, from the collection of Frank J. Barrett, r.; Aerial view of Williams River, Richard J. Ewald

06, Corduroy road, illustration from the collection of Frank Barrett, Jr.; Chain ferry, in *The Connecticut River and the Valley of the Connecticut*, by Edwin M. Bacon, op.cit.

07, Map of early turnpikes, illustration by Frank J. Barrett, r.; Haverhill Corner, photo by Frank J. Barrett, Jr.

08, Hinsdale's Auto Pioneer, Richard J. Ewald

09, Early White River Junction, in Bacon, op.cit.; Rail-ɔad notice, from the collection of Frank J. Barrett, Jr.

10, Fairlee Depot, Adair D. Mulligan; Railroad accident, rom the collection of Katharine Blaisdell

11, Ashley's Ferry and Orford-Fairlee covered bridge, an-que postcard views from the collection of Frank J.Barrett, r.; Old Ferry Road sign, Richard J. Ewald

12, Cornish-Windsor and Vilas Bridges, Richard J. Ewald

13, Lebanon arch, from the collection of Frank J. Barrett, r.; Morey Bridge restoration, Adair D. Mulligan

14, Concrete bridge, Richard J. Ewald; Horse and buggy, rom the collection of Katharine Blaisdell

15, Lyme's southern entry, c. 1916, from the collection of rank J. Barrett, Jr.; 2002 view, Adair D. Mulligan

16, Arch Bridge, from the collection of Frank J. Barrett, r.; farm overpass, Adair D. Mulligan

17, Bicyclist, ArtToday; Bedell Bridge and toll house, photo y Brad Smith, from the collection of Frank J. Barrett, Jr.

18, Flying Yankee Folder, courtesy of Carl Lindblade; Rail rail bridge and North Stratford depot, Adair D. Mulligan

19, Futuristic view of White River Junction, from the col-ction of Frank J. Barrett, Jr.

20, Sign clutter, courtesy of LandWorks

CHAPTER 8 - ARCHITECTURE

21, Connecticut River Valley porch, Adair D. Mulligan

22, Saxton's River church, Richard J. Ewald; Lebanon Queen Anne and Fairlee porch, from the collection of Frank Barrett, Jr.

23, Chesterfield Town Hall, Richard J. Ewald

24, Connecticut River Valley porches, Richard J. Ewald; Connected farmstead, Rev. Frederick W. Greene, in *Jaffrey Then and Now, Changes in Community Character*, by Rob-rt B. Stephenson and Catherine L. Seiberling, op.cit.

25, Greek Revival and Bank Block detail, Richard J. Ewald; N. Fairlee scene, from the collection of Frank J. Barrett, Jr.

26, Lebanon City Hall and Rogers Hotel, collection of rank J. Barrett, Jr.; Coös Co. Courthouse, Warren Bartlett

127, Fairbanks Museum, courtesy of Fairbanks Museum; Morrill house, courtesy VT Dept. of Historic Preservation

128, Old South Church, Richard J. Ewald

129, Shattuck Observatory, from the collection of Frank J. Barrett, Jr.; Upjohn churches, Richard J. Ewald

130, Samuel Morey House and Lyme Congregational Church, Richard J. Ewald

131, Lyme horse sheds and Unitarian Church in Chester, Richard J. Ewald

132, Rockingham Meeting House, Richard J. Ewald

133, Alpenglo Farm outbuilding, Adair D. Mulligan; Sky Farm, from the collection of Sharon F. Francis

134, Two early cape houses, Adair D. Mulligan

135, Fence painting in Guildhall, photo by Edith Tucker, courtesy of the *Coös County Democrat*

136, Latchis Hotel and Putney Tavern, Richard J. Ewald

137, Guildhall Library, Lyme Center Academy, and fund-raising projects, Adair D. Mulligan

138, Architectural detail in Hartford and barn, Adair D. Mulligan; Ornament courtesy of the Lyme Historians

139, Alumni Hall in Haverhill, Adair D. Mulligan

140, Fountain at Mountain View Grand, photo by Jill Brooks, courtesy of the *Coös County Democrat*

CHAPTER 9 - CIVIC LIFE & THE ARTS

141, Keene Square, from the collection of Frank J. Barrett, Jr.

142, Angel at Westminster cemetery, Richard J. Ewald

143, Rebellion in Western New Hampshire, illustration based on a map in Jerold Wikoff's *The Upper Valley: An Illustrated tour along the Connecticut River before the Twentieth Century*, Chelsea Green Publishing Co., 1985.

144, Bradford library, collection of Frank J. Barrett, Jr.

145, Chase House, Richard J. Ewald

146, Constitution House, Richard J. Ewald

147, Town Meeting, photo by Jennifer Hauck, courtesy of the *Valley News*; Eureka Schoolhouse, Richard J. Ewald

148, Bradford school and Norwich church, antique post-card views from the collection of Frank J. Barrett, Jr.

149, Parrish, courtesy American Precision Museum

150, Rudyard Kipling, courtesy of the Howard Rice collec-tion, Marlboro College, Marlboro, VT.

151, Matt Brown in his studio, and the Hopkins Center at Dartmouth, Adair D. Mulligan

152, Stark's Rangers, Brunswick Town House, courtesy of Brendan Whittaker and Brunswick Bicentennial Committee

153, Woodsville Fire Department, from the collection of Katharine Blaisdell; Colebrook Festival, Edith Tucker

154, Pie auction, photo by Jim Sheridan, courtesy of the Upper Valley Land Trust

155, Snow roller, from the collection of Frank J. Barrett, Jr.; cat in Guildhall store window, Adair D. Mulligan

156, Post Mills hall and school, from the collection of Frank J. Barrett, Jr.

Chapter 10 - Tourism & Recreation

157, Rusticators near Wells River, from the collection of Frank J. Barrett, Jr.

158, John Ledyard, in Bacon, op.cit.; Smith's Hotel, from the collection of Katharine Blaisdell; White River Junction station, from the collection of Frank J. Barrett, Jr.

159, Bethlehem Depot, from the collection of Frank J. Barrett, Jr.; Woodsville Stage, from the collection of Katharine Blaisdell

160, Steamboat on Lake Morey and hiking campers, from the collection of Frank J. Barrett, Jr.; Fisherwomen courtesy of Lisa and Tim Savard, Lopstick Lodge, Pittsburg, NH

161, Alden Inn and Windsor House, antique postcard views from the collection of Frank J. Barrett, Jr.

162, Huntley's Inn, Claremont, from the collection of Frank J. Barrett, Jr.; The Balsams, Richard J. Ewald

163, Mt. Washington Hotel centennial, photo by Edith Tucker, courtesy of the *Coös County Democrat*

164, Thayer Hotel, Richard J. Ewald; Riverdale Cabins, from the collection of Frank J. Barrett, Jr.

165, Hay Estate, courtesy of the Friends of the Hay Refuge; Camp Wyoda bugler and Camp Lochearn boating scene, from the collection of Frank J. Barrett, Jr.

166, Deer hunters, courtesy of Lisa and Tim Savard, Lopstick Lodge, Pittsburg, NH; White River Tavern, from the collection of Frank J. Barrett, Jr.

167, Hikers and snowmobile signs, Richard J. Ewald

168, Appalachian Trail signs and hiker, Adair D. Mulligan

169, Pisgah State Park signs, Richard J. Ewald; kayaker, photo by Edith Tucker, courtesy of the *Coös County Democrat*

170, Landing, Adair D. Mulligan; Child in canoe, Bob Linck

171, Tourist photographers, Richard J. Ewald; riverfront condominium and sign, Adair D. Mulligan

172, River scenes, crew team, Adair D. Mulligan

173, Bicycles on car, Richard J. Ewald; children in costume, Adair D. Mulligan

174, Clark's Tavern, Richard J. Ewald; former Grafton Inn, Frank J. Barrett, Jr.

175, Bob-house, Richard J. Ewald; Byway logo courtesy the Connecticut River Byway Council; Orford pamphlet courtesy Orford Historical Society; newsletter cover courtesy of the Lyme Historians

176, Paddlers, photo by Edith Tucker, courtesy of the *Coös County Democrat*

Chapter 11 - Community Profile

177, On the Common, Richard J. Ewald

178, Horse and buggy, from the collection of the Lyme Historians; North Main Street Newport, from the collection of Frank J. Barrett, Jr.

179, Lambert Ridge and Ely Depot, Adair D. Mulligan

180, White River Junction panorama, from the collection of Frank J. Barrett, Jr.; Jaffrey children, Rev. Frederick V. Greene, in *Jaffrey Then and Now*, op. cit.

181, Trinity Church, Cornish, NH, and log truck, Richard J. Ewald; Blow-Me-Down Mill, from the collection of Frank J. Barrett, Jr.

182, Putney quilt, Richard J. Ewald; page from *Valley Quest*, published by Vital Communities of the Upper Valley

Appendix A. Watershed Towns

183, Littleton Main Street, from the collection of Frank Barrett, Jr.

Appendix B. Agencies and Organizations

185, Stocking salmon, Bill Byrne of MassWildlife

188, First Cutting, photo by Carol Vredenburgh, courtesy of the Upper Valley Land Trust

189, Wells River Brass Band, from the collection of Katharine Blaisdell

191, Early postcard view, from the collection of Frank Barrett, Jr.; 2000 view, courtesy of Carola Lea; 2002 view, Adair D. Mulligan

Appendix C. A Sampler of Architectural Styles

All photos, Adair D. Mulligan

Watershed address: Connecticut River at Second Connecticut Lake, elevation 1870 feet, 8 miles from the source, and 402 miles from the sea. Circa 1908. From Bacon, op. cit.

❊ Index ❊

benaki, 48–*49*
benaki shelter, *51*
dams, Herbert, 150
dams Grist Mill, 90
gricultural land, loss of, 78–79
gricultural villages, 61–63
griculture
   animal breeding, 75–76
   arrival of the railroads and, 73
   Community Supported Agriculture (CSA) farms, 78
   creation of glacial and floodplain soils, 74–75
   dairy farming, 74, 76–77
   development as a threat to, 78
   erosion and soil depletion as threats to, 79
   farm economics as a threat to, 80
   farmers' markets, 78
   farmstead architecture, 77, 132–33
   The Grange and, 77
   impact on cultural landscape, 71–72
   introduction of Morgan horses, 75
   lack of public awareness as a threat to, 79
   loss of prime agricultural land as a threat to, 78–79
   loss of the farming tradition as a threat to, 79
   maple sugar, *77–78*
   market policies as a threat to, 79–80
   opportunities for action, 80–82
   questions worth asking, 82–83
   roadside stands, 78
   sheep, 73, 75–76, 111
   soils, 74
   sources of information, 83–84
   stone walls, *75*
   working farms open to the public, 77
ir pollution, 14
ir travel, 106, 114
lcott, Louisa May, 151
lden Inn, *161*
lpenglo Farm, *133*
lpine communities, 30, 36
lumni Hall, *139, 174*
merican Builder's Companion, The, 128
merican chestnut, 31–32
merican elm, 32
merican Indians
   Archaic Period, 48

archeological sites, 50–51
Contact Period, 48–49
cultural borrowings from, 52
erosion as a threat to archeological sites, 52
evidence of early habitation, 46–47
historic markers, 51–52
impact on the land, 47
lack of public support as a threat to archeological sites, 52
looting as a threat to archeological sites, 52
opportunities for action, 52–53
Paleo-Indian Period, 47–48
petroglyphs, *46*, 51
questions worth asking, 54
raids on frontier settlements, 58–59
soil disturbance as a threat to archeological sites, 52
sources of information, 54
trails, 102, **103**
Woodland Period, 48
American Precision Museum, *94*, 127
American shad, 21, 24
American Transcendentalist Movement, 37–38
amphibians, 25
animal breeding, 75–76
animal life. *See* natural communities
Appalachian Sulphides, *89*
Appalachian Trail, *167–68*
Archaic Period, American Indian, 48
Arch Bridge, *116*
archeological sites, American Indian, *47, 49,* 50–51, *53*
architecture, historic
   architectural styles, 122–23, 192–201
   building materials as indicators of period and style, 123
   building types, 126
   commerce/trade buildings
      Bank Block, *125*
   Connecticut River Valley porch, *121*, 123–*24*, *125, 158*
   context-rich habitats, 125
   "continuous" farm architecture, 124–*25, 133*
   definition of historic, 125
   domestic buildings
      early 19th century Greek Revival duplex, *121*
      Federal home of Samuel Morey, *130*
      Gothic Revival home of Justin Morrill, *127*

domestic buildings (cont.)
   Greek Revival, *125*
   Latchis Hotel, *136*
   piazza, *122*
   Queen Anne residence, *122*
   Rogers Hotel, *126*
education/research buildings
   Fairbanks Museum and Planetarium, *127*
   Guildhall Public Library, *137*
   Lyme Center Academy, *137*
   Shattuck Observatory, *129*
   farmstead, 77, *132–33*
government buildings
   Brunswick Town House, *152*
   Chesterfield, NH Town Hall, *123*
   Coös County Courthouse, *126*
   Lebanon City Hall, *126*
historic buildings as storytellers, 121–22
historic districts, 63, 131
historic preservation and, 124
historic sites, structures, and objects, 126
importing of building ideas and fashions, 123
industrial buildings, 132
lack of information as a threat to, 134
meeting houses
Rockingham Meeting House, 131–32
National Historic Landmarks, 126–28
notable architects, 128–29
opportunities for action, 135–39
questions worth asking, 139
religious buildings
   Congregational Church, *122*
   Immanuel Episcopal Church, *129*
   Lyme Congregational Church, *130*
   Old South Church, *128*
   St. Luke's Episcopal Church, *129*
   Unitarian Church, *131*
"remuddling" as a threat to, 134
scarcity as a threat to, 134
sources of information, 139–40
time as a threat to, 134
artists, 149–51
arts
   cultural centers, 151
   notable artists and authors, 149–51
   opportunities for action, 153–54
   questions worth asking, 154
   sources of information, 155–56
   upper Connecticut River Valley as a center for, 149

Ascutney, Mt., *11*, 168
Ashley's Ferry, *111*
Atlantic salmon, *24, 43*
"Aunt Sally" (steamboat), *104*, 108
Audubon Society of New Hampshire, 29
authors, 149–51
automobiles
   arrival of, 105
   impact on tourism, 159–60
   as a threat to everyday transportation
     environments, 117
   as a threat to traditional settlement patterns, 64

B
bald eagle, *21, 27*, 35
Balsams, The, *162, 163*
"Barnet" (steamboat), 108
Barnet town plan,**59**
Barns, *71, 124*, 132-3, *138*
bass, 23
Bayley, Jacob, 106
Bayley-Hazen Road, 106–7
bear, *29, 42*
Bear Pond Natural Area, *45*
beaver, 29, *30*
Beaver Brook Falls, *9*, 170
Bedell Bridge, *117*
Belknap, Jeremy, 157
Bellows Falls, VT, 92–93, 109–10
Bellows Falls Canal Company, 108
Benjamin, Asher, 128
Ben Thresher's Mill, *90*
bicycle trails, 169
Bierstadt, Albert, 151
Billings, Frederick, 37, 127
Billings Farm and Museum, 77
Birch Meadow Farm, *116*
birds, 25–28
black-throated blue warbler, *37*
Blow-Me-Down Mill, *181*
boats and boating, *104, 106*, 108, *111, 160, 165*, 169–
   170, *176*
bobcat, 29
bogs, 34
boreal spruce-fir forests, *20, 30*, 33, *38*
boundary, 142-4
Brattleboro, VT, 60, *63*
Brick Store, *96*
bridges, 105, 111–14, *116, 117*

Brockway Mills Gorge, 170
brook trout, 22–23
Brown, Matt, *151*
brownfields, 97–*98*
Brunswick Springs, 162–63
Brunswick, VT, *152*
Bulfinch Row, 129–30
Burtch-Udall-Boyd Homestead, 130
business. *See* industry/commerce
Buttermilk Falls, 170

C
Camp Lochearn, *165*
Camp Stark, 146
Canaan, NH, 60
Canadian border crossings, 146
canals, 102, 104, 108
catamount, 29–30
cellars, 61
cell towers, *98*
Chase, Salmon P., 128, *145*
Chesterfield, NH Town Hall, *123*
churches, *6*, *59*, *61*, *122*, *128*, *129*, *130*, *131*, *132*,
    148-9, *181*
civic life
    adoption of Vermont Constitution, 145
    education, 147–48
    establishment of political boundaries, 142–44
    evolution of regional culture, 141–42
    granting of town charters, 142
    notable political personalities, 145–46
    opportunities for action, 152–53
    organizations and traditions reinforcing political
        stability, 144
    questions worth asking, 154–55
    religion, 148–49
    sources of information, 155
    threats to, 162
    Town Meetings, 146–47
    Westminster Massacre and, 145
Claremont, NH, Broad Street, *32*
Clark's Tavern, *174*
"Clermont" (steamboat), 108
climate change, 40
Clinton, George, 142
coal, 89
cobblestone tiger beetle, *25*
Cohass Meadows, 72, *75*
Colburn Park, *60*

Cold Spring Trout Ponds, 23
Colebrook archeological site, 50
Comerford Dam, *92*
commerce. *See* industry/commerce
community profiles
    checklist, 178–82
    suggestions for generating, 177–78
Community Supported Agriculture (CSA) farms, 78
Congregational Church, *122*
Congregationalists, 148–49
Connecticut River
    as an American Heritage River, 4, 7
    at Brattleboro and Hinsdale, *62*
    bypassing an old oxbow, *34*
    between Guildhall, VT and Lancaster, NH, *3*
    as it leaves Fourth Lake, *22*
    jurisdiction of, 3
    at Maidstone, VT, and Northumberland, NH, *11*
    as a spawning stream, 21
    between Thetford and Lyme, *8*
    as a tourism/recreation resource, 169–70
    as a unifying force, 3
    as an international flyway, 21
    at Vernon, VT, *15*
Connecticut River Birding Trail, 26
Connecticut River Byway, 4, 161, 171
Connecticut River Corridor Management Plan, 15
Connecticut River Rapids Macrosite, 35
Connecticut River Valley/Watershed
    area encompassed within, 1, 3, 183–184
    diversity of, as a natural community, 20
    expressions of natural and cultural unity in, 3–4
    map of, **2**
    sprawl in, 4–5
Connecticut River Valley porch, 123–*24*, *125*
Connecticut River Watershed Council, 41
conservation, natural resource. *See* natural communities
consolidation, as a threat to industry/commerce, 97
Contact Period, American Indian, 48–49
contamination, 41
Conte Refuge. *See* Silvio O. Conte National Fish &
    Wildlife Refuge
Coolidge, Calvin, 62–63, 127, 146
Coös County Courthouse, *126*
copper, 11, 89–90
Corinth Center, VT, *55*
Cornish Colony, 150
Cornish-Windsor Covered Bridge, *112*–13
cottontail rabbit, 29

Country Builder's Assistant, The, 128
courthouses, *126, 139*
covered bridges. *See* bridges
coyote, 30
Crawford Depot, 164
Crawford House Artist's Studio, 164
Crown Point Military Road, 106
cultural landscape, evolution of, 5–6
Currier's Camps, *160, 166*

D
Dams, 2, 15, 21-2, 24-5, *30, 33*, 36, 57, 63, 91, *92*
Dartmouth College, 31-32, *129*, 142, 148, *151*, 158, 166
deer, 28
depots, *104, 110, 118, 159, 179*
development
    as a threat to agriculture, 78
    as a threat to the natural environment, *14*
Diamond International Company, 166
disinvestment, as a threat to industry/commerce, 97
Dix House, 163
Domes of the Yosemite, 151
downtown revitalization, 96–97
Dresden, 143
Dresden School District, 147–48
dwarf wedgemussel, *24*–25, 35
Dwight, Timothy, 31

E
education, 147–48
Elizabeth Mine, 89–90
Enoch Hale Toll Bridge, *102*
environmental protection, changing definition of, 6–7
Episcopalians, 149
erosion
    as a force in shaping the landscape, 11
    as a threat to agriculture, 79
    as a threat to American Indian archeological sites, 52
    as a threat to the natural environment, *14*
Estey Organ Complex, 96
E.& T. Fairbanks Scale Works, *95*
Eureka Schoolhouse, *147*
exotic species, displacement by, 40

F
Fairbanks Scale, 95
Fairbanks Museum and Planetarium, 27, *127*
Fairlee, VT, *13*
farm economics, 80

farmers' markets, 78
farming. *See* agriculture
farming tradition, loss of, 79
feldspar, 12
Fellows Gear Shaper Company, 95
Fells, The, *165*
ferries, *106*, 111
Fifteen Mile Falls, 33, 92
First Cutting, *80*
fish, 22–24
fisher, 29
fishing, 23, *39, 160, 175*
flooding, *13, 14*, 36, 90, *75*
floodplain forests, 35
floodplain soils, 13, 74–75
fluted spear points, *47*–48
Follett, James O., 113
fords, 111
forests
    communities, 33–34
    history of, 30–32
    old growth, 36–37
Fort at No. 4, *47*, 49, *50*, 51, *53, 58*
Fort Dummer, 56, 58
Fort Hill Site, 51
forts, frontier, 58
Fourth Lake, 34
Fourth New Hampshire Turnpike, 107
Free Will Baptists, 149
Frost, Robert, 75
Fulton, Robert, 108

G
Garland Mill, 91
Geese, *21, 25*
general stores, 96
geography. *See* natural environment
geology. *See* natural environment
George II (king of England), 142
Gilbert, Clinton, 160
glacial erratics, 12
glacial soils, 74–75
glaciers, 12
global economy, 97
Goddard, Ely, 89
gold, 89
gouges, *48*
government. *See* civic life
Grafton, VT, 61

Grafton Hotel, 162
Grafton Turnpike, 107
grand hotels, 163–64
Grange, The, 77
granite quarrying, 88–89
Grant Brook, 26, *61*
Great Meadow, 26
Green Mountain National Forest, 37
Green Mountains, 11
grouse, *33*
Guildhall, VT, *57, 61*–62
Guildhall Public Library, *137*

H
habitat, loss of, 40
Hale, Henry S., 163
Hamilton Falls, 170
hang-gliding, 114
Hanover High School, 166, *172*
Harris, Fred, 166
Hartness, James, 94, 114
Hartness House, 95
Hartness State Airport, 114
Haverhill Corner, *107*
Hay, John M., 165
Hay Estate, *165*
Hazen, Moses, 107
Hemenway, Abby Maria, 151
hemlock, *40*
Herrick's Cove, 25
hiking, 167–68
hill towns, 60–61
historic buildings. *See* architecture, historic
historic districts, 63, 131, 202
historic markers, American Indian, 51–52
historic preservation, changing definition of, 6–7
Hitchcock, glacial Lake, **10**, 12–13, 74
Hopkins Center, *151*
hot-air ballooning, 114
Hunt, William Morris, 151
Hunter Site, *50*
Huntley's Inn, *162*
hydroelectric power generation, 91–92

I
ice storm (1998), *32*
Immanuel Episcopal Church, *129*
Indian Stream Republic, 144
industrial buildings, historic, 132

industry/commerce
    arrival of the railroads and, 87
    brownfields as a threat to, 97–*98*
    cell towers, *98*
    consolidation and disinvestment as threats to, 97
    general stores, 96
    global economy as a threat to, 97
    hydroelectric power generation, 91–92
    impact on cultural landscape, 85–86
    inventors and entrepreneurs, 95–96
    "Main Street" commercial centers, 87–88, 96–97
    mining, 87, 88–90, *89*
    national chain retailers as a threat to, 98
    opportunities for action, 99–100
    paper manufacturing, 92–93
    precision manufacturing, 87, *88*, 94–95
    quarries, 88–89
    questions worth asking, 100
    revitalization of downtown areas, 96–97
    sources of information, 100
    textile manufacturing, 93
    timber industry, 72–73, 86–*87,* 90–91, 92–*93*
    water-powered mills, 90–91
Inn at Sugar Hill, 160
inns, *126,* 158, 161–64, *166, 174*
insects, 25
International Paper Company, 38, 92–93
Interstate 91, *105*
interstate highways/interchanges, 105, 114–15, 116
inventors and entrepreneurs, 95–96
iron foundries, 88

J
Jaffrey, NH, *64, 180*
Jarvis, William, 75, 93, 111
John Hay National Wildlife Refuge, 165
Johnson, Elizabeth Captive, 59
Johnson, Susannah, 59
Jones and Lamson Machine Company, 95

K
kayaking, 170
Keene Square, *141, insert*
Kilburn, Benjamin, 95
Kilburn, Edward, 95
King Philip's War, 49
Kipling, Rudyard, 128, *150*–51

L

Lake Hitchcock, **10**, 12-13, 34, 74
Lancaster, NH, *70*
Lancaster Rotary Club, *176*
landscape scale conservation, 38
land use regulations and policies, 66
Latchis Hotel, *136*
Lawrence, Richard S., 94
Lebanon, NH, 60, *113, 126, 155*
Lebanon City Hall, *126*
ledge communities, 36
Ledyard, John, *158*
light rail systems, 110
lime kilns, 88
Lindbergh, Charles, 114
logging, 37, 72-73, 86-*87,* 90-91, 92-93
Long, George, 108
long house post mold outline, *49*
loon, common, 28
looting, as a threat to archeological sites, 52
Lovejoy Tool Company, 95
Lyme, NH, 60, 61, 177, *178*
Lyme Center Academy, *137*
Lyme Center tannery, *61*
Lyme Congregational Church, *130-31*
Lynx, Canada, 30, *insert*

M

MacKaye, Percy, 150
"Main Street" commercial centers, 85, 87-88, 96-97
mammals, 28-30
Man and Nature, 37
maple sugar, *77-78*
Maplewood Hotel, 163
marbled salamander, *25*
market policies, as a threat to agriculture, 79-80
Marsh, George Perkins, 37, 127
Marsh-Billings-Rockefeller National Historic Park,
    37,77,127
marsh hawk, 28
Martin, Chris, *27*
Mascoma River headwaters, *179*
Mead, Larkin, 151
Mead, William R., 151
meeting houses, 131-32
"Mending Wall," 75
Meriden Bird Club, 27
Merino sheep, 73, 75-76, 111
mica, 12
Miller, William, 149

mills, 57, 85, *86,* 90-1, *93, 181*
minerals/mining, 11-12, 87, 88-90, *89*
mineral springs hotels, 158, 162-63
mink, 29
Monadnock, Mt., 11, 12, 168
Monadnock Mills, 93
monadnocks, 11
Montshire Museum, 39, *43*
Moore Reservoir/Dam, *33,* 34, 170
moose, 28-29
Moose Festival, *153*
Morey, Lake, *160*
Morey, Samuel, 104, 108, 130
Morgan, Justin, 75
Morgan horses, 75
Mormons, 149
Morrill, Justin S., 127-28
Morris, Lewis R., 145-46
Morse, Susan, 29, 42
Mothers and Daughters Club, 150
mountain lion, 29
Mountain View Grand Hotel, *140,* 163-64
Mount Sunapee State Park, 36, 169
Mt. Ascutney, 11
Mt. Washington Hotel, *163*
Mt. Wantastiquet, 36, 38
mussels, *24,* 25

N

national chain retailers, 98
National Historic Landmarks, 126-28
Native Americans. *See* American Indians
natural communities
    air pollution as a threat to, 14
    animal life
        amphibians, 25
        anadromous fish, 24
        aquatic macro invertebrates, 24
        birds, 25-28
        insects, 25
        mammals, 28-30
        reptiles, 25
        resident fish, 22-24
    climate change as a threat to, 40
    community types
        alpine communities, 30, 36
        calcareous riverside seep communities, 36
        forest communities, 33-34
        ledge communities, 36
        old growth forests, 36-37

community types (cont.)
    rare communities, 35–36
    riparian habitat and floodplain forests, 35
    scour communities, 36
    wetland communities, 34
competition for clean water as a threat to, 41
Connecticut River as a spawning stream, 21
Connecticut River as an international flyway, 21
conservation
    creation of public lands, 37, 38
    early pioneers in, 37–38
    economics of, 39–40
    establishment of Silvio O. Conte National Fish
        and Wildlife Refuge, 38–39
    landscape scale conservation, 38
    natural heritage programs, 39
    organizations, 39
contamination as a threat to, 41
development as a threat to, 14
displacement by exotic species as a threat to, 40
disturbance, 32
diversity of Connecticut River watershed, 20
extinction of species, 21
factors shaping, 20
forest history, 30–32
interdependency of, 19–21
loss of habitat as a threat to, 40
natural succession, 32
opportunities for action, 41–44
plant life 32–33
questions worth asking, 44
recent efforts to restore and preserve, 22
riparian environments as, 20
sources of information, 44–45
natural (physical) environment
    erosion, 11, *14*
    floodplain soils, 13
    geologic history, 8–10
    glacial Lake Hitchcock, 10, 12–13
    glaciers, 12
    minerals, 11–12
    monadnocks, 11
    opportunities for action, 15–16
    plate tectonics, 10–11
    quarries, 11
    questions worth asking, 17
    sources of information, 17–18
    water pollution as a threat to, 13–14
Naulakha, 151
Newfane, VT, 61

"New Connecticut," 142-3, 145
Newport, NH, Main Street, *178*
northern hardwood forests, 33–34
northern harrier, 28
northern pike, 23
Norwich Congregational Church, *59, 148*
Norwich University, 148
Nulhegan River basin, 33

O
Old Constitution House, 145, *146*
Old South Church, *128*
Ompompanoosuc River flats, 26
Orford, NH, *13*
osprey, 28
Otis, Elisha Graves, 95
Otis Elevator Company, 95
oxbows, *34*

P
Paleo-Indian Period, American Indian, 47–48
paper manufacturing, 92–93
Park Hill Meeting House, 132
Parris, Alexander, 128
Parrish, Maxfield, *149*–50
Partridge, Alden, 148
pegmatite, 12
peregrine falcon, *27*
petroglyphs, *46*, 51
phragmite, *40*
physiography. *See* natural environment
pickerel, 23
Pine Park, 36–37
pink ladyslipper, *20*
Pisgah Wilderness State Park, 169
Pittsburg, NH, *20, 22, 37,* 62, 144
Plainfield, NH, 25
plant life. *See* natural communities
plate tectonics, 10–11
Platt, Charles A., 150
Plymouth Notch, 62–63, 127
politics. *See* civic life
population, 57
Porter, Rufus, 149
Porter, Russell W., 95
Post Mills Hall and School, *156*
potash, 73
precision manufacturing, 87, *88,* 94–95
pride of place, 7
Prospect, Mt., 28

Proulx, Annie, 6
Province Road, 107
public lands, creation of, 37, 38
public transportation, lack of viable, 64
Pumpkin Festival, *173*
Putney Mountain, 28
Putney Tavern, *136*

Q
quarries, 11, 88–89
quartz, 12
Quechee Gorge, 13, 168
quilts, *182*

R
railroads
    development of, 109–10
    growth of tourism and, 158
    impact on industry/commerce, 87
    impact on physical/cultural landscape, 104–5
    wrecks, 110
Randolph, VT, 61
raptors, 27–28
recreation. *See* tourism/recreation
religion, 148–49
"remuddling" *vs.* remodeling, 134
reptiles, 25
Retreat Meadows, 25, *175*
Ridge, The, 129–30
riparian buffer, *16, 42*
riparian habitat, 35
Rivendell Interstate School District, 148
Riverdale Cabins, *164*
river towns, 63
road and bridge design standards, 115–16
road crew (1899), *155*
roadside stands, 78
roads/turnpikes, early, 102, 106–8, **107**
Robbins and Lawrence Armory and Machine Shop, 94
Robbins' cinquefoil, *36*
Rockefeller, Laurance S., 37, 127
Rockingham Meeting House, 131–*32*
Rocks Estate, 29
Rogers Hotel, *126*
Rogers Rangers, 51, *152*
Roman Catholics, 149
round barns, *71,* 133
Route 10, *115*
Russell, William A., 92–93

S
Saint-Gaudens, Augustus, 128, 150
Saint-Gaudens National Historic Site, 128, *insert*
Saint Regis Paper Company, 166
salamanders, *25*
salmon, 22-4
Samuel Morey Bridge, *113–14*
Sanborn, Charles, *60*
schools, 147–48
scour communities, 36
sculpin, 22
Second Connecticut Lake, *20*
Second New Hampshire Turnpike, 107
setback habitat, 25-6
settlement
    agricultural villages, 61–63
    automobiles as a threat to traditional settlement
        patterns, 64
    cellar holes, 61
    community character, 64
    creation of town commons and greens, 59–60, *61*
    1810 populations, 57
    18th century, 56–57
    frontier forts, 58
    hill towns, 60–61
    historic districts, 63
    Indian raids, 58–59
    lack of awareness as a threat to traditional settlement
        patterns, 66
    lack of viable public transportation as a threat to
        traditional settlement patterns, 64
    land use regulations and policies as a threat to
        traditional settlement patterns, 66
    19th century, 57–58
    opportunities for action, 67–68
    questions worth asking, 68
    river towns, 63
    sources of information, 68–70
    sprawl as a threat to traditional settlement
        patterns, 65–66
Seventh Day Adventists, 149
Shakers, 149
Shapleigh, Frank H., 164
Sharon, VT, *5*
Shattuck Observatory, *129*
sheep's milk cheese, *76*
Shingle Style church, *6*
silky dogwood, *35*
silver, 89

Silvio O. Conte National Fish and Wildlife Refuge, 20,
    38–39
16th New Hampshire Regiment, *57*
skiing, 160–61, 166–67
Skitchewaug Site, 50–51
Sky Farm, *72, 133*
Smith, Joseph, 149
Smith's Hotel, *158*
Smith & Son, *88*
snowshoe hare, 29
soapstone, 89
Society for the Protection of New Hampshire
    Forests, 29, 37, 39
soil depletion, 79
soil disturbance, as a threat to American Indian
    archeological sites, 52
Source to the Sea Cleanup Day, *41*
southern oak-pine forests, 33
Spaulding brickyard, 95–96
sprawl
    as a threat to tourism/recreation, 172
    as a threat to traditional settlement patterns, 65–66
Springfield, VT, *73*
Springfield Telescope Makers, Inc., 95
St. Johnsbury, VT, 109
St. Johnsbury Athenaeum, 127, 151
St. Luke's Episcopal Church, *129*
stagecoach, *101*, 158-9, 164
stagecoach inns, *158, 161, 174*
state parks, 169
steamboats, 104, 108
Stellafane Observatory, 95, 127
Stone, Harlan F., 146
Stone, Livingston, 23
stone walls, 61, *75*
Sugar River, *4*
Sullivan Machinery Company, *85*
summer children's camps, *165-6*
summer people, *157,* 160, 165–66
Sumner's Falls, 50

T
talc, 11, 89
Tannery Falls, *138*
taverns, 158, 161–62
textile manufacturing, 93
Thayer's Inn, 163, *164*
Thetford Center, 60
Third New Hampshire Turnpike, 107
Thoreau, Henry David, 38, 168

"Thy Templed Hills," 150
timber industry, 72–73, 86–*87,* 90–91, *92–93*
Tipping Rock, *12*
topography. *See* natural environment
tourism/recreation
    bicycle trails, 169
    on the Connecticut River, 169–70
    Connecticut River Byway, 171
    construction of railroads and, 158
    efforts to promote, 159
    grand hotels, 163–64
    hiking, 167–68
    impact of increased automobile use, 159–60
    impact on farm base in late 1800s, 159
    inns and taverns, 158, 161–62, *164, 166, 174*
    kayaking, 170
    lack of coordination, infrastructure, respect,
        appreciation for differences, and awareness as
        threats to, 172–73
    mineral springs hotels, 158, 162–63
    opportunities for action, 173–75
    outdoor recreation today, 167
    questions worth asking, 175
    rail trails, 110, *118,* 169
    sources of information, 175–76
    sprawl as a threat to, 172
    state parks, 169
    summer people, 160, 165–66
    tourist cabins and roadside attractions, 164–65
    transplantation of English Romantic movement
        across the Atlantic, 157–58
    winter sports, 160–61, 166–67
tourist cabins, 164–65
town charters, 142
town commons and greens, *57,* 59–60, *61, 177*
Town Meetings, 146–47
transportation
    air travel, 106, 114
    automobiles, 105
    bridges, 105, 111–14
    canals, 102, 104, 108
    community origins and, 101
    early roads and turnpikes, 102, 106–8, **107**
    fords and ferries, 111
    interstate highways, 105, 114–16
    lack of informed public involvement as a threat, 116
    lack of maintenance and funding as a threat, 116
    light rail systems/trolleys, 110
    Native American routes, 102, **103**
    opportunities for action, 117–18

transportation (cont.)
   overemphasis on automobiles as a threat, 117
   questions worth asking, 118–20
   railroads, 104–5, 109–10, 116
   region "firsts," 101–2
   remnants of historic modes, 115
   road and bridge design standards as a threat, 115–16
   sources of information, 120
   steamboats, 104, 108
Trinity Church, *181*
trolleys, 110
trout, 22-24
Tullando Farm, *83*
Tullando Royal Maxima, *76, 82*
turkey, *27*
turkey vulture, 28
Tyson village, 88

U
Union Station, *158*
Unitarian Church, *131*
United Inhabitants of Indian Stream Republic, 144
Universalists, 149
University Grange, *77*
Unredeemed Captive, The, 58
Upjohn, Richard, 129
Upper Valley Land Trust, 39, 45, 80, 170
uranium, 12

V
Valley Quest, *67, 182*
Vermont Constitution, 145
Vermont Copper Mining Company, 89
Vermont Institute of Natural Science, 28
Vermont Youth Conservation Corps, *39*
Vermont Land Trust, 39
Vernon Dam, *92*
Vilas Bridge, *112*, 113
Vital Communities of the Upper Valley, 182

W
Waits River, *86*
Washington, George, 143
water, competition for, 14, 41
waterfalls, *9*, 170
waterfowl, *21*, 25-6
water pollution, as a threat to the environment, 13–14, *16*

water-powered mills, 90–91
Webber, Frances W., 23
Webster, Daniel, 109
Weeks, John Wingate, 37, 38, 146
Weeks Act, 37
Weeks State Park, 27
Wells River, VT, *13, 14, 97*
Wentworth, Benning, 142
Western Abenaki, 48–*49*
West Lebanon, NH, *65*
Westminster, VT, 60
Westminster Massacre, 145
West Mountain Wildlife Management Area, 33
Weston, VT, 165–66
West River, 170
wetland communities, 34
Wheelock, Rev. Eleazar, 148
Whipple archeological site, 50
White Mountain National Forest, 37
White Mountains, 11
white pine, 31
White River Junction, VT, *109, 119, 180*
White River Tavern, *166*
Wilder-Holton House, 130
Wilder Wildlife Management Area, 26
Wildflowers, *20, 36*
Williams, Rev. John, 58
Wilson, Clark James, 95
Windsor, VT, **63,** *94*
Windsor House, *161*
winter sports, 160–61, 166–67
wolf, 30
wood duck, *26*
Woodland Period, American Indian, 48
Woods Public Library, *144*
Woods School Building, *148*
Woodsville Fire Department, *153*
Woodsville Stage, *159*
Wyoming Valley Dam, *91*

Y
Young, Ammi Burnham, 128–29
Young, Brigham, 149

Z
zoning, 68, 134–35

New Hampshire & Vermont ‡ *History, Culture & Environment*

THE CONNECTICUT RIVER is the heart of this story. It flows through space, and it flows through time, connecting people and communities that share both a common heritage and prospects for the future.

Proud to Live Here is designed to stimulate new appreciation for the natural and cultural heritage of this remarkable river valley, and inspire new motivation to learn and to act. The book asks some basic questions:

What are the layers of change beneath the present moment?

How did this place come to be the way it is?

What important parts of the river's story are worth remembering and retelling?

What are the special places worth saving?

And, most importantly, how do we go about all this?

Proud to Live Here is written for everyone:
Old timers and newcomers,
Farmers and village dwellers,
Teachers and students,
Citizens and officials,
Visitors from afar who journey to appreciate this valley of breathtaking beauty, and
All who live here.

Vermont and New Hampshire paid tribute to the river and its watershed in the 1980s by establishing commissions to preserve and protect its resources, advise on growth and development, and cooperate with the other state. Working together since 1990 as the Connecticut River Joint Commissions, they continue a tradition of bi-state friendship and cooperation in the valley. Both commissions are advisory and have no regulatory powers, preferring instead to promote public involvement in decisions that affect the river and its watershed.

CONNECTICUT RIVER JOINT COMMISSIONS INC

The Connecticut River Joint Com
PO Box 1182, Charlestown NH

ISBN: 0-9728056-0-5

www.crjc.org